Goforth Solutions
PO Box 3151
Oxford, MS 38655

Visit our websites at www.Media-Shift.com and www.StephenGoforth.com
Online correspondence may be directed to StephenGoforth@gmail.com

Second Edition: August 2010

Cover design: Kathi James
Book design: Kathi James
Copy Editors: Brent Inman, Dan Lounsbury, Alex McDaniel

ISBN-10 0615383858
ISBN-13 978-0-615-38385-9

Printed in the United States of America

media shift

Journalism in a Connected World

social media
Twitter
film
interactive journalism
facebook
augmented reality
television
radio
newspaper

mashup
e-reader
hyperlocal
hacker journalism
YouTube
tablet
iTunes
crowdsourcing
interactive TV
ambient
awareness

Stephen Goforth

CONTENTS

INTRODUCTION

The Shape of the Future

When facing new ideas and challenges, some people lean forward. Some people lean back. When change hits, we decide whether to move into it or become defensive.

The media are undergoing their own rapid combustion. The shift stings and impassions. This brief volume is devoted to helping the burn glow brighter by encouraging proactive thinking about the future of media, and journalism specifically. The format is simple for most chapters: A review of today's landscape sandwiched by a glance back (the *Timeline*) and a look forward (*Trends*).

The goal is to first understand each medium's trajectory by identifying innovators who challenged the status quo and the compelling ideas that have brought us to where we are now. A given past suggests a particular future. It defines the possibilities and limitations. Let's pick up that passion and critical thinking as we launch into a digital lifestyle.

Our goal is not to be ahead of the curve but on the curve. There is the danger of twisting in the wind by following each new lurch of technology that promises to change the media landscape. The sparkling novelties can distract us from developing those fundamental building blocks of journalism: compelling storytelling, accurate reporting, and sharp writing.

William Bridges wrote in his book, *Transitions*, "The future is not delivered like the morning paper. The future comes looking like something else." Take ownership over your own career and media philosophy now rather than allowing yourself to become a victim of circumstance, so that as new technologies rise up, you are not swept along with each new wave, or caught hiding your head in the sand. Allow for ambiguity where we do not have definite answers. According to social psychologist Erich Fromm, "Creativity requires the courage to let go of certainties." Embrace uncertainty and love the possibilities.

Special thanks go to my copy editors, Brent Inman, Dan Lounsbury and Alex McDaniel; my graphic designer Kathi James; the Journalism faculty at *Ole Miss*, and the *Student Media Center* staff; Arvinder Kang and Robbi Crockett for advice; and my inspirations, John, Anna and Mark as well as my parents, Wilbur and Jane Goforth, who started me on this media adventure.

Stephen Goforth
Oxford, Mississippi

ONE
Mass Communication

Awash in the Glow of Media

There is a saying, you don't know how much you value something until it is gone. What would you be willing to give up first: Your TV or access to the Internet? Would you first give up your cell phone or your computer?

Not long ago, access to television was more important than access to the Internet. A desktop computer would outrank a cell phone. College students now overwhelmingly say they prefer Internet access, and won't give up their cell phones. Our media experience is evolving rapidly, allowing some innovative companies to gather significant influence. This isn't the first time technology has disrupted the business landscape. Think of Ford's automobile or the Intel chip.

New technology gains traction when it makes it easy to do something we already are doing. Facebook simply made it easier to do the socializing we were already in the process of doing. The more friction-free something is while offering value, the more of it we do. This can put tremendous power in the hands of a few people. A few years ago, there were cries that *Microsoft* was too powerful because it controlled so much that was vital to accessing the Web. Now *Google* tempts users by offering its services for free in return for gathering information about them. *Google's* motto "Do no evil" hasn't prevented some people from imagining the worst. A popular fictitious flash movie called *EPIC 2015*, created by two journalism students offers a chilling projection of the world in 2015 when a fictional future company is created by the merger of *Google* with *Amazon*, creating a Goliath called *Googlezon* (find the video by searching *Googlezon* on *YouTube*). This Orwellian colossus gathers information on individual's behaviors and activities by employing algorithms and computers to reveal their digital experiences. Is this where we are headed? Is *Googlezon* around the corner? While some Internet companies struggle to make money, *Google* and *Amazon* are doing well financially. By following the money and connecting with solid business models, you'll gather valuable clues as to where technology may take us next.

Culture Quiz

How well do you know the American culture? Try this short quiz and find out.

1. True or false: Teen pregnancy and out-of-wedlock birthrates are higher than a decade ago.

2. True or false: The number of teens who SAY they are having sex is less than 50%.

3. What percent of all U.S. families are headed by two parents, that is, a married mother and father: 37%, 50% or 68%?

4. The rate of juvenile crime has risen, stayed about the same, or dropped over the last 20 years?

5. Which of these three states has the lowest divorce rate: Mississippi, Oklahoma, or Connecticut?

6. Who is most likely to be divorced: Evangelical Christians, Catholics, Atheists or non-Christians?

7. How tall is the average American woman: five foot three or five foot seven? And how much does she weigh: 132 pounds or 152 pounds?

(Answers at the end of the chapter)

The more we watch TV and movies, the more likely we expect cars to blow up when they crash and white collar businessmen to be greedy crooks.

Some media experts tell us the reason we may offer the wrong answers to these questions is that we have bought into stereotypes reinforced in the media. We expect there to be more out-of-wedlock pregnancy and crimes. We misjudge the size of a typical woman. The more we watch TV and movies, the more likely we expect cars to blow up whenever they crash and white collar businessmen to turn out to be greedy crooks.

Media critic Marshall McLuhan is said to have asked, "Does a fish know it's wet?" His answer was "no." The fish's existence is so dominated by water that only in the absence of water is the fish aware of its condition. We are like the fish, so fully saturated by media in our everyday lives that we are often unconscious of their presence and influence. The media impact our view of the world in ways we don't even realize. Media help define us and shape our realities.

Before going further, let's step back to look at the fundamental elements of media and culture, beginning with what goes into making "communication" happen between them.

The Elements of Communication

For communication to take place, there must be a starting point and ending point. That is, a source and a receiver. Communication can be described as simply the transmission from a source to a receiver. What runs between the source and receiver is a message delivered by way of a medium. Put that all together and here's what you have: Communication is the transmission of a message through a medium from a source to a receiver. This is the model described by Wilbur Schramm in his 1954 book *The Process and Effects of Mass Communication*.

A medium is just one transmission (a speaker's voice would be an example). When the message is carried to a large number of receivers, then media or mass media are creating the multiple transmissions. (*Medium* is singular while *media* is plural). When this process loops back around (when you yawn in response to a lecture) then there is "feedback."

Given those parts of communication, here are the definitions we will work with:

> *Communication* is the process of shared meaning.

> *Mass communication* is the "process of shared meaning between mass media and their audiences."

Communication can be altered in several ways:

› The number of *people involved* (a family discussion versus a stadium packed with people).

› The number of *identical messages* (The ubiquitous Mickey D's ad versus two friends gossiping once).

› The *speed* of the feedback (TV executives have to wait to get ratings; they are not instantaneous).

› The *distance* between the source and the receiver (two people chatting face-to-face is different from someone writing a blog, and someone later posting a response on that blog).

Culture

The final piece of the puzzle is the *place* a medium "does its thing." We call it culture. Though there are many definitions of culture, here is the one we'll use:

> Culture is the behavior of members of a given social group, learned and maintained through communication — including mass communication.

Culture is not the same as the *climate.*

The climate of a university can be altered by a new president taking charge. If he declares, "Anyone can park in any space on campus," that would change the climate of the school. Attitudes toward football, drinking and church are part of the culture and will not easily change.

Culture does some good things for us, such as giving answers to questions like:

> "How close do I stand to another person when we talk?"

> "When do I burp?"

> "When should I wear a dress or tie?"

On the other hand, there are some negative effects. Culture can give us inappropriate expectations such as, "All women should be thin." Culture can encourage us to cling to stereotypes like, "Someone wearing a turban is a Muslim, and could be a terrorist."

The mass media support culture by telling stories (how can you pick out the bad guy in a movie?) and serving as forums (places where we debate ideas). The media serve as an outpost where people can get their cultural bearings. Journalism can provide a useful knowledge cartography for that exploration.

Some people believe media change culture. Others insist media are neutral. The side you choose in the debate will go a long way toward determining your view on many issues we will deal with in coming pages.

Mass Media Trends

MASS MEDIA TREND: MEDIA MULTI-TASKING

Do you work for 20 minutes and then feel compelled to check your Facebook account, e-mail or the latest celebrity news? At the end of spending hours on the Internet, do you feel like you haven't accomplished anything?

In his book *The Shallows: What the Internet is Doing to Our Brains*, digital skeptic Nicholas Carr says media multi-tasking has rewired our brains. We are more shallow and easily distracted because of our frenetic digital life, and this phenomenon, Carr says, can be measured at a neurological level. He decries the "state of distractedness that defines the online life." Carr worries we will replace "deep reading" with "power browsing."

We are constantly connected. Americans soaked up information an average of nearly 12 hours per day in 2008, according to researchers at the University of California at San Diego. This includes more than 100,000 words and 34 gigabytes at an average day. The traditional media, led by television, still dominate.

During the second quarter of 2009, *Nielsen* says TV consumption hit an all-time high of 141 hours per month. It was 139 hours per month during the same period a year earlier. Internet use is about the same over the same period (about 26 hours per month). Where are we getting all of that time? Apparently, we are simultaneously consuming many different kinds of media. We are media multi-taskers. According to *Nielsen,* 57% of American Internet users say they watch TV while browsing the Internet. About 9% of the time, prime-time TV viewers are *multiscreening* — surfing while watching TV, according to *Integrated Media Measurement.*

These days, the generational divide in the workplace isn't defined primarily by what you wear or the music you like, it's how you communicate.

These days, the generational divide in the workplace isn't defined primarily by what you wear or the music you like, but how you communicate. Young workers stay in a constant whir of socializing. The popularity of texting has given rise to what can be called a *culture of availability.* While we are physically present with other people, we also make ourselves available digitally to a completely different group of people. This hypersocializing can reduce interpersonal skills and cut productivity. But there are benefits, such as developing multi-tasking abilities and knowing how to get to the essence of an issue.

In years past, when students walked out of class, they could be seen chatting with one another while exiting buildings. Now their heads are bowed, absorbed in pressing tiny keys. They are glued to miniature screens waiting for incoming transmissions. Or else their heads are tilted to the side, as they enjoy the intimacy of a cell phone. As technology has changed, the way we relate and connect to one another has changed as well. If we choose, we can stay cloistered in a cone of distraction. A 2010 Zogby poll showed just how far many are willing to go. The survey found one in ten Americans under the age of 50 say they would be willing to implant a device in their brain to be connected to the Internet.

Some social observers say the rise of digital media has increased something called *isolated connectivity*. We are more isolated yet more connected than ever before. We know people through our Internet correspondence and yet we don't really know them. We know the people who pass through our space and yet we don't really know them in the same way we know our Internet companions. The digital age has created a new group of friends with whom we have digital intimacy through incessant online contact. These quick snippets of minutiae form an *ambient intimacy* or *ambient awareness*. Together, like pixels on a screen, they paint a portrait of friends and family we were not aware of in everyday life. Users gain a new sense of how someone thinks and the rhythms of their lives.

> *We are more isolated yet more connected than ever before.*

MASS MEDIA TREND: CONVERGENCE

Convergence is the erosion of traditional distinctions among media, the combining and coordinating of various media. Normally, we think of convergence as a newspaper reporter bringing a camera along with her on a story, or a TV reporter writing for the Internet while putting together video for the TV newscast. But it can go even further. The advertisement below probably sounded appealing to journalists and public relations specialists coming out of college until they read further down.

> "Are you looking for an exciting opportunity to make a real impact with your business and marketing writing talents? A dynamic, entrepreneurial (organization) is looking for an experienced copy writer and desktop publisher to lead aspects of both internal and external written communications."

> "The twist: while you are writing copy you will also fill the role of security guard. We will buy your uniform. You won't carry a gun. The security guard spends most of the shift seated at the reception desk, and there will be very minimal security duties. Practically the entire shift you will be able to focus on writing copy — you'll just happen to be wearing a uniform."

Will wearing the hat of a security guard or other side duty be necessary for writers to stay employed in the future? And if so, what does this say about the trustworthiness of media outlets?

As news organizations move to the Internet, we're finding more people put faith in what they read online. A broad 2009 *Ad Week* survey covering consumers in 50 countries found 70% trusted content they read over the Internet more than opinions found in newspapers, television and magazines, according to *Ad Week*.

Will New Media eventually replace Old Media or will the two cousins live happily side-by-side? Perhaps there's a lesson in the past. This isn't the first time they've crossed swords.

The Wall Street Journal calls 1949 the year of the "new media crisis." Network radio had dominated the entertainment landscape for a quarter century. Television was up and coming in the late 1940's, but losing money. The shift came in 1949 when technological advances made it possible for viewers in many cities to watch network TV live. Although TV became more powerful, radio didn't go away. The airwaves shifted from drama and comedy to music. Radio survived. Our current media shift leaves the future of old media in doubt once again and those who champion it will have to discover another saving shift for it to endure.

The news business has continuously endured the throes of reinvention. Its fluid history combined with today's constant technical experimentation suggests not a single solution or path but a range of partial remedies.

MASS MEDIA TREND: CUTBACKS AND NEW BUSINESS MODELS

The average American family will spend nearly $1,000 in 2010 on cable television, Internet connections, and video games. That's up from about $770 in 2004, according to *The New York Times*. Annual cell phone charges add another $1,000 to the 2010 total.

While the American family is spending more than ever to stay connected, the media industries are cutting back. More than 30,000 jobs were cut in 2008, according to an *Ad Age* analysis of Department of Labor employment statistics and news reports. That's about 3.5% of the total media work force of 858,000.

Is this just a result of the weak economy? Or could it be that as people exchange information, videos and other information online, they have decided the professional media is not needed as much any more?

Thanks to budget cutbacks, many news organizations are turning reporters into a self-contained newsroom. *Backpack journalism* is where a reporter acts as a one-man-band who researches, reports, shoots, edits and narrates each piece. These *all-platform journalists* post headlines and upload videos, write short and long stories and act as photojournalists. Their job is to work seamlessly in a *cross platform environment*.

Besides giving more work to fewer people, there are other ideas as to how to pay for online journalism in the new media era:

> *Micropayments* (a small cost for access to each story)
>
> Subscriptions (like *WallStreetJournal.com; The New York Times*, starting in 2011; and global analysis from *Stratfor.com*)
>
> Dependence on large individual donors (such as *ProPublica.com* which investigates corruption and now has a annual newsroom budget of around $10 million and some 36 reporters and editors.)
>
> Non-profits (including *The Daily Beast* backed by media mogul Barry Diller, and *The Watchdog Institute*, an investigative journalism organization spun off from *The San Diego Union-Tribune*)
>
> Sites offering premium memberships give readers who are willing to pay for the privilege special access and perks. *Global Post*, for instance, offers subscribers conference call briefings by freelance correspondents in more than 50 countries, plus the opportunity to vote on story topics they would like to read about.

There are also for-profit companies now funding non-profit companies. However, the IRS is concerned that in these arrangements the work of the non-profit may only benefit the for-profit. The federal government says the non-profit must be more than just a shell used to escape taxes, since non-profits get special benefits that for-profits do not.

A novel attempt to fund journalism comes from *Spot.Us*. The nonprofit website lets journalists pitch their ideas directly to readers who can decide whether to fund a story. The venture has begun in San Francisco and Los Angeles.

MASS MEDIA TREND: GLOBALIZATION

Will distant, anonymous foreign corporations, each with vast holdings in a variety of nonmedia businesses, use their powers to shape news and entertainment content to suit their own goals?

A job posting read, "We seek a newspaper journalist based in India to report on the city government and political scene of Pasadena, California, USA." The new employee would watch Pasadena City Council meetings over the Internet and file reports. But could someone, half a world away, really be able to cover local zoning debates and votes on garbage pickup? Or does it even matter, as long as the reporter takes accurate notes and writes well? How would you feel if you discovered that your local newspaper was being written in India? Would you feel cheated or would it not matter, as long as the information is accurate? We'll talk about outsourcing more in the chapter on newspapers.

MASS MEDIA TREND: FRAGMENTATION

Broadly written magazines like *Life* and *The Saturday Evening Post* thrived before the advent of TV and radio. We now have specialty magazines like *Ski* and *Internet World*. In *niche journalism* specific audiences are targeted with content designed exclusively for them. The tightening of brand focus naturally leads to tightening of ambition.

Radio formats and TV networks have also moved toward programming designed to reach more targeted audiences. This is known as *narrowcasting* or *niche marketing*. The positive side of fragmentation is greater diversity of voices in the digital conversation. The negative side of the coin is that it discourages national, common, unifying experiences and leads to less social cohesion.

MASS MEDIA TREND: CONSUMPTION ON DEMAND

There has been a shift from appointment consumption (you'll get to see it when we decide to show it) to consumption on demand (I'll watch it when I'm ready). Traditional media have operated as a one-way street. News was gathered, produced and delivered to you. Information consumption was overwhelmingly passive, with the telephone being the only interactive medium. Now, the formal one-size-fits-all news format is no longer satisfying. The process is more of a dialogue. When we go online, each of us becomes our own editor, our own gatekeeper. We select the kind of news and opinions we care most about. Some observers are calling this emerging news product *The Daily Me*.

How do people behave when they are in control of the content? *Newsweek*'s editor says 500 words is the max that people are willing to read on the Internet. Eighty percent of readers

While Americans say they believe in the marketplace of ideas, our behavior may suggest we like to embed ourselves in a hermetically sealed echo chamber.

won't even read page 2 of an eight-page Internet story. *CNN.com* aims to keep its stories between 600 and 800 words and doesn't continue stories on the next page.

Journalists have always wrestled with whether to give audiences what they *want* or what they *need*. Now, traditionalists fear the move to the Internet will mean the number of public interest reporters will decline because the information isn't sexy like novelty stories and celebrity news. Many journalists fear that the public won't look for quality information, but rather information that confirms prejudices. While Americans say they believe in the marketplace of ideas, our behavior often suggests we like to embed ourselves in a hermetically sealed echo chamber. Defenders of traditional media see the rise of the so-called *Daily Me* as a bedtime lullaby, luring Americans into a false self-confidence that sees the world in black-and-white without shades of gray.

MASS MEDIA TREND: HYPERCOMMERCIALISM

Hypercommercialism is the increase in commercial time in a typical broadcast or cable show and the use of brand names in songs for payment. The trend also includes rising product placement and brand entertainment where product brands are part of the entertainment program and play an essential part in the show. For instance, *Extreme Home Makeover* uses only *Sears* tools. We'll talk about this more in the chapter on advertising.

Pause for Discussion: How Much Influence?

Is it worth it for advertisers to spend billions of dollars this way? If you say yes, you are also saying you are influenced by the media. Does this mean media are not merely a reflection of culture, but are driving it? The side of the fence you choose in this debate will, for instance, help you decide whether you'll let your kids watch provocative cable shows or attempt to shield them from the media.

MASS MEDIA TREND: NANOSTORIES

Susan Boyle, the frumpy English singer, became an overnight sensation when she displayed her remarkable singing voice on *Britain's Got Talent* and told her interviewers she'd never been kissed. Her video raced around the Internet. She became a symbol of the average person, simple and unspoiled. But Boyles' next TV appearance was weeks away. There was nothing to feed the machine. Soon, attention moved away from her to the next conversation stopper. At the time, her rise to fame was a *nanostory*. Bill Wasik (the creator of flash mobs) defines nanostories in his book *And Then There is This: How Stories Live and Die in Viral Culture* as a "short-lived media phenomenon that is driven by the sheer quantity and speed of the contemporary conversation."

This type of buzz becomes fuel for conversation because of its value within social relationships. In the news business, *buzz news* has also been referred to as *water cooler stories*. Producers ask themselves, is this story something that would be shared around the water cooler at work? These stories often have a novelty aspect to them.

As we begin to find out more about which stories most attract web surfers, journalists will be tempted to use the number of page views to guide their story choices. Should we allow the *hive mind* to select stories even if it steers toward instant digestibility and sensationalism?

Avoiding the snare of culture's nanostories may be the only way for journalists to keep the creative juices flowing and stay productive. As Wasik suggests, "The challenge is to try to find ways to partially unplug ourselves. To carve out spaces in our lives away from information. Away from the sort of constant buzzing of the hive mind."

For Next Time

Think about what books have influenced you and the ones you have particularly enjoyed. What books should be required reading in college?

Answers to Culture Quiz

1. The teenage pregnancy rate has declined steadily since 1990, except for a spike in 2006 and 2007, according to *Pew Research Center* survey.

2. The number of teens who say they are having sex is less than 50 percent. According to the *National Youth Risk Behavior Survey* it was 47.8% as of 2007, down from 54.1% in 1991.

3. 68% of children live with two married parents; 3% live with two unmarried parents; 26% live with one parent and 4% live with no parent present.

4. Arrests of young people for violent crimes fell by 20% from 1997 to 2006. The number of people under 18 arrested for murder dropped 42% during the same time period.

5. The divorce rate is lowest in Connecticut, then Mississippi, and Oklahoma.

6. There's a 26% chance that Evangelical Christian adults who've been married have also been divorced, compared to a 28% chance for Catholics, a 30% divorce rate for atheists and a 38% chance for non-Christians, according to a survey by Barna Research Group.

7. The average American woman is five feet, three inches and three-quarters, and she weighs 152 pounds.

Books

Book Timeline

1455 German Johannes Gutenberg prints his first book, the *Latin Vulgate Bible.* As Gutenberg's press reaches across Europe, the Bible is translated into local languages. Poorly-produced copies of the Bible and mediocre literature soon thrive, leading to claims that the printing press must be controlled to avoid chaos and loss of intellectual life. Martin Luther complains, "The multitude of books is a great evil. There is no measure of limit to this fever for writing." Comparisons are being made between the effect of the printing press to the advent of the Internet.

1638 *First printing press* arrives in the American Colonies.

1640 The *first book* is printed in the American Colonies by locksmith Stephen Daye. *The Whole Booke of Psalmes* later becomes known as *The Bay Psalm Book* because it serves as the hymnal of the Massachusetts Bay Colony. Nearly 300 pages, the 1,700 copies are filled with errors. Fewer than a dozen survive today.

1732 Almost 90 years later, Ben Franklin's *Poor Richard's Almanack* is published.

1740 The first true novel is published in America: Samuel Richardson's *Pamela.*

Pamela is the story of a housemaid whose master, Mr. B, makes unwanted advances toward her. She rejects him many times and her virtue is eventually rewarded when he shows his sincerity by proposing an equitable marriage to her. In the second part of the novel, Pamela tries to adjust to upper-class society and build a successful relationship with her husband. The story is widely mocked for its perceived lewdness and inspires at least two parodies.

At this time, printing requires the permission of the colonial government. Many printers are imprisoned, including Ben Franklin's brother, for what they publish.

1776 Anti-British sentiment reaches a climax as pamphlets stir dissent. The most famous pamphlet is *Common Sense* by Thomas Paine. Published anonymously, it sells 120,000 copies in the first three months after release, even though there are only 400,000 adults in the U.S. This means more than one out of four people buy a copy. It is a best-seller, not just in the colonies but in Europe as well. More than any other publication it may be described as the writing that sparks the American Revolution, putting the blame for the suffering of the colonies directly on the reigning British monarch, George III.

Born in England, Paine was fired from his job as an excise officer because he started fighting for higher wages. Paine's immigration to America in 1774 was sponsored by none other than Benjamin Franklin. In Philadelphia, Paine became a journalist and essayist.

1860   *Dime novels* become available for ten cents a copy. The first stories are about Indians and pioneers.

Early 1900s — Book sales take off because of lower costs and greater literacy. Classics from the 1800's fuel the fire, like *The Scarlet Letter* (1850), *Moby Dick* (1851) and *Huckleberry Finn* (1884).

1935   Inexpensive *paperback* versions of successful hardcover books begin coming out.

1939   Ernest Vincent Wright ties down his typewriter's letter E key, so he can't use it while writing a book called *Gadsby*. According to *Mental Floss* magazine, the 50,000-word novel did not contain the letter E except in the introduction and a note at the end. Wright believed that a great author could work around just about any restriction. He dies later this year.

1947   A group of ancient manuscripts written on papyrus and leather parchment are found in caves near the Dead Sea. The manuscripts containing portions of the Bible were written or copied between 250 B.C.E. and A.D. 68.

1960   Paperback books surpass hardcover book sales. Today, about 2 of 3 books sold in the U.S. are paperbacks.

1971   Work begins at the *University of Illinois* on the first digital library called *Project Gutenberg*.

Activist Abbie Hoffman releases *Steal This Book* and many people do. It's one of the most stolen library books and he doesn't mind. It includes information on stealing credit cards and growing marijuana with the intention of bringing down capitalism. The book becomes a best-seller, making an embarrassed Hoffman a successful capitalist himself.

1988   Police attempt to arrest Vietnam vet Gustav Hasford for book theft on the same night he attends the Oscars (he co-wrote *Full Metal Jacket* which was up for an Academy Award). Hasford accumulated some $3,000 in fines from 87 overdue books taken out of a California library. Those missing volumes along with 10,000 books stolen from libraries around the world are later found in his storage unit. Hasford doesn't win an Oscar that year and the bibliophile is later sentenced to six months in prison for his crime.

1995   Jeff Bezos launches online book retailer *Amazon* out of his garage in Bellevue, Washington. His parents sink a substantial portion of their life savings into the effort. "We weren't betting on the Internet," his mother would later say. "We were betting on Jeff." By the end of the decade, Jeff's parents are billionaires.

1998   J. K. Rowling's *Harry Potter and the Sorcerer's Stone* arrives in the U.S. It is released a year earlier in the UK as *Harry Potter and the Philosopher's Stone*.

2002   A Japanese man publishes the first cell phone novel. *Deep Love* tells the story of a teenage prostitute in Tokyo. It becomes so popular that it is eventually printed in book form and sells several million copies. It is adapted for film, television and comics.

2006   The *Sony Reader* becomes the first electronic reader (or e-reader) introduced in the U.S. It is followed the next year by *Amazon's Kindle*.

2009   Massachusetts prep school, *Cushing Academy*, decides to rid itself of more than 20,000 books, replacing its library with a digital learning center. The headmaster tells the *Boston Globe*, "When I see books, I see outdated technology."

New York University announces plans to digitize all of its holdings in its main library.

Amazon sells more digital books than paperback books on Christmas Day.

2010   Stanford University builds a new engineering library with 85% fewer books on the shelves after a survey shows the vast majority of the previous collection had not been taken off the shelves in five years. The library director says he anticipates one day not having any books at all.

Books Today
READING THE CLASSICS

St. John's College believes in the classics so much, that its curriculum is based solely on classic works. No modern textbooks are used. Its students are required to read what are considered to be the important works of Western civilization, from Aristotle to Einstein.

Reading classic books can bring memorable characters to life and is still worthwhile even if you don't love the material. Exposing yourself to great writing puts great ideas by great minds in your head and develops a better understanding of effective communication. Reading a wide variety of books sharpens your critical thinking skills.

Books are valuable for the ideas they contain and how those ideas can mold our thinking and affect our actions. Reading fires the imagination, more than TV and film, which can be passive. The purchase and reading of books is much more an individual and personal activity than consuming the advertiser-supported media.

Exposing yourself to great writing puts great ideas by great minds in your head...

Here are some recent books that have had an impact on my thinking:

• *Hope for the Flowers* by Trina Paulus (a children's book about hope)
• *The Road Less Traveled* by M. Scott Peck (a psychologist writes about growth)
• *Love in the Western World* by Denis De Rougemont (the myth of romantic love)

- *Predictably Irrational* by Dan Ariely (our decision-making is not always rational)
- *The Black Swan* by Nassim Taleb (the impact of the highly improbable)

In Taleb's *The Black Swan*, his chapter entitled *The Narrative Fallacy* suggests an idea that's relevant to journalism.

> "If I asked you how many cases of lung cancer are likely to take place in the country, you would supply some number, say half a million. Now, if instead I asked you how many cases of lung cancer are likely to take place because of smoking, odds are that you would give me a much higher number (I would guess more than twice as high). Adding the because makes these matters far more plausible and far more likely. Cancer from smoking seems more likely than cancer without a cause attached to it — an unspecified cause means no cause at all."

When a narrative is added to a set of facts, we tend to think the events described are more likely to have happened. Humans are wired to attach significance to information wrapped in stories. This is why journalists should put a face on articles and TV stories. Show the audience who is being impacted by the story and why. Give readers and viewers a reason to care about those numbers, committee votes and public initiatives. The audience will stay engaged if you take them beyond a list of dry facts and figures to the emotion at the heart of a story.

Humans are wired to attach significance to information wrapped in stories.

WHO'S READING

A 2002 *National Endowment for the Arts* survey found the number of American adults who read a book in the previous 12 months was about 115 million. This was a little *less* than half of all Americans at that time. In 2008, the number increased to 119 million, which is a little *more* than half the population (there were about 19 million more Americans by 2008).

While 54% of all Americans in the 2008 survey say they read for pleasure, the numbers for college-age adults 18-24 drops about four percentage points.

Are you proud of your reading habits? Why or why not?

BANNING BOOKS

Ray Bradbury's futuristic classic, *Fahrenheit 451*, depicts a time when all books have been banned. Readers memorize passages because possession of a book is a crime. Existing books are set on fire. Bradbury says he selected the title *Fahrenheit 451* because he believed that was the temperature at which book paper burns.

In January of 2010, a Southern California school district banned a dictionary from fourth and fifth grade classrooms after a parent complained about a child possibly reading the definition for oral sex. Merriam Webster's 10th edition was quickly returned to bookshelves after an outcry from around the country.

An Indianapolis school board suspended a teacher after she assigned students *The Freedom*

Writers Diary before getting approval from administrators. The collection of essays written by teenagers contains profanity and sexual overtones. The teacher said she tried to obtain the proper authorization, but frustrated with not getting an official answer for months, she went to the students' parents and received written permission from 149 of them, with one objection. The book was eventually made into a movie.

Pause for Discussion: Censorship or Education?

Was the teacher right in using the book or should she have worked only within the system? Is this more a case of school board censorship or of insubordination by the teacher?

WHAT BOOKS DO FOR CULTURE

- Books *foster social change*, like *Uncle Tom's Cabin* by Harriet Beecher Stowe. Our defenses are down when we read stories, making us more open to new ways of thinking.

- Books *contain facts*. Encyclopedias give us a place to check the truth. When *Scrabble* players debate a word, they grab a dictionary to settle the dispute. Books build a common body of knowledge that can be shared across generations.

- Books *provide windows into the past*. They reflect the time in which the author lived better than the electronic media can do in movies. What would do a better job of transporting you back into Jane Austen's 18th-century world described in *Pride and Prejudice*: watching the 1995 or 2006 films based on the book or actually reading her book itself?

- Books *encourage personal development*. *Our Bodies, Ourselves* is an example. This early 1970's book helped women make more informed decisions about their health care.

A classic is something that everybody wants to have read but nobody wants to read.
—Mark Twain

Besides social change, books make a remarkable difference in the lives of people. Sociologists at the University of Nevada reviewed 20 years of data on 73,000 people and found a child born into a family of average education but with 500 books in the house would, on average get three more years of education that a child in a home with no books.

CHALLENGED BOOKS

In common-law tradition, censorship refers specifically to the government's prior restraint of publication. Identifying a book as *challenged* is a broader concern since it includes books already published. Since 1982, the *American Library Association* has kept a list of books frequently challenged by private citizens to keep out of public libraries or schools. Most of the challenges concern the appropriateness of the books for school children.

The ALA list of Top Ten challenged books from 2007 and 2008 include:

- *The Gossip Girl* series, by Cecily von Ziegesar
- *The Kite Runner*, by Khaled Hosseini
- *The Golden Compass*, by Philip Pullman
- *The Adventures of Huckleberry Finn*, by Mark Twain

- *The Color Purple*, by Alice Walker

Can you imagine any situation in which censorship would be justified?

The protectors of Margaret Mitchell's *Gone With the Wind* tried to stop publication of Alice Randall's book *The Wind Done Gone* which tells the story from a slave's point of view. Lawyers for the Mitchell trust argued Randall borrowed passages, characters, and her plot from *Gone With the Wind*, violating the copyright of Mitchell's 1936 classic about the Civil War. A judge agreed and blocked publication, but an appeals court overruled him, saying it amounted to "unlawful prior restraint in violation of the First Amendment." The lawsuit continued, even as the book was published and spent weeks on best-seller lists. Randall said her work was nothing more than a parody featuring a unique perspective from Scarlett O'Hara's slaves. After a year, a settlement was reached where a contribution to a historically black school in Atlanta was made by Randall's publisher.

BOOK BURNING

Does book burning still take place today? In June, 2008, members and supporters of several churches in Shreveport, Louisiana gathered to toss copies of Harry Potter books and pornography into a fire. About 30 people showed up.

Members of *Grace Baptist Church* in Canton, North Carolina gathered on Halloween, 2009 to burn Bibles that were not the *King James Version*, as well as music and books from evangelical authors like Rick Warren and Billy Graham because the authors have used Bibles other than the *King James Version*.

Can you think of a situation in which book burning would be justified? How about this one: A used book store owner in Kansas City, Missouri discovered he couldn't even give away some of his books to libraries and thrift stores. His solution: create a bonfire for books to protest our society's decreasing respect for the printed word. He told the crowd that gathered, "This is the funeral pyre for thought in America today." After about 50 minutes, the fire department showed up and put out the blaze.

Was the book store owner making a bold statement by turning the act of book burning on its head or was he doing the very thing he was supposedly protesting against?

Book Trends

BOOK TREND: HOLLYWOODIZATION

The book publishing industry is entwined with the global media and entertainment industry. Mergers and acquisitions in the industry (leaving *Barnes & Noble* and *Amazon* standing above the rest) have driven publishing into the arms of the entertainment giants. Besides lowering costs this puts companies such as *Viacom*, *Time Warner* and *News Corp* in a better position to develop material that has both book and film potential. They can turn more profit from books that become movies than from best-sellers than remain only print products.

BOOK TREND: PRINT-ON-DEMAND

Writers no longer must depend on publishers. Using inexpensive technology, print-on-demand developed in the late 1990s. Color laser processing allows the printing of as many or as few books as the author desires. A number of companies now offer as little or as much help as a writer wants. *Amazon* offers self-publishing services through *CreateSpace. Author Solutions* is one of the largest self-publishers operating *iUniverse, AuthorHouse, Trafford Publishing, Xlibris* and *Wordclay.*

BOOK TREND: BOOKS ON THE INTERNET

Time spent reading tripled between 1980 and 2008, according to a study conducted at the University of California at San Diego.

The image of bookstores was revitalized by the addition of coffee and snack bars, cushioned chairs and sofas. Now booksellers are grappling not only with falling consumer spending, but heavy competition from online booksellers. The Internet is changing the way books are distributed and sold. New technology is giving writers fresh outlets in the form of *e-publishing* (the publication of books initially or exclusively online), and *d-books* (books downloaded in electronic form from the Internet to a computer or handheld PDA).

Here's what online readers are saying they enjoy most:

> Mysteries 46%
> Other Fiction 40%
> Thrillers 32%
> Science Fiction 29%
> Romance 23%
> Source: *National Endowment for the Arts*

You can't tell a book by its cover if there isn't one.

One of the reasons romance titles are popular in electronic editions may be that e-readers have no cover displaying the owner's particular guilty pleasure.

This also means publishers will lose sales that come from seeing several people reading the same title. You can't tell a book by its cover if there isn't one. Makers may add functions to allow users to show what they are reading in public.

Google says it wants to create the library of the future by bringing millions of books online in a massive Manhattan Project of cultural digitization. The search giant plans to scan orphaned and out-of-print books and sell them online and create a research program to explore the digital humanities using the *Google Book* library. The company has digitized more than 12 million books in over 300 languages. The effort has slowed because of two class-action lawsuits filed by U.S. authors and publishers. At this writing, a proposed settlement is being considered by a New York judge. Through its *Google Editions* store, the company already offers digital editions of books from publishers with which it has distribution deals. Meanwhile, the *Internet Archive* has created a system for helping people find digital books on the Internet. The service is called *BookServer.*

BOOK TREND: DIGITIZED BOOKS

Many people don't enjoy reading on computers because a backlit screen causes eye fatigue. The Internet is a grazing medium. Books tend to be a longer-term experience. Enter the electronic book (e-reader) and tablets (like the *iPad*). You can download books, daily newspapers and magazines. Unlike printed newspapers that require paper milled from many trees, e-readers are environmentally friendly. The digital revolution is rewriting the rules of the book industry.

A decade ago, *Wired* magazine cofounder Kevin Kelly pitched publishers with the idea of writing a book proclaiming reading is dead. He's since changed his mind, according to *Fortune* magazine. Instead, Kelly predicts reading will change forms "embedded into screens that are full of moving images… like subtitles in a movie." That's what readers are getting from some digital devices.

The first two e-readers to hit the market were the *Sony Reader* which has been out since 2006 and the *Kindle*, produced by *Amazon*. Both are designed to make the electronic reading experience more like that of traditional books. Forrester Research estimates that by the end of 2008, *Amazon* and *Sony* had combined sales of one million e-readers in the U.S. The lesser known *Cool-er* doesn't view magazines or newspapers but holds 800 books and is less expensive. The *Sony Reader Pocket Edition* is even smaller and less expensive, but holds only 350 books. Newspaper publisher Hearst Corp. developed its own e-reader called *Skiff* and then sold it to *News Corp* in 2010.

If you want something smaller than an e-reader, lots of sites offer classics for your cell phone for free, and many others charge only 99 cents. A hot new book might cost you the cover price, but you can find plenty of book downloads for your iPhone and other devices for practically nothing. Plus, it's environmentally friendly. No trees are harmed during the production.

Electronic books accounted for just 1.3% of the approximately $23.9 billion made in U.S. book sales during 2009, according to the *Association of American Publishers*. Still, that was 176.6% over the previous year. E-books are forcing authors, publishers, and retailers to reinvent their business models. For the first time, *Amazon* sold more digital books than paper books on Christmas Day, 2009. *Idea Logical Co.* predicts digital books could make up as much as half of all sales by the end of 2012. Some observers believe that in just a few years nearly all college text books will be delivered to students through some sort of digital device like an e-reader.

In early 2010, Apple introduced its *iPad*, provides a reading experience like an e-reader. Apple's *iPad* bookstore will operate as a storefront for book publishers, with Apple taking a 30% bite out of each sale. Book lovers wanting to read will prefer the lighter and less expensive e-readers, but most users will want to do more than just read. This is where the iPad's appealing video experience may succeed. Read more about it in the chapter on magazines.

Are books as we know them going away? *Amazon* founder Jeff Bezos told *The Wall Street Journal's* D Conference, "Physical books won't go away, just as horses won't go away. But in the future the majority of books will be read electronically." Less optimistic is Jaron Lanier who writes in his book *You Are Not a Gadget* that the process will splinter the information into fragments, obscuring the context and authorship of each fragment. In the end, Lanier tells us, there will be only one book.

For Next Time

What do you read first when you pick up a newspaper? Which section gets your attention? What do you never bother to read? Most students say they read the front page headline. After that, they may dive into the Sudoku, cartoons or sports — if they take the time to read a newspaper at all.

J B

Newspapers

Newspapers Timeline

Photo courtesy Library of Congress

1690   Boston bookseller and printer Benjamin Harris prints the first daily newspaper. *Publick Occurrences Both Foreign and Domestick* lasts one edition. Four days after it appears, the governor and council of Massachusetts issue an order forbidding its publication. What did they find objectionable in the paper? *Publick Occurrences* spoke about "barbarous" human rights abuses and a sex scandal involving the King of France. The paper reported that the monarch was said to "lie" with his daughters-in-law.

1704   *The Boston News-Letter* becomes the first newspaper to publish multiple issues.

1721   Ben Franklin's brother, James, is jailed for printing scandalous libels.

1729   Ben Franklin takes over a failing newspaper in Philadelphia and renames it *The Pennsylvania Gazette.*

1734   The publisher of the *New York Weekly Journal* is jailed for criticizing the governor. In a landmark decision, a jury acquits publisher John Peter Zenger. His defense is that truth triumphs accusations of libel. The role of a free press begins taking shape in the American colonies. While her husband spent time behind bars, Anna Catherine Zenger took over the paper, becoming one of the first women newspaper publishers in the country.

1783   *The Pennsylvania Evening Post* becomes America's first daily newspaper. It lasts only 17 months.

1787   Thomas Jefferson writes, "Were it left to me to decide whether we should have a government without newspapers, or newspapers without a government, I should not hesitate a moment to prefer the latter."

1801   There are about 20 daily newspapers in the U.S.

1808   The first Spanish-language newspaper in the U.S., *El Misisipi* begins publication in New Orleans in both English and Spanish. The first issue covers Napoleon's invasion of Spain.

1827   The first African-American-owned newspaper is published under the banner, *Freedom's Journal.* On the front page is written, "We wish to plead our own cause. Too long have others spoken for us." *Freedom's Journal* was published weekly in New York City. It included the biographies of prominent African-Americans; international, national, and regional news; and editorials about slavery, lynching, and other injustices. *Freedom's Journal circulated* in 11 states, Haiti, Canada and Europe.

1830   Tabloid-style newspapers are referred to as the penny press. News is written to appeal to the lowest common denominator.

1840   Margaret Fuller becomes the first female journalist hired by a major U.S. daily, *The New York Tribune.*

1847   An African-American newspaper called the *North Star* begins publication under the direction of editor Frederick Douglass.

1848   Six New York papers pool efforts to collect news from people disembarking from foreign ships in New York harbor.

1851   *The New York Times* debuts for a penny a copy.

1856   The group of six newspapers mentioned above becomes the first news-gathering and distribution organization, the *New York Associated Press.*

The first Native American newspaper, the *Cherokee Phoenix*, begins publication in Georgia and the first daily African-American newspaper, the *New Orleans Daily Creole*, begins publication in the Crescent City.

1887   Stunt journalist Nellie Bly pretends to be insane in order to write a story about the Women's Lunatic Asylum in an effort to get a job at a New York paper owned by Joseph Pulitzer. Her tactics prove wildly successful and are imitated by other reporters in her day. These antics are considered inappropriate by today's papers.

1880   The U.S. Census counts more than 11,000 newspapers. By 2006, the number drops to only 2,344.

1900   The *Associated Press* wire service is established. Many stories printed in the newspaper or read on *CNN* and *FOX News* originate from the AP. The name "wire service" comes from the way in which stories were first distributed: telephone wire. Members of the *Associated Press*, such as *USA Today, Yahoo Finance* and *CNN*, pay annual fees for the right to use AP-produced stories and photos. The members also provide some of their own stories to the AP for use by other members.

Early 1900's   Yellow Journalism (a name derived from a popular cartoon called *The Yellow Kid*) becomes popular. Newspapers owned by William Randolph Hearst and Joseph Pulitzer fight over the strip and eventually feature different versions of *Yellow Kid* drawn by different cartoonists. The term becomes synonymous with what the two papers emphasized at the time: sensational sex, crime, and disaster news.

1905   *The Chicago Defender* starts publishing. The African-American paper reaches a remarkable circulation of 280,000 in 15 years and is banned throughout the South. At least two of the paper's distributors are murdered.

1907   *United Press* begins operation.

1947   Newspapers begin experimenting with fax editions.

1952   In the film, *Deadline U.S.A,* Humphrey Bogart plays a newspaper editor whose struggling paper is on the auction block. "It's not enough any more to give 'em just news," Bogart rants. "They want comics, contests, puzzles. They want to know how to bake a cake, win friends and influence the future. Ergo, horoscopes, tips on the horses, interpretation of dreams so they can win on the numbers lottery. And, if they accidentally stumble on the first page, news!"

1972   *The Washington Post* breaks the Watergate scandal, leading to the resignation of President Nixon.

1981   The plight of an 8-year-old heroin addict wins Janet Cooke and *The Washington Post* a Pulitzer Prize, until it is revealed the story is not true.

1982   Gannett Co. launches *USA Today*. Its colorful graphics and easy-to-read sections filled with short stories are inspired by television. A decade will pass before the paper becomes profitable.

1983   *The Knight Ridder* newspaper chain starts offering expensive, online news terminals on which you can read news stories. More than a dozen daily newspapers play with the technology, called *Viewtron,* for several years, but can't make enough money to justify its continued use.

1994   A strike shuts down San Francisco's daily newspapers. Strikers and management create rival dailies on the Web: *The Free Press,* and *The Gate.* These are among the first pure Web newspapers in the U.S.

2008   Microsoft CEO Steve Ballmer predicts that with some exceptions, "There will be no newspapers, no magazines, that are delivered in paper form" by 2020.

2009   The number of newspaper editorial employees falls to 40,000, according to *The New York Times.* That's about the same as in 1971 after reaching a high of 60,000 in 1992. *The Project for Excellence in Journalism* estimates the newspaper industry's annual reporting and editing capacity is down 30% since 2000.

Newspapers Today

During this nation's history, the printed news has provided citizens with information about their community and government. Reading your local newspaper helped to make you an informed citizen.

The surveillance role is probably the most important function of a newspaper.

The Newseum, a Washington Museum dedicated to news, provides a way to look at the front pages of newspapers across the country each day. Readers can view a gallery of newspaper front pages at *Newseum.org*, or use a map of the U.S. that shows local newspapers as a user's mouse rolls over the city of origin.

COLLEGE PAPERS

Some of the most motivated college students can be found at their campus newspaper. These go-getters understand the need to not only make decent grades, but to create a track record of what they can do. During job interviews, applicants will be asked to provide samples (articles, videos, audio, photographs) of work in support of what their degree says they can do. Student media is a great place to sharpen the skills learned in the classroom and create examples of your talents.

During job interviews, applicants will be asked to provide samples of work in support of what their degree says they can do.

When students make mistakes on tests and papers, the professor is typically the only person who sees the errors. But when those in student media make mistakes, the whole campus, and now through the Internet the whole world, knows about it. The pressure to perform under deadline and constant scrutiny gives students a chance to see what the "real world" will be like and make their mistakes before entering the field professionally. Here are some examples of headlines and leads that the student writer probably wishes to take back.

A female faculty member had won a prestigious grant from the National Endowment for the Sciences. The student reporter didn't finish writing the story until 3 a.m. when she wrote the unfortunate headline: "(Name of instructor) is well endowed."

Brigham Young University's *The Daily Universe* once captioned a photo from the Latter Day Saints General Conference that read: "Members of the Quorum of the Twelve Apostates and other general authorities raise their hands in a sustaining vote Saturday morning..." Of course, it should have been "Apostles."

A few years ago, a reporter wrote a story about a community meeting led by the mayor. It began, "The mayor said at yesterday's pubic meeting..."

One college newspaper headline read, "1 Dead; 9 Killed in Pileup."

In September, 2009, *Harvard University's* campus newspaper ran an advertisement questioning the reality of the Holocaust. *The Harvard Crimson* later said it was published in error.

The student newspaper at *Brown University* found itself embroiled in controversy, not from a typo but an ad. The paid advertisement in *The Brown Daily Herald* was titled, "Ten Reasons Why Reparations for Slavery is a Bad Idea—and Racist Too." Some students said the ad was offensive and should never have run. Others called it an issue of free speech and censorship. Student protestors at the Providence, Rhode Island school swiped all the newspapers they could find and pounded on the doors of the *Herald's* offices, demanding the staff, which had barricaded itself inside, turn over the few remaining copies and publish for free an article against the ad.

Pause for Discussion: Fighting the Good Fight?

Would you have run these ads? Were the students right to take newspapers? To get into the newspaper's office? What are the pros and cons of a newspaper taking an active role on an issue? Is it ever a good idea for college journalists to take up a cause and fight for it in print?

Journalism Gone Wrong

The New York *Daily News* headline read, "Sugar as Addictive as Cocaine, Heroin, Studies Suggest," and the first paragraph told readers, "…sugar — as anyone who mainlines sweets can attest — can be just as habit-forming as cocaine." Really?

This sounds dramatic, but it is completely misleading. The main study cited in the article involved rats and only suggested sugar can have some of the same effects as hard drugs (such as withdrawal symptoms). That's a long way from saying it is as habit-forming or that the research applies to humans.

Here's another headline to ponder. "Bras Shown to Cause Cancer." The info in this story was based on an old 1991 study that was inconclusive and an outdated 1995 book that the American Cancer Society says is scientifically unsound.

The makers of a 2009 documentary called *Starsuckers* fed Britain's competitive tabloid press phony news tips to see whether the information would be disseminated without fact-checking. Sure enough, the false stories about Amy Winehouse (a blown fuse singed her signature hairdo) and Guy Ritchie (received a black eye while attempting to juggle knives) were printed. These blunders form the basis of the movie's theme, that the culture of celebrity has undermined social values and journalistic standards. Dignity and truth are left behind in the pursuit of popular figures.

What are the pros and cons of a newspaper taking an active role on an issue?

Is this typical of news outlets? Do they hype or completely misrepresent medical news because they don't understand the information or just because they want to attract more viewers? A *Pew Research* survey found that less than a third of Americans (29%) say news organizations "generally get the facts straight," while nearly two-thirds say they believe news stories are often inaccurate (63%) and politically biased (60%).

Pause for Discussion: Faking It

Jayson Blair was a *New York Times* reporter who admitted lying about many of his stories and plagiarizing his work. What was the first lie? Blair made up the name of a source. One little word. Then it snowballed. It's the small omissions that lead one astray, making it easier to justify doing something bigger. Blair had to be a very good writer to earn his position at *The New York Times*, but he took a chance and threw away his career just to make it easier on himself. And what's Blair doing today? He's become a life coach.

Do you think what Blair did is common in the news media or a cautionary tale that sticks out because it is an exception to the rule?

Civic Journalism

In the 1987 movie *Broadcast News*, an anchorman is told he had "crossed the line" and lost his objectivity for crying during an interview with a date rape victim. "The line," he blasts. "They keep moving the little sucker!"

Not all journalists strive to remain unbiased. Some journalists advocate interpretive reporting which tries to explain the story by placing the facts into a broader context. This stands in contrast to *objective journalism* (or empirical journalism) where reporters try to inform the public without taking sides. A step further away from objective reporting is *civic journalism* (also known as *advocacy* or *public journalism*), where reporters take up a just cause and serve as the voice of a community's conscience.

Civic Journalism is what journalism students at *Northwestern University* are doing in the *Innocence Project*. Started in 1999, it gives undergraduate students firsthand experience in investigating wrongful convictions. Anthony Porter was less than 50 hours from execution before being exonerated with evidence developed by the *Project*. He was released from death row February 5, 1999 and promptly hugged the professor and students involved in his release. This is what supporters of civic journalism talk about when they say they want to make a difference.

In the balanced view, the media are looked on as a public utility like the power company.

Publishers in the early days of America made no pretense of objectivity. Each political party had its own paper touting its own agenda. The partisan press filled publications with anonymous stories about political figures. As the *Associated Press* expanded and began gathering news for more papers with varying political viewpoints, it needed to publish neutral reports. This helped to put forward the goal of impartial journalism.

Do newspapers and broadcasters have the right to show bias? In the balanced view, the media are looked on as a public utility like the power company. According to the *theory of social responsibility*, the media hold a public trust and have a civic duty to remain neutral.

An Atlanta alternative newspaper fired a veteran news reporter in February, 2010 for trying to be objective. The editor of the *Atlanta Progressive News* says Jonathan Springston was let go because he insisted on clinging to the "notion that there was an objective reality that could be reported objectively."

Here are some criticisms against the effort to be unbiased:

> It can't be done. No one can really be objective.
>
> It prevents journalists from advocating a pro-public stance.
>
> It doesn't allow journalists to decide the most important stories to pass along.
>
> It encourages passivity among reporters.
>
> It lends credibility to debunked and extremist views.
>
> It doesn't allow for give and take with the audience.
>
> The public assumes bias and the pretext of objectivity is deceptive.
>
> There is disagreement over the definition of objective journalism.

Those who support objective journalism could say it is the *method* that should be objective and not the *journalist*. Because we cannot achieve complete objectivity does not prove it is not a worthy goal. The American journalistic standard arrived with the scientific method, and like the scientist aiming to discover the truth, having some bias does not mean he cannot arrive at the truth through a tested and effective approach.

Newspaper Trends

NEWSPAPER TREND: CITIZEN JOURNALISM

More than eight out of ten Americans have a mobile phone, according to the *International Association for Wireless Telecommunication*. The BBC says there are an estimated two billion camera phones in circulation worldwide. All those devices mean someone, an average citizen or group of citizens, will likely be armed with the means to rapidly transmit vivid images of news as it happens. When they step into the role of journalist we call it *citizen journalism*.

Citizen journalism may not be the best term for this trend because it suggests a limitation by placing what is emerging in relation to what has gone before, something like "horse-less carriage." Perhaps *civic media* may be more useful, in that it suggests a more actively engaged citizenship. Some prefer *participatory journalism* or *pro-am journalism* (professional-amateur) to underscore the blend of reader contributions with traditional reporting

There's a sense in which citizen journalism turns professional editors into *journalism citizens*. It has blurred professional journalists' sense of identity. They no longer hold the powerful place in the news information system that they once held. New York University professor Clay Shirky says the traditional media are based on a "filter, then publish" model while new media often operates on a "publish, then filter" model.

Supporters of *user-generated content* say it empowers the little guy, while detractors claim you won't see the same kind of sustained digging you get from investigative journalism's professional and well-trained operations.

Most newspaper and broadcast news editors say American journalism is in decline. A Pew Research Center survey also found about half of them believe their employers will go out of business in the next few years if they do not find new sources of revenue.

Regardless of where the news business is going, citizen journalists are having an impact. The effects of the 2004 Indian Ocean tsunami were so widespread, traditional journalists couldn't immediately cover it all. But those living where the disaster struck, along with many of the tourists who survived, dispersed images of the devastation.

Few of the images reaching us now that show protests in faraway lands are taken by professional journalists. The demonstrations in the days following the disputed 2009 Iranian presidential election were seen around the world, thanks to images provided by protestors. The foreign press was kept away from the rallies, but protesters filmed and photographed the events themselves.

Social media played an important role during January, 2010, in spreading news about the Haiti earthquake. Reporters on the ground enriched their coverage with user-generated content which partly made up for the lack of information coming from the affected areas.

Some sites are now devoted to citizen journalism, such as *Orato.com*. The name of the site comes from Latin for "I speak." Started in 2005, *Orato* "encourages anyone to publish their own experiences with newsworthy events." AOL is offering a citizen journalism approach on its site called *Patch* and while *The Huffington Post* employs a 70 member editorial staff, the site depends on 6,000 uncompensated bloggers.

Citizen journalism platform *AllVoices* received $3 million in funding in January, 2010 from *VantagePoint Partners*. The site lets its community of 275,000 citizen reporters file from their smart phones.

Related to citizen journalism is *open source reporting*. This moves the public even further into the newsroom by revealing story ideas early in the reporting process and inviting their input.

NEWSPAPER TREND: GLOBALIZATION

One way newsrooms are saving money is outsourcing work to parts of the world where labor is cheaper than in the U.S. *The Miami Herald* and *The Sacramento Bee* began sending some of their advertising production work to India in 2007. The next year, the *Herald* and *The Orange County Register* began outsourcing part of their copy editing and design to a company based in New Delhi. Chapter one offered an unusual example of outsourcing. An advertisement asked for someone in India to cover city council meetings for a website devoted to news in Pasadena.

NEWSPAPER TREND: CONVERGENCE

Many in the industry have resisted the digital change, reminiscent of a 1930's *New York Times* editorial that complained the typewriter undermined the art of "writing with one's own hand." But there's no holding back the technology.

Most newspapers have reacted by focusing on cutbacks to save money. Stories, page count, sections, international and national news and the number of days of publication are all shrinking. There are fewer words on smaller, thinner pages. Some papers refuse delivery to distant suburbs. Many papers are focusing on local news and sports, letting wire services provide stories of national and international news. Along with science and general business reporters, car and film reviews have been pushed overboard.

Traditional newspapers are also trying to reinvent themselves by converging with the very technologies that threaten their existence. And there is some success for newspapers going online. *The New York Times* site draws 22 million visitors a month. Some 10% of the traffic comes from *Twitter*. *The Times* online edition attracts about ten times as many readers as the print edition. The problem, however, is that there are more places to advertise and reach the Internet crowd. Plus, online links obscure quality brand names that produce quality material like *The New York Times*. It is difficult for broad-based news publications that have traditionally relied on ink and paper to change the internal culture to digital. News operations that start as dot-coms have the advantage of being native to the Internet. The thinking and outlook of employees and management are more pliable and adapt more freely to the constant online change than organizations steeped in an understanding of effective communication from a generation ago.

Newspapers are encouraging community publishing — pages built by local schools, clubs, and nonprofit groups. Another localizing strategy is for online papers to build and maintain message boards and chat groups. Many papers have started their own blog sites, inviting readers and journalists to talk to one another. HD cameras are capable of producing a high-enough quality frame grab to run in the average daily newspaper. The *Dallas Morning News* and the *San Jose Mercury News* use them quite often. But the marriage of newspapers to the Web has not yet proven financially successful for the older medium.

The problem isn't that readers aren't willing to use online newspaper content; it's that a huge and important part of the audience, the young and Web-savvy, simply are not coming to newspaper sites. One reason young people don't gravitate to newspaper websites is that most function like a newspaper rather than the Web: static and not interactive. The numbers for newspaper sites are improving. They pulled in an average monthly audience of 72 million unique visitors in the last quarter of 2009, according to Nielson Online. That's an increase of more than 5% over the fourth quarter of the previous year. Newspapers still have the edge over local TV rivals for eyeballs. The *Media Audit* found the audience for major daily newspapers was bigger in 73 of 95 markets than local TV sites.

NEWSPAPER TREND: FALLING CIRCULATION AND REVENUE

While the average age of the newspaper reader is going up, circulation dropped more than 8% in the six months ending March 31, 2010, compared to the same period a year earlier, according to the *Audit Bureau of Circulation*. Some of this may be due to newspaper closures and not just decreasing readership. Among the top 25 newspapers, 10 had declines in weekday circulation of more than 10%.

The Pew Research Center says the Internet has passed newspapers to become the third most popular news platform, behind national and local TV news.

The bottom line isn't encouraging either.

Newspapers have never made much money from news. They've made money from the special interest sections on topics such as Automotive, Travel, Home & Garden, Food & Drink and so forth.

The Internet has cut into newspapers' bread and butter: classified ads. Someone living in a large city would most likely skip newspapers and first post an apartment to rent or car to sell on *Craigslist*. The site publishes about 40 million classified ads each month. At the same time, newspaper revenue from classified ads has fallen significantly, according to the *Associated Press*:

    2000 – $20 billion or 40% of revenue that year

When popular culture suggests an image of a dying industry, it can help to speed up the process of decline.

2008 - $10 billion or 25% of revenue that year

Nearly one-quarter of the newspaper industry's annual advertising sales evaporated between 2007 and 2009, according to *The Associated Press*. The income is not expected to go back up.

The *Associated Press* itself draws a great deal of its revenue from newspapers. About 1,500 newspapers are currently part of the AP, but the organization is losing members due to financial cutbacks. The wire service made around $700 million in 2009, down from $748 million in 2008.

An episode of FOX's long-running animated TV show *The Simpsons*, offered this comment on the state of newspapers. With derision in his voice, an animated Dan Rather introduces a "print journalist from *The Washington Post*." Neighborhood bully Nelson Muntz points at him and cries, "Ha, ha! Your medium is dying!" Principal Skinner yells at the student and scolds, "Nelson!" "But it is," Nelson pleads. Skinner doesn't disagree: "There's being right and there's being nice."

Comedian Stephen Colbert introduced an interview with a newspaper lobbyist by explaining to younger viewers that a newspaper is like "a blog that leaves ink on your hands and covers topics other than how much you love *Fall Out Boy*." During the interview, the *Newspaper Association of America* president tries to explain to Colbert why his industry is not dead while Colbert interrupts by coughing and wheezing, pretending to be a dying newspaper, and complaining about blood in his stool. Stephen Whitty, of the *Star-Ledger* writes, "The traditional newspaper reporter is a dinosaur and the tar pits are around the corner."

When popular culture suggests an image of a dying industry, it can help speed up the process of decline. Perceptions often become realities because the expectations of large groups are powerful.

If printed newspapers actually disappear from American life, it will not be any harder for teachers to explain them to young students than to explain a typewriter, a telegraph, or any other obsolete technology.

Perhaps newspapers are not completely dying but are in transition, becoming smaller, less culturally significant and less profitable organizations. The business model is a hard sell in a digital environment. Google offered this assessment to the FTC (Federal Trade Commission) regarding the loss of newspaper revenue:

> The large profit margins newspapers enjoyed in the past were built on an artificial scarcity: Limited choice for advertisers as well as readers. With the Internet, that scarcity has been taken away and replaced by abundance. No policy proposal will be able to restore newspaper revenues to what they were before the emergence of online news. It is not a question of analog dollars versus digital dimes, but rather a realistic assessment of how to make money in a world of abundant competitors and consumer choice.

How you approach newspapers' financial problems will differ depending on whether you assume we are losing a government watchdog essential to democracy or whether Americans are just losing one of many delivery systems for information. Some journalists who believe the former have called on the federal government to intervene, but most Americans oppose any kind of subsidy for newspapers from taxes or fees. A Rasmussen poll showed 84% of respondents rejected the idea of putting a 3% tax on mobile phone bills while 76% didn't like the idea of a tax on consumer electronics.

NEWSPAPER TREND: LAYOFFS

The presses literally stopped at nearly 150 newspapers in 2009. The *Chicago Sun-Times* declared bankruptcy in the first quarter 2009. At the same time, the *Seattle Post-Intelligencer* stopped printing. Even *The New York Times* is struggling.

The American Society of News Editors says 13,500 editorial jobs were cut at U.S. newspapers between 2007 and 2010. The *Gannett Company* (publisher of *USA Today*) cut 10,000 jobs during 2007 and 2008. In 2009, the firm eliminated 4,500 more U.S. newspaper jobs and cut salaries in its broadcast division. Major U.S. cities may soon have no community conversation in print.

Comedian Jon Stewart sent one of his *Daily Show* correspondents to *The Gray Lady* (a nickname for *The New York Times*) to question staffers why they preferred "aged news." The executive editor was asked, "What's black and white and red all over?" "A newspaper," he replied. "No. Your balance sheets." Ouch. Have newspapers become no more than documentation stuck in a moment of time?

Print journalists, dislodged from a salaried position, are scrambling to put together a freelance income while building their personal brand.

The shrinking newsroom has opened new doors for some journalism students. Several universities have arrangements with local newspapers to use the work of student journalists. *Florida International University* students are helping to fill the gap at *The Miami Herald*, *Palm Beach Post* and *South Florida Sun-Sentinel*.

NEWSPAPER TREND: AD REVENUE DOWN

Newspaper ad revenue (both print and online)

Year	Billions	% Change
2004	$48.2	4.50
2005	$49.4	2.47
2006	$49.3	-0.32
2007	$45.4	-7.90
2008	$34.7	-17.70
2009	$27.6	-27.20

Source: *The Newspaper Association of America (NAA)*

Advertising revenue fell more than 27% in 2009 for newspapers. Classified ads are down more than two-thirds since 2000.

Some hope that moving online will save newspapers, but online revenue, which had been growing by double digits, fell 1.8% in 2008 and more than 11% in 2009. Online ad revenue has started picking up again in 2010.

The news business is certainly in turmoil. But here's the good news: Where there is chaos, there is opportunity.

A survey by *Rasmussen Reports* found 65% of Americans say they expect daily newspapers will be gone in a decade and 17% say it will happen in three years. Considering only readers age 18-29, the number who expect newspapers to be extinct in ten years jumps to 83%.

Does this mean you should not go into journalism? The news business is certainly in turmoil. But here's the good news: Where there is chaos, there is opportunity. An uncertain situation leaves the door open to new possibilities for those who are adaptable.

The Bloomberg Model

Some observers expect some sort of *Bloombergization* of news. The Bloomberg news and data company creates its revenue by using news gathering to support the main goal of selling information terminals. Similarly, Microsoft builds Internet Explorer without the intention of making profits from the browser but to support the company's Windows operating system. The gathering of news and information by newspapers (which does not make a profit) may be worthwhile in situations where the effort supports some larger company goal.

Smallville

Small papers are suffering, though not as much as the big newspaper publishers. A media business analyst at the *Poynter Institute* in Florida says the circulation of community news-papers is holding up because of their in-depth coverage of local communities, while larger papers have trimmed local coverage because of budget cuts.

On average, eight out of ten people read a local weekly paper each week and share it with more than two other readers, according to *National Newspaper Association Readers*. Only about one out of ten say they read local news often-to-very often online and of those that do, most found local news on the local newspaper's website.

The survival of small town newspapers may be similar to how AM stations have survived in large cities. In cities like Atlanta, Chicago and LA there are AM stations among the top three in ratings. These are news-talk formats that reach commuters who want traffic, weather and local news. The formula doesn't have the same impact in smaller cities with different needs. Likewise, newspapers in small towns may be in a better position to survive because of the unique circumstances in which they operate. While sites dedicated to particular communities within large cities may find their niche, small cities may not be able to support such ventures, leaving the door open for papers that reflect the local culture. And there is less media competition.

A benefit of a paper connected with a newspaper chain over a small newspaper is its insulation from the decisions of a single advertiser or a small group of advertisers. When a critical advertiser makes a strong economic threat to reduce or stop advertising all together, a small paper may be tempted to compromise news coverage that might be critical of the advertisers.

Nonprofits

Nonprofit news organizations may sell their stories to a variety of outlets including radio, television, local Internet sites and newspapers rather than to only one news organization. These third-party vendors sell the journalism they produce and also raise funds from foundations, businesses and individuals. San Francisco's *Bay Citizen* is one example of this model in action. In a similar fashion, *Spot.Us* is a news site that raises funds from online readers to fund journalists to produce specific stories. Between 2006 and 2010, more than $140 million of nonprofit money has flowed into new media efforts, according to *J-Lab*.

NEWSPAPER TREND: ONLINE PAYMENTS

While people are paying for music downloads, video games, and fantasy sports information, there's a question of whether there is some content they simply won't pay to read, even small sums through *micropayments* (charging just a little bit a lot of times).

A 2009 *Forrester Research* study found there doesn't seem to be a one-size-fits-all solution for publishers looking at erecting a *pay wall* (payment is required before the site can be accessed). Researchers found 80% of those surveyed said they would not pay for online content. An *American Life Project* put the figure at 19%. Three months after erecting its pay wall, Long Island daily *Newsday* had only 35 subscribers. The *London Times* puts its content behind a $3-a-week pay wall and immediately lost all but 10% of its online readership.

Although 8% in the *Forrester* study preferred an online subscription and multichannel subscription, only 3% preferred micropayments. The impediment to either a subscription or micropayment system is that most websites do not have the names and credit card information of their users. New users would have to make a considered decision about whether to pay for the service. The cable and telephone companies are ahead of the game because they already possess the banking information of their customers and are ready for a metered payment system. Eventually, your phone may replace your credit card and keys to become your personal remote control to life. Another option may be in the works from *Google*. The search giant plans to launch a pay wall system for publishers, called *Google Checkout*, that will provide news organizations with the technology to build any type of subscription service.

According to the same survey, 11% of respondents thought their newspaper subscription was "surprisingly inexpensive" while 28% felt their newspaper subscription was too expensive.

A successful micropayment strategy may require a concerted effort from multiple papers grouped around a toll collector. Should publishers come to an agreement on a system for collecting payments, the effort may send up anti-trust red flags to regulators. There is also the possibility taking this route may only be trading print dollars for digital dimes.

If you are highly motivated to read financial news, perhaps you'll pay for *The Wall Street Journal* or *Consumer Reports Online*. These sites have carved out an important content niche, offer quality content that's original and created a compelling online presence. But would you be willing to pay for *USA Today* or *The Boston Globe*? It's worth a shot to see if folks want to pony up for the *Globe* but the motivation may not be there for general interest stories. And if readers, who've gotten used to free information, can still get bits of free information elsewhere, will they even be aware of what they are missing? Some will pay. So, it's a matter of whether the group that's willing to go for micropayments is large enough to keep things going for newspapers. Some sites, like *Consumer Reports* and *The Wall Street Journal*, have used the alternative subscription business model effectively. Those publications are focused on specific information for highly motivated groups. *E & E Publishing* is making a significant amount of money by selling environmental news to high interest clients without any social networking.

Despite the lingering questions about paying for online news, it's better to try than watch your product bleed online. The history of cable television offers some hope. In 1992, critics questioned whether HBO could survived as a paid cable network. Viewers had watched free television shows for years, yet the network not only survived but thrived and saw the rise of many imitators.

A new brand of media firm called *Content Farms* is based on the notion that neither online revenue from ads or subscriptions will cover the cost of reporting, so journalists will simply have to accept less pay. Critics say Content Farms force freelancers to take on more work than is reasonably possible, thus swamping the Internet with mediocre content.

NEWSPAPER TREND: TABLETS

Newspaper enthusiasts are hoping tablets, like Apple's *iPad*, will herald a new day for publishing. Apple founder Steve Jobs fanned the flames of enthusiasm when he said, "Anything that we can do to help the news-gathering organizations find new ways of expression so that they can afford to keep their news-gathering and editorial operations intact, I'm all for."

The *iPad* vividly displays newspapers, books, websites and videos. Critics deride the device as simply an oversized *iPod Touch*. But sales are brisk. Apple reportedly sold two million units in the first two months of release. Others are on the way. Hewlett-Packard and Dell are expected to put out less expensive tablets soon.

Tablet sales could eat into sales of laptops (the industry's biggest profit maker) and challenge Microsoft's dominance because manufacturers are embracing mobile operating systems for the new devices.

In the next few years, we are likely to consume news on a colorful and mobile personal device offering stories that are incremental to what we read, rather than just repetitive or random. The device will know the identity of our friends and what they are reading and what they think is important. Its GPS and radio network will know what is going on around us and will tie this information to the news we receive as well as its targeted display ads.

...even if newspapers begin delivering material in a smooth block of glass and metal it seems unlikely readers will be persuaded by shiny and flickering lights to suddenly start paying for the same old content in a significant way.

However, even if newspapers begin delivering material in a smooth block of glass and metal it seems unlikely readers will be persuaded by shiny and flickering lights to suddenly start paying for the same old content in a significant way. Newspapers often fail to produce enough distinctive work to convince readers it's worth paying as much for. Look for a push from papers toward more locally-focused and more clearly-defined topics. The economics will make it a necessity for survival.

MY ADVICE: WEAR SUNSCREEN

Before writing off newspapers as a lost cause, consider how old and new media may work together.

A *Chicago Tribune* columnist wrote a piece in the late 1990's that's become known as *Wear Sunscreen*. She imagined what advice she might give to students at a commencement. It starts like this:

> Ladies and gentlemen of the class of '97: Wear sunscreen. If I could offer you only one tip for the future, sunscreen would be it. The long-term benefits of sunscreen have been proved by scientists, whereas the rest of my advice has no basis more reliable than my own meandering experience. I will dispense this advice now.

She goes on to present some common sense advice that rang true with readers, like "Don't be reckless with other people's hearts. Don't put up with people who are reckless with yours." The article made the rounds in an email, wrongly attributed to American novelist Kurt Vonnegut, Jr. as an address to a graduating college class at an Ivy League school.

The message was intensified when it was set to music, renamed *Everybody's Free (To Wear Sunscreen)* and released on an album by an Australian film director. One of Brazil's biggest advertising agencies added video. The result is remarkable. You can watch it on *YouTube* by searching for *sunscreen*.

Perhaps this is our future. Various creators around the globe (Chicago, Australia and Brazil) come together to build on the work of the other (text, music, video) in order to make a bigger impact.

Step out of the comfort zone to discover your own passion. Take ownership over your career and future.

Echoing the sentiment in the *Sunscreen* column, let me encourage every student to step out of the comfort zone to discover your own passion. Take ownership over your career and future. Not only will people pay you money for what you enjoy doing, you'll be able to genuinely approach it with enthusiasm. If you only slide by, you'll wind up taking what you can get in order to pay bills. And you may be miserable.

Many middle-aged people are sad and disappointed with their lives. It started in college when they passively took tests, did the "required" work but didn't launch out. They missed their best chance to figure out what they were good at doing. Don't look back and go, "I *wonder* what would have happened if I had tried that thing that I wasn't sure about but *really* wanted to try." Open yourself up to paradigm shifts. And prepare to run into road blocks on the pathway. There will always be someone or something you'll have to work around. Don't let them stop you. Be persistent.

For Next Time

What magazines do you pick up over the course of a month? Do you subscribe or borrow someone else's copies? Are your choices different from those of other members of your family?

Magazine Timeline

1731   *The Gentleman's Magazine*, published in London, is the first publication to use the word "magazine" in its title.

1741   *American Magazine* becomes the first magazine published in the U.S. The publication is doomed without an organized postal service or means of distribution. Only three issues are printed. Benjamin Franklin's *General Magazine* comes out three days after *American Magazine* debuts. Franklin's publication lasts six issues.

1821   *The Saturday Evening Post* appears. It continues for 148 years.

1825   Some 100 magazines ae in operation, helped by social movements like abolition and labor reform.

1828   *Ladies' Magazine* debuts under the editorial leadership of Sarah Joseph Hale, a widow with five children.

1841   The first modern detective novel, Edgar Allen Poe's *Murders in the Rue Morgue,* is first offered in serialized form in *Lady's and Gentleman's Magazine*. Subscriptions rise from 5,000 to 25,000, thanks to Poe's contributions. Charles Dickens also first offered many of his classic works this way.

1850   The number of U.S. magazines is up to 600. Specialist writers begin taking hold and illustrations fill the pages.

1879   Following the Civil War, magazines take off because *The Postal Act of 1879* permits mailing magazines cheaply. This cost reduction of magazines, along with widespread literacy, the railroad, the popularity of women's magazines about suffrage, and how-to publications for homemakers drives the growth.

1883   *Ladies' Home Journal* arrives. Within 20 years it becomes one of the first magazines to reach a circulation of one million. It is essentially the same magazine that it is today, dealing with woman's concerns such as health, family, relationships and some controversial issues. Early editions included articles on venereal disease and premarital sex.

1885   3,300 magazines published in the U.S.

1888   The National Geographic Society starts *National Geographic Magazine*.

1900   200,000 families subscribe to one or more magazines.

1906   Theodore Roosevelt gives his "muckrakers" speech, insulting magazines for digging up dirt. Publishers wear the label proudly, viewing themselves as agitators of change, targeting the powerful on behalf of the poor. The label comes from a character in John Bunyan's *Pilgrim's Progress* who delighted in raking up filth. Support for social reform from their investigative journalism eventually turns to sensationalism and in increase in yellow journalism.

1910   *The Crisis* is founded as the NAACP's official magazine.

1923   *TIME* magazine begins publication.

1927   *TIME* magazine picks its first *Man of the Year*: Charles Lindbergh.

1933   *Newsweek* magazine debuts.

1938   Radio advertising revenue surpasses magazines.

1945   John H. Johnson borrows $500 from his mother to start *Ebony* magazine. She pawns her household furniture for the money. Johnson goes on to become the first African-American to appear on *Forbes'* 400 Rich List.

1950   32 million families subscribe to one or more magazines, up from 200,000 just 50 years prior.

1953   The first issues of *TV Guide* and *Playboy* magazine hit the newsstands. The first child of Lucille Ball and Desi Arnaz graces the cover of one, while Marilyn Monroe is on the cover of the other.

1956   *Collier's* declares bankruptcy and the advent of television begins to erode magazine readership. Magazines do not have moving pictures or visual and oral storytelling.

1967   *Rolling Stone* debuts with John Lennon on the cover as part of a trend toward special interest publications.

1969   *The Saturday Evening Post* closes.

1971   *Look* closes.

1972   *Life* closes.

1974   *People* magazine debuts with Mia Farrow on the cover.

1990   *Entertainment Weekly* hits newsstands.

2009   Consumer magazines total about 9,400, four times the number produced in 1980

Magazines Today

How many magazines count you as a subscriber? Which ones? Are the magazines you read different from your family's or do you pick up their copies to read?

A magazine is a printed periodical published less frequently than a newspaper, but containing more long-form articles, typically targeted at a narrow audience, printed on higher-quality paper stock than newspapers, but aimed at a broader geographic area. Despite these differences, the technological and journalistic histories of newspapers and magazines are interwoven.

Some people involved in new media deride magazines as nothing more than glorified blogs, just vertical collections of content focused on individual interests. Yet the number of magazine titles grew from 13,541 in 1988 to 19,532 in 2007, according to the *National Directory of Magazines*. Some 23 million magazines are sold every week. More than 9 out of 10 people with some college experience subscribe to one or more magazines.

Magazine expert Samir Husni is known as *Mr. Magazine*. As a consultant trying to get magazine staffs to think outside of the box, during past presentations he has tapped on a publication with a wand and suggested something like this: "Now the magazine is a person. Tell me about her. How old is she? What are her interests, her routines?" Thinking of the publication as a person along with the typical reader's demographics and tastes help to reveal whether they are a good match.

Thinking of the publication as a person along with the typical reader's demographics and tastes help to reveal whether they are a good match.

Some magazine publishers insist they are now in the content business and no longer concerned with how a customer gets the information, whether printed or online. Husni says content is only one part of what makes a magazine what it is. Ink on paper and all the other aspects of what goes into making a magazine creates a unique experience. Husni doesn't deny the digital age "is helping us to create new platforms and new media." But the digital experience is not identical to the one created by ink on paper. Mr. Magazine says, "Magazines are not just content providers, they are experience makers." Print and digital may discover themselves to be cousins finding separate places in the world to survive and thrive.

The changing media landscape is forcing magazines to rethink their tactics for keeping readers and finding new ones. Since magazines cannot publish quickly enough to stay on the news curve, there is a move toward interpreting rather than simply reporting the news of the day. *TIME*'s managing editor says his magazine's strategy in the new digital age is:

- Curate over Create (*curate* means to organize or oversee.)

- Me Today (consumers establish their own priorities and create their own front page headlines and stories.)

- The User (emphasis is now on the user not the information provided.)

- Beautiful Objects (Magazines must become beautiful objects, more upscale.)

Do you think *TIME*'s strategy is working? *TIME* lost about 4,500 ad pages in 2009, according to *Publishers Information Bureau*.

TYPES OF MAGAZINES

Magazines are typically one of three types:

1. Consumer magazines. These are grouped by editorial content and can be broken down into major specialty areas like news (*Time*), fashion and celebrity (*People*), women (*Redbook*), families (*Family Circle*), sports (*Sports Illustrated*), ethnic (*Ebony*), medical and health (*Prevention*), political

(*National Review*), farming (*Farm Journal*) and lifestyles (*Real Simple*).

2. Business-to-Business or Trade magazines. These magazines are aimed at specific professionals such as doctors (*American Medical News*).lawyers (*ABA journal*), welders (*Welding Journal*), etc.

3. Custom magazines. These magazines are often provided for free, periodicals are designed to promote or enhance the use of a company's product such as the in-flight magazines provided by airlines for passengers.

Magazine Trends

MAGAZINE TREND: FALLING SALES

The *Pew Research Center* says newsstand sales were down 9% for the entire year of 2009 after a tumble of 11% the previous year. Newsstand sales combined with subscriptions fell 9.1% during the last six months of 2009, according to the *Audit Bureau of Circulations*. Total magazine ad pages fell 9.4% from the first quarter of 2009 to the first quarter of 2010, according to the *Publishers Information Bureau.*

GfK MRI says the overall consumer magazine audience in the U.S. remained steady between Spring 2009 and Spring 2010 which could be a sign the market is stabilizing. Some women's fashion and beauty titles posted big gains while some celebrity and health magazines enjoyed some audience growth. These advances were offset by double-digit percentage drops at major publications like *Newsweek, TV Guide* and *Parenting.*

Newsstand sales are often a more timely indicator of a magazine's vitality than subscriptions, which tend to lag and can be driven by discounts.

Here's a list of the top 10 newsstand magazines. Most are down from the year before. The percentage in parenthesis shows the difference between 2008 and 2009.

Single-copy circulation (2009)

1.	*Cosmopolitan*	1.7 million	(-4.6%)
2.	*People*	1.3 million	(-11.4%)
3.	*Woman's World*	1.1 million	(-6.6%)
4.	*First*	1 million	(-8.0%)
5.	*Us Weekly*	843k	(1.94%)
6.	*In Touch Weekly*	746k	(-14.2%)
7.	*Family Circle*	695k	(-15.9%)
8.	*O, the Oprah Magazine*	667k	(-0.03%)
9.	*In Style*	657k	(-13.7%)
10.	*Glamour*	588k	(-9.3%)

Source: *Audit Bureau of Circulations*

The total circulation numbers are better. Most large-circulation magazines saw slight declines in overall circulation, off a little more than 1% from the same period the year before. However, many people receive some publications (such as *AARP the Magazine*) because they are members of the organization. It's unlikely subscribers read this type of magazine with as much interest as someone would who has paid only for the publication.

Circulation of Leading U.S. consumer magazines (2009)

1.	*AARP the Magazine*	24.4 million	(1.4%)
2.	*AARP Bulletin*	24.1 million	(-0.8%)
3.	*Reader's Digest*	7.6 million	(-8.2%)
4.	*Better Homes and Gardens*	7.6 million	(-0.04%)
5.	*Good Housekeeping*	4.6 million	(-0.08%)
6.	*National Geographic*	4.6 million	(-9.1%)
7.	*Woman's Day*	3.9 million	(1.3%)
8.	*Family Circle*	3.8 million	(0.08%)
9.	*Ladies' Home Journal*	3.8 million	(0.2%)
10.	*AA Westways*	3.8 million	(0.0%)

Source: Audit Bureau of Circulations

When circulation drops, advertising sales are sure to follow. American magazines lost more than 58,000 pages of ads during 2009, according to *Publishers Information Bureau*. That's about a quarter of the total number of ad pages. The advertising and circulation decline has forced some magazines such as *Domino* and *Conde Nast's Portfolio* to close. *Reader's Digest* filed for bankruptcy. *Barclays Capital* projects magazines will continue to suffer ad revenue declines in 2010. On top of this, magazine publishers are facing projected price increases of up to 10% for paper and ink during 2010.

So what's a magazine to do? We've already discussed *TIME* magazine's new strategy. *Newsweek* offered a redesign in early 2009. The hope is that the most desirable demographic for advertisers (affluent, highly-educated) will continue purchasing.

Some magazines are blurring the line between advertising and editorial with what's called advertorials. This is material designed to look like editorial content but is actually paid advertising.

A 2009 *Forrester Research* study offers a glimmer of hope. Nearly a fifth of respondents (19%) thought their magazine subscription was "surprisingly inexpensive" while fewer (15%) said their magazine subscription was too expensive.

MAGAZINE TREND: ONLINE

Some online magazines or Webzines, now have interactive features. *Slate* and *Salon* are examples of this type. *Slate* is a *Washington Post* publication offering analysis of current events and political news. Some industry observers consider *Slate* and *Salon* communities rather than magazines. Two other similar online entities, *The Daily Beast* and the *Huffington Post* don't refer to themselves as magazines at all, viewing their material as curated news and opinion.

Although *The Onion* has been called a Webzine for its style, the satirical publication filled with fake news actually started as a college newspaper in the 1980's at the *University of*

Wisconsin-Madison. In 1996, it moved to the internet, and video came later. In August, 2009, two Bangladeshi newspapers took seriously an *Onion* article, republishing its outrageous claim that the moon landings were faked.

A survey by the *Columbia Journalism Review* found only a third of magazines say their websites make money. Most upload their entire print editions online without charge. One-out-of-ten put some of their publication behind a pay wall and 4% put all or nearly all their print product behind a wall.

The same survey discovered ammunition for those who believe the editorial quality has fallen. Online copy editing standards were looser than those for the print edition at nearly half of the magazines while 11% did not copy edit online-only articles at all and 17% did no fact checking for online articles.

Consumer Reports Online is one of the few success stories in the online magazine world with some 600,000 subscribers reading reviews of products. Online magazines have generally not fared well in the digital world, partly because computer screens and small mobile devices cannot match the clarity of the printed page. This may change with the advent of tablets like the *iPad.*

MAGAZINE TREND: TABLETS

Magazine publishers have created an online presence and are eyeing other digital outlets for their products. The financial model for Sony's *e-reader* and Amazon's *Kindle* were developed without input from magazine publishers. Publishers only see a small portion of the revenue when someone purchases a copy of *GQ* on *iTunes* or *Fortune* on the *Kindle.* They are also prevented from reaching the buyer with their marketing.

Publishers hope to have better success with tablet computers (or slates) like the *iPad* which promise opportunities to reimage magazine covers and the entire user experience. Publishers are moving aggressively to reinvent themselves on these devices with the goal of maintaining the eye-catching graphics of traditional magazines with the immediacy of multimedia.

There are already *iPhone* versions of *Esquire, GQ, TIME* and *Entertainment Weekly. Tablets* are larger in size than phones but smaller than a typical computer with hybrid functions borrowed from e-readers, smart phones and laptops. The iPad tablet has been called "iPhone on steroids." Some may offer stellar photography that morphs into video or two-way video. Digital magazines on tablets contain interactive ads on the level of video games, suggesting magazines are now in the business of creating experiences. They may well end up evolving into competition for television as well as enhancing print publications like newspapers and magazines.

Media producers are embracing the *iPad* as a multi-layered consumption machine. Simply moving printed texts to tablets is not enough. Publishers will have to embrace multimedia and community. Imagine *National Geographic* offering not just sharper digital images but leaving readers with the feeling they've just traveled to Africa. The opportunities presented by an *iPad* are likely to stimulate experimental creativity at magazines.

Months before the first tablets were due on the market, *Wired* and *Sports Illustrated* were already working on tablet versions of their print editions.. *Hewlett-Packard* has a touch-screen tablet in development. Microsoft is reportedly working on a color tablet device called *Courier*. Dell is offering a tablet called the *Streak*. Google is exploring the possibility of offering their own version of a tablet soon and Nokia (the world's biggest cell phone maker) may jump in the digital book market with its own version of an *iPad* designed to function as e-reader.

Tablets are unlikely to take over the roles of smart phones, televisions and personal computers in our lives, but they may find a place as portable video players and magazine racks. Price will certainly play a part in deciding the place of slates. More than a third of those responding to a survey by consumer electronics company *Retrevo* said *iPads* are overpriced and 58% say they don't need one. Lower price tags on models from Apple competitors may open the door for a larger swath of consumers to pick up a tablet.

One advantage of printed magazines over tablets is the cover. Publically reading *The New Yorker* or *Atlantic Monthly* serves as a way of indicating (or attempting to indicate) one's social awareness and aspirations. Of course, the discretion of *iPad* may also hide a reader's particular indulgence as well.

For Next Time

Which movies do you think are the best of all-time? Which are among your must-see films? What movies are showing now in theaters that you'd like to see?

Film Timeline

1896 Thomas Edison builds the first motion picture studio in New Jersey and calls it *Black Maria*, a common name for a police paddy wagon. The *Edison Vitascope* premieres in New York City and the American movie business is born.

The same year a film called *The Kiss* generates a great moral outcry because of a climactic smooch.

1902 French filmmaker Georges Melies begins making movies that tell a story such as *A Trip to the Moon*. Thanks to his narrative motion pictures, Melies is the first to use special effects and is often called the "first artist of the cinema."

1903 Not to be outdone, the next year Edwin Porter releases his 12-minute film *The Great Train Robbery*. It is the first movie to use editing, intercutting of scenes and a mobile camera. It is also the first Western. The film is shown in hundreds of nickelodeons, where the price of admission is, of course, five cents.

1915 D.W. Griffith releases *The Birth of a Nation*. A 3-hour epic, the production takes six weeks in rehearsal and nine weeks of shooting with a cast of thousands at a cost of $125,000. Admission price is $3. The most influential silent film ever made, it remains the most popular and profitable movie ever made until 1939's *Gone with the Wind* unseats it. Despite the popularity of Griffith's film, it draws protests for including a racist portrayal of African-Americans and a sympathetic treatment of the *Ku Klux Klan*.

1922 A series of Hollywood scandals and concern over movie content leads to the creation of the *Motion Picture Producers and Distributors of America* (MPPDA). The goal is to improve the image of the film industry.

1926 Warner Brothers releases the first *Talkie*. Historians argue whether it was *Don Juan* in 1926, *The Jazz Singer* in 1927 or *Lights of New York* in 1928. *The Jazz Singer* is mostly silent; *Don Juan* is really just synchronized music and sound effects; *Lights of New York* is the first fully all-sound movie.

1928 Mickey Mouse is introduced in the animated hit, *Steamboat Willie*.

1931   A movie called *The Front Page* starts a trend depicting reporters as hard-working and scoop-addicted, with machine gun dialogue and cynical attitudes. Journalism appears exciting, important and downright fun.

1934   The *Motion Picture Production Code* (MPPC) is released. Among other things, the code forbids the use of profanity, bedroom scenes with unmarried couples, skimpy costumes, ridiculing public officials and religious leaders. It outlaws words — like God and nuts.

1946   Movie attendance peaks in the U.S. Seven years later, ticket sales will fall by nearly half due to the popularity of television. At first the movie industry boycotts the new industry, blacklisting some actors who take TV roles. Hollywood attitudes change when it becomes clear that television can provide new life to movies that have finished their theatrical runs.

1947   A congressional committee investigates possible communist influences in Hollywood. Those who are called to testify but refuse to answer questions are *blacklisted*, banned from working in the film industry.

1966   The *Motion Picture Association of America* (MPAA) begins a ratings system. It ranks films based on adult content with designations including *G, M, R,* and *X*.

1975   Steven Spielberg begins the era of the special effects summer blockbuster with *Jaws*.

1976   The film *All the President's Men* shows how reporters from *The Washington Post* break the Watergate scandal, leading to the resignation of President Nixon. Journalists are depicted as truth-seeking crusaders, an image that will give way in film to that of reporters as mostly gossip-obsessed nuisances.

1995   *Disney's Toy Story* is the first major release to be produced entirely on computers. Five years later, The Coen brother's film *O Brother, Where Art Thou?* is given a nostalgic feel by editing with Apple's *Final Cut Pro*, the most popular video software program used by journalists.

1997   The movie that becomes the top domestic grossing film of all time is released. *Titanic* makes more than $600 million in the U.S.

2003   DVD sales of theatrical releases begin earning more than domestic box office sales. This leads to a rising problem for Hollywood — DVD piracy.

Film Today

A famous line in the movie *Citizen Kane* is uttered by a powerful businessman played by Orson Welles. "I think it would be fun to run a newspaper." Many critics consider it the best movie ever made because of its technical innovation related to lighting, camera shots and special effects. Notably, Kane's obituary in the movie is not written by a print journalist, but by a newsreel reporter. On the next page are some of the other top picks.

American Film Institute Top Movies

1. *Citizen Kane* (1941)
2. *The Godfather* (1972)
3. *Casablanca* (1943)
4. *Raging Bull* (1980)
5. *Singin' In The Rain* (1952)
6. *Gone With The Wind* (1939)
7. *Lawrence of Arabia* (1962)
8. *Schindler's List* (1993)
9. *Vertigo* (1958)
10. *The Wizard of Oz* (1939)

Source: AFIs 100 Years.. 100 Movies January 2, 2010 from http://www.afi.com/tvevents/100years/movies.aspx

ESPN's Top Sports Movies of All-Time

1. *Bull Durham* (1988)
2. *Rocky* (1976)
3. *Raging Bull* (1980)
4. *Hoosiers* (1986)
5. *Slap Shot* (1977)

Source: Page 2's Top 20 Sports Movies of All-Time http://espn.go.com/page2/movies/s/top20/fulllist.html

What would you have on your list of must-see films? Here are some other quotes from movies, and trivia questions about films.

MOVIE TRIVIA QUESTIONS INVOLVING COLLEGES

1. The fictitious school is Faber College. What's the name of the movie?

2. The fictitious school is South Central Louisiana State University. What's the name of the movie?

3. In the *Indiana Jones* movie series, where did the hero earn his degree?

4. In the film *Election*, starring Matthew Broderick and Reese Witherspoon, which college did Tracy Flick attend?

5. What university law school did Reese Witherspoon attend in *Legally Blonde?*

Here's the movie line. What's the name of each movie?

1. "Life is like a box of chocolates."
2. "Show me the money!"
3. "We're on a mission from God."
4. "I'll be back."
5. "Snakes! Why does it always have to be snakes?!"
6. "Go ahead. Make my day."

7. "Phone home."
8. "If you build it, he will come."
9. "My father made him an offer he couldn't refuse."
10. "I'll have what's she's having."
11. "I'm mad as hell, and I'm not going to take it anymore!"
12. "May the Force be with you."
13. "Every time you hear a bell ring, it means that some angel's just got his wings."
14. "Wanna know how I got these scars?"
15. "You know how they say we only use 10 percent of our brains? I think we only use 10 percent of our hearts."

(Answers are at the end of the chapter)

TOP GROSSING FILMS OF ALL TIME (domestic)

1. *Avatar* (2009) $748 million
2. *Titanic* (1997) $601 million
3. *The Dark Knight* (2008) $533 million
4. *Star Wars* (1977) $461 million
5. *Shrek 2* (2004) $441 million

Source: Domestic Grosses, Box Office Mojo January 18, 2010 from http://boxofficemojo.com/alltime/domestic.htm

But what if the numbers are adjusted for ticket price inflation? The price of admission years ago would have cost a fraction of what it does now. So if you put all movies on the same playing level, which one wins?

TOP GROSSING FILMS: ADJUSTED (domestic)

1. *Gone with the Wind* (1939)
2. *Star Wars* (1977)
3. *The Sound of Music* (1965)
4. *E.T.: The Extra Terrestrial* (1982)
5. *The Ten Commandments* (1956)
14. *Avatar* (2009)

Source: Domestic Grosses, Adjusted for Inflation, Box Office Mojo December 20, 2009 from http://boxofficemojo.com/alltime/adjusted.htm

While making movies sounds exciting, it's a risky business. A whopping 70-80% of films fail to make money.

Pause for Discussion: Fave Flicks

What's your all-time favorite movie? Or at least, the name of a film you really like? What have you seen recently? Would you recommend it?

Movie Trends

MOVIE TRENDS: REPURPOSING

Movie-makers tend to return to the same themes over and over again. More than three-fourths of all movies deal with crime, sex or love, according to research by *The Payne Fund*. Once a combination of elements proves successful, it's tempting to keep drawing from that same well. TV producers seem blissfully unaware that no remake of a previous hit series has ever itself become a hit on network television. Making movies based on television hits has a better track record. That's probably why we see a great deal of repurposing on both the big and little screens. Here are some examples of how Hollywood has reformatted material for a movie:

> Sequels: *Mission Impossible, Shrek.*
> TV Remakes: *Brady Bunch, Star Trek.*
> Books: *Harry Potter, The Twilight Saga.*
> Comic Book stories: *X-Men, Men in Black.*
> Video-Games: *Tomb Raider, Grand Theft Auto.*
> Merchandise Tie-Ins: *The Lion King, Toy Story*

TV producers seem blissfully unaware that no remake of a previous hit series has ever become a hit itself on network television.

MOVIE TRENDS: CONVERGENCE

Now movies are available from satellite, cable, video-on-demand, pay-per-view, DVDs, video cassettes and even your cell phone. The audience for the small screen will affect how movies are shot, and ultimately what you watch. The more users are comfortable seeing video on their mobile phones, the more likely journalists will need to shoot with that screen in mind. This will probably mean fewer wide shots and more close-ups.

As a way to combat illegal downloads and pressure from DVD sales, the film industry is increasingly moving toward simultaneous international releases of major movies. Convergence not only means more outlets for movie viewing, but films originating on the Internet. Diablo Cody wrote a blog, earning enough attention to get a book contract. Her narrative was eventually made into a movie, the widely acclaimed *Juno.*

MOVIE TRENDS: DIGITAL FILMS

Hollywood movie studios have embraced digital cinema, both from a financing and a creative perspective. The slow transition to green screens (where an actor is placed in front of scenery like a weather forecaster on television), CGI (computer-generated imagery) and digitized animation took a leap forward with James Cameron's 3D sci-fi epic *Avatar* (2009). The trend toward completely digitized entertainment is bolstered by *Disney's Pixar* studio and *DreamWorks Animation* which have a release schedule dominated by the technology.

MOVIE TRENDS: DOCUMENTARIES

Documentaries have broken through the commercial barrier to become financially profitable. Success stories for the genre include Al Gore's environmental treatise, *An Inconvenient Truth*; the *French Documentary, March of the Penguins*; Michael Moore's *Fahrenheit 9/11*; and the fast-food exposé, *Super Size Me*.

MOVIE TRENDS: TABLETS

The ultimate goal of tablets (such as the *iPad*) might be playing high-definition movies on a color laptop screen and to double as a flat screen to play high-definition movies on a color screen.

For Next Time

If you were marooned on a desert island and could have only three music releases with you, what would you put on your list of must-have albums?

MOVIE TRIVIA ANSWERS

1. Faber College is a the fictional school in *Animal House*.
2. South Central Louisiana State University is the fictional school in *Waterboy*.
3. Indiana Jones attended the University of Chicago and taught at Marshall College until the third film in the series which put him at Barnett College.
4. In the film *Election*, Tracy Flick attended Yale.
5. In *Legally Blonde*, Reese Witherspoon attends Harvard.

Here's the movie line, what's the name of the movie?

1. "Life is like a box of chocolates." *Forrest Gump* (1992)
2. "Show me the money!" *Jerry Maguire* (1996)
3. "We're on a mission from God." *Blues Brothers* (1980)
4. "I'll be back." *The Terminator* (1984)
5. "Snakes! Why does it always have to be snakes?!" *Raiders of the Lost Ark* (1981)
6. "Go ahead. Make my day." *Sudden Impact* (1983)
7. "Phone home." *E.T.: The Extra-Terrestrial* (1982)
8. "If you build it, he will come." *Field of Dreams* (1989)
9. "My father made him an offer he couldn't refuse." *The Godfather* (1972)
10. "I'll have what's she's having." *When Harry Met Sally* (1989)
11. "I'm mad as hell, and I'm not going to take it anymore!" *Network* (1976)
12. "May the Force be with you." *Star Wars* (1977)
13. "Every time you hear a bell ring, it means that some angel's just got his wings." *It's a Wonderful Life* (1946)
14. "Wanna know how I got these scars?" *The Dark Knight* (2008)
15. "You know how they say we only use 10 percent of our brains? I think we only use 10 percent of our hearts." *Wedding Crashers* (2005)

Radio, Recording, and Popular Music

Radio Timeline

1877   Thomas Edison patents his "*talking machine*," but only one recording could be made of any given sound. The first recording is of the nursery rhyme, *Mary Had a Little Lamb*.

1887   German immigrant, Emile Berliner solves the one recording problem (above) a decade later with the development of the flat disc *gramophone*. The phonograph serves as a musical time machine, allowing sound of the past to be heard in the present.

1896   Guglielmo Marconi, the *Father of Radio*, is able to send and receive wireless telegraph code over a distance of two miles.

1901   Marconi successfully transmits across the Atlantic Ocean.

1903   Canadian Reginald Fessenden invents the first audio device that picks up wireless voices. His 1906 Christmas Eve broadcast is the *first public broadcast of voices*.

1912   The emerging radio technology disperses news of the *Titanic's* sinking much faster than any previous, similar event. It's the first use of radio to cover a major breaking news story. The disaster spurs the development of radio communications and disaster planning. Among other things, ships carrying 50 or more people were required to have a 24-hour radio watch. Radio is first thought of as a way for ships to communicate with each other and with people living on coastlines to improve safely, not as a method of entertaining the masses.

1920s to 1950s   Radio becomes the dominant entertainment and information source in the U.S. until the advent of television. This period is referred to as *The Golden Age of Radio*.

Here's how it happened:

LIBRARY OF CONGRESS

1920   *KDKA* in Pittsburgh, the first commercial radio station in the U.S., makes its initial commercial radio broadcast, announcing the results of the presidential election that put Warren G. Harding in the White House.

The FCC later uses *K* as the first of four identification letters for radio stations located west of the Mississippi River while those east of the Mississippi River are given the letter *W* as their first call letter. Stations already on the air but located east of the Mississippi (such as *KDKA*) are allowed to keep their letters.

1921   Boxing launches radio. While the first real broadcast came in 1920, the event that gets radio "on the map" happens a year later.

Jack Dempsey, the heavyweight champion of the world, is set to fight decorated French Army veteran Georges Carpentier (*Jorge Car-pon-tee-ay*). Promoter Tex Rickard declares it the "Battle of the Century," pitting an undisciplined American who avoided the draft against a hero of World War I, a French pilot admired on both sides of the Atlantic. It is leaked to the press that Carpentier has a mystery punch and an "evil eye." Writer George Bernard Shaw even claims that Carpentier is "the greatest boxer in the world."

The outdoor stadium in New Jersey where the fight is to be held seats 91,000 people, but the promoter has an idea to make more money. Rickard decides to put the contest on the radio. Only a few people have radios at the time, but Rickard gets around this by outfitting theaters and halls with radio receivers tied to crude loudspeakers; he charges a fee to get inside. Rickard sets up a temporary radio transmitter with the help of RCA. Crowds gather from Maine to North Carolina, from New York to Cleveland. Dempsey badly beats the Frenchman in the fight, knocking Carpentier out in the second minute of the fourth round. Carpentier never fights again for that title. But the fight is an amazing success, boxing's first million-dollar gate, pulling in an astounding $1.6 million.

Radio is launched. Hundreds of thousands of people hear the broadcast, catching a glimpse of what radio can do for them — which is to put them in the seat of big events, rather than reading about it the next day. They can hear the excitement while it happens.

A few months later, *KDKA* offers the first broadcast of a baseball game between the *Pittsburgh Pirates* and the *Philadelphia Phillies*. By Christmas time, demand for home radio equipment soars. It is the *Playstation* of its day.

1921   A business model has yet to emerge for the new technology. *Radio Broadcast* magazine sponsors a $500 contest asking for the best essay on "Who is to Pay for Broadcasting — and How?"

LIBRARY OF CONGRESS

1926   RCA, supplier of the 1921 boxing match, now forms the first major broadcast network in the U.S. The new corporation's initials are NBC (*National Broadcasting Company*). TV comes later for NBC. The network makes its mark through sporting events, running the first live World Series, the first college football game, etc. The company later makes so much money during the Great Depression of the 1930's that it moves into Rockefeller Center in midtown Manhattan.

1927   The *Columbia Broadcasting System* (CBS) is formed. ABC doesn't begin broadcasting until 1945.

The Radio Act of 1927 creates the *Federal Radio Commission*, a forerunner of the *Federal Communication Commission* (FCC).

Mid-1920s   Major European colonial powers start using *shortwave radio* to connect with their various colonies in Africa, Asia and the Middle East. They use what's known as *skip* (bouncing the signal off the ionosphere) to get the broadcast signals to travel long distances. Some people begin listening to distance stations at night to see what far-flung signals they can pick up with the help of skip. The hobby becomes known as DXing which is telegraphic shorthand for distance. Shortwave has never been big in the U.S. but for many parts of the world it has served as a lifeline to the outside world. For many people living in repressive regimes, it is their way to find out what really is going on — even in their own country.

1933   Inventor Edwin Armstrong patents what would become *FM radio*. By 1937, he finances construction of the first FM radio station. But RCA goes to court to stop him. A lengthy legal battle ultimately gets the FCC to change the broadcast rules so that Armstrong's FM network could not survive. Less than 20 years later (1954) Armstrong jumps to his death from a 13th-story building in New York. Decades will pass before FM emerges to dominate the U.S. radio landscape, but many of his lawsuits are settled shortly after his death, leaving his widow a fortune.

FM's slow implementation allows AM radio to take off in the 1930's, becoming the major source of entertainment and news in America.

Radio has the physical presence that TVs now enjoy in American homes. Wooden radio sets come to look like fancy living room furniture. And what did everyone listen to? Shows featuring one celebrity with one sponsor. Jack Benny, for example, steps out of character on his show to pitch *Jell-O,* and *Campbell's Soup* is the single sponsor of the *Burns and Allen Show*. Dramas, comedy, and music fill the airways of the 1930's. In 1933, the *William Tell Overture* becomes the theme song for *The Lone Ranger,* which runs on radio for nearly 3,000 episodes.

By the mid-1930's women dominate the daytime radio lineup as both creators and listeners, with the rise of the "radio soap." Soap operas like *The Guiding Light*, and comedy from Abbott and Costello become popular.

Nearly every one of these shows has someone on staff who does nothing but sound effects to give the listener a sense of actually being there. These noise artists never get recognition. Radio networks make money from these shows, but also agree to broadcast religious content and political talks "in the public interest." Music doesn't become a focus until later.

1934   The federal government establishes the FCC (*Federal Communications Commission*) to regulate broadcasters. A guiding principle is that the airwaves belong to the public.

Not just anyone can start a new broadcast station. Here are the FCC requirements. The licensee must:

1. Be a U.S. citizen
2. Be of good character
3. Have enough financial resources to build and keep the station in operation
4. Have the technical ability to operate the station according to FCC regulations

The *Communications Act of 1934* prohibits the FCC from censoring radio programs, but some in Roosevelt's administration believe that radio stations should be physically controlled by the government. Radio transmitters can become targets during war, so the government needs to guard against sabotage, they argue. Instead of taking over radio, FDR decides voluntary censorship for radio and newspapers is the way to go.

Not long ago, political leaders debated whether the government should run the media or not. This might be hard to imagine in today's climate, but the programming freedoms enjoyed by the media were not assured when broadcasting got its start.

1935   There are 62 radio stations in the U.S. and all but four are part of either the NBC or CBS networks.

1937   FDR offers a series of *fireside chats* to the country. The most-listened-to speech comes during March of this year. To put it in perspective, his talks have less than half the audience of a Joe Louis fight.

1938   *War of the Worlds*, the dramatic presentation of the science fiction classic, is adapted for radio broadcast by Orson Welles. The radio drama sounds realistic and offers news reports of a Martian invasion of Earth. Numerous announcements tell listeners it is only a drama, but many still panic, taking steps to protect themselves and revealing the power of radio. Welles plays a newspaper owner in the ground-breaking film *Citizen Kane* three years later.

Radio advertising revenue surpasses magazines.

1940   The U.S. Census shows nearly every household has a radio.

1941   Radio news becomes a force on December 7th, 1941 when Japan attacks the U.S. at Pearl Harbor. Most Americans hear about it from radio news bulletins interrupting regular programming or from people who hear the bulletins.

World War II sees the rise of the *radio journalist,* like Edward R. Murrow, reporting from the front lines.

While the German army is smaller and its tanks inferior to France's at the start of World War II, the German Blitzkrieg succeeds because its tanks are equipped with a technology the French tanks lack: radio. Clay Shirky writes in his book, *Here Comes Everybody,* that Panzer commanders could share intelligence and make quick decisions while French commanders "regarded tanks as a mobile platform for accompanying foot soldiers. The Germans, on the other hand, understood that the tank allowed for a new kind of fighting, a rapid style of attack."

1945   Fewer than 1000 AM radio stations are in operation.

1946   World War II is over and so is the supremacy of network radio. TV takes off, and within a decade, TV sets claim the spot in the living room once occupied by radio sets. Radio soon makes its way into cars and becomes the medium of choice for commuters during their drives to and from work.

Sony is founded in the ruins of postwar Japan. The consumer electronics company will create the first *Walkman* (1979), compact disc player (1982), and *PlayStation* console, (1994) which changes the way media is produced, packaged and consumed.

1948   *Columbia* creates a record album that revolves at a speed of 33 1/3 rpm (revolutions per minute). At the same time, *RCA* comes out with its 45 rpm. An example of technology driving culture, short songs become the norm on radio since 45's can only fit about three minutes of music into their grooves. Record companies prefer this length since distribution to radio stations is cheaper.

1949   The ratings service for radio is founded as *ARB*, becoming *Arbitron* during the 1960s.

About 85 million radio sets are in use throughout America. More than two-thirds of teens say they own a radio. But TV makes its mark. A survey of people living in the nation's capital finds the time they spend listening to the radio each day falls from three hours and 42 minutes to less than half an hour.

1951   KOWH-AM in Omaha schedules music in *dayparts*. Network radio in the 30's and 40's emphasized a different show every half-hour while radio in the 50's is built on a continuous, consistent sound.

1955   *Rock and Roll* hits radio with Chuck Berry's *Maybellene*, a country song played on an electric guitar, sung in a blues style, but toned down for an audience of white suburban teenagers. It reaches #5 on the pop chart.

The same year, radio finds Elvis. Teens want to hear the new rock music over and over. This leads to the creation of the *Top 40* format. The 40 most popular songs (all about 3 minutes long) are played over and over again. Depending on the number of commercials, radio programmers can repeat those 40 songs about every three hours.

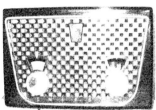

HAMMONDCAST

1957   The first *transistor radio* is introduced. This means kids can carry in their pockets what was once a piece of furniture.

1958   More radios are sold for cars than for homes. Seven out of ten new cars have radios.

1960   AM radio stations now number about 3,600, more than three times the total existing in 1945. Two-thirds of them are profitable, compared with only a quarter of FM stations.

1967   Congress passes the *Public Broadcasting Act,* creating *The Corporation for Public Broadcasting* (*CPB*). The name of the *CBP* television vehicle is *PBS* (*Public Broadcasting Service*). The name of the *CBP* radio vehicle is *NPR* (*National Public Radio*).

1978   *WKRP in Cincinnati* premieres on CBS, a sitcom following the misadventures of a small radio staff. In an early episode, later named one of the greatest in television history by *TV Guide* magazine, live turkeys are dropped from a helicopter as a PR stunt. Unable to fly, the birds plunge to their deaths (off camera) as shoppers run for their lives. The station manager later mutters, "As God is my witness, I thought turkeys could fly." The episode, based on a true story, captures the free-wheeling nature of radio broadcasters.

The student radio station at Nebraska's *Wayne State College* holds an annual turkey drop shortly before Thanksgiving in honor of the TV series. The tossing of pumpkins, TVs and even toilets from the fire escape of a third-floor dorm is a yearly ritual. Students donate two cans to a food bank in order to watch the destruction as items smash on the ground below. A trophy topped by a turkey, along with frozen turkey pot pies are handed out to those who donate items to be dropped and make the best splattering on the tarp.

1979   AM cannot match the fidelity and stereo offered by FM, so the number of FM listeners passes the number listening to AM radio.

1980   *Compact discs* hit the market.

1981   *MTV* is introduced. The first video played on MTV is *Video Killed the Radio Star* by the Buggles. Among the lyrics, "We can't rewind, we've gone too far... video killed the radio star."

1990   Most people are listening to radio in their cars, and three out of four are tuned to FM.

1996   The *Telecommunications Act of 1996* overhauls the broadcast rules set up in 1934 by the FCC. The legislation is intended to speed up the growth of technologies by allowing companies to enter each other's markets. Instead, it leads to media consolidation.

Auto-Tune is invented, a quirky little side note in the history of music. *Auto-Tune* is a downloadable studio trick that can take a vocal and instantly nudge it onto the proper note or move it to the correct pitch. It's like *Photoshop* for the human voice.

Here's how it came about. Andy Hildebrand had figured out a way to save oil companies a lot of money using a mathematical formula. He came up with a way to map out potential drill sites. Hildebrand retired at the age of 40, thanks to his invention's remarkable success. At a dinner party one night, a guest asked him to invent a box that would allow her to sing in tune. Hildebrand took up the challenge. He tinkered with his math formula for a few months and *Auto-Tune* was born.

Auto-Tune was used in a way Hildebrand never intended on Cher's 1998 hit, *Believe*. In the first verse, Cher sings "I can't break through" and it sounds as if she's standing behind an electric fan. Music producers discovered if you set the gadget to zero, it finds the nearest note and changes the output pitch instantaneously. There's no natural transition between notes. It makes the singer sound jumpy and automated. Hildebrand says, "I never figured anyone in their right mind would want to do that." The technique was picked up by Forheem Najm (better known as T-Pain), Lil Wayne and others.

Most contemporary music is composed on the program Pro Tools, and nearly every song is tweaked using *Auto-Tune*. This means songs are harder to distinguish from each another. Many producers say this makes singers lazy.

Aretha Franklin was criticized for being "pitchy" at the 2009 Obama Inauguration, as if she were auditioning for *American Idol*. But that's because she was really singing. Her voice was not bouncing through a computer. In other words, music listeners are getting used to hearing singing that is dead on pitch, changing audience expectations.

After watching *American Idol*, we may assume that the "right way" to sing is to be dead on pitch. Ringo Starr is off pitch on the song *With a Little Help from My Friends*. Should we fix that? Just about every blues song slides into notes as opposed to hitting them dead on. Norah Jones has some misses on *Don't Know Why* from her album *Come Away with Me*. Are those flaws? Or do they give the song character and authenticity?

As you march into the world of the media, you'll have ample opportunity to smooth out human flaws using computers. You are doing that already if you use spell check. So how far do you go?

If you would like to try it yourself, *Auto-Tune* has an app for your *iPhone*.

1997   Most public TV stations agree to follow the *Common Carriage Agreement*, which means they will carry PBS programs at night in the same order the shows are sent out.

2000   Music company sales peak at nearly 800 million albums. By 2007, sales will fall to little more than 500 million.

2001   XM satellite radio launches. The service is subscription-based, like cable television, allowing it to escape content restrictions placed on AM and FM radio by the FCC.

2002   Sirius satellite radio launches.

2003   *Apple* opens a digital jukebox called *iTunes* and rocks the music industry with 99-cent pricing for songs.

2007   *Arbitron* introduces the *Portable People Meter*. Replacing radio's ratings system where listeners keep written records of what they listen to, the *People Meter*, a cellphone-size device, relays exactly which stations people are hearing down to the second. Some critics claim it undercounts minorities, which *Arbitron* denies.

As a result of the new system, in 2009 stations in New York and Los Angeles switch formats from talk to Top 40, because *People Meter* ratings show that male-oriented chat isn't doing as well as previously believed under the old diary system.

2008   XM and Sirius merge under the name *Sirius XM Radio*.

The number of commercial radio stations reaches more than 11,000.

The number of new releases increases to 106,000 compared with 44,000 in 2005, according to Nielsen SoundScan. Yet little more than a third (35%) of album sales comes from new releases, the lowest since Nielson began tracking the data in 1991.

2009   A poll by the *Pew Research Center* finds rock and roll the most popular style of music in the U.S. In a similar survey in 1966, a greater number of Americans picked it as the style of music they most disliked.

Sales of individual tracks top $1 billion, according to RIAA, but album sales (including digital) are down by 23%, to $6 billion. Listeners prefer individual songs to buying the whole package.

Radio & Music Today

Next to watching television, listening to music is one of America's favorite pastimes. Playing air guitar as a teenager or sharing special songs as a couple are common experiences built around rhythms and melodies that we adopt as expressions of who we are and what we feel.

Imagine you are lost on a desert island and can have only three albums with you. What would you put on your list of "must have" music? Chances are good the music you select will come from one of the four big music companies: EMI, Sony, Universal or Warner Music. Of the 63 albums that sold more than a quarter of a million units in 2009, according to *Nielsen's Soundscan,* all but two were issued by a major music company. Still, more artists than ever are putting out albums online so that most of the revenue for the music companies no longer comes from legacy artists and their catalogues. In the 1990s, best-selling albums sold at least 15 million copies. In 2007, the top-selling albums sold only 3.7 million. Forrester Research says music company revenue will fall to $9 billion in 2012 after topping out at $14 billion in 2000 because listeners are buying individual songs over albums. The record business is in trouble. The music business is not.

Any idea what artists and albums are the best-selling of all-time? Some are sure to surprise you. It's a reminder that some pockets of culture are much larger than you imagine when they are outside your personal radar. If your friends don't listen to these artists, and the medium you consume doesn't play them, they don't seem so important, but if you want to see the big picture, don't allow your connection to segments of our culture blind you to their significance to others.

Imagine you are lost on a desert island and you can have only three albums with you.

All-Time Top Selling Artists

1. Beatles
2. Garth Brooks
3. Elvis Presley
4. Led Zeppelin
5. Eagles
6. Billy Joel
7. Pink Floyd
8. Barbra Streisand
9. AC/DC
10. Elton John
11. Michael Jackson

PORIUS

Source: Top Selling Artists, *Recording Industry Association of America (RIAA) January 2, 2010*
From http://www.riaa.com/goldandplatinumdata.php?table=tblTopArt

All-time Top Selling Albums

1. *Thriller*, Michael Jackson
2. *Eagles/Their Greatest Hits 1971-75*, Eagles
3. *Led Zeppelin IV*, Led Zeppelin
4. *The Wall*, Pink Floyd
5. *Back in Black*, AC/DC
6. *Double Live*, Garth Brooks
7. *Greatest Hits Vol.I & II*, Billy Joel
8. *Come On Over*, Shania Twain
9. *The Beatles*, The Beatles
10. *Rumours*, Fleetwood Mac

Source: Top 100 Albums, Recording Industry Association of America (RIAA) January 2, 2010
From http://www.riaa.com/goldandplatinumdata.php?table=tblTop100

Radio introduced us to many of our favorite artists. While we may identify with a particular style of music, the intimate relationship listeners once had with local DJs has been replaced by computer-driven formats operated by large corporations.

Current rules allow a company to own a maximum of eight radio stations in the same market. Among the larger radio companies today are *Clear Channel, Cumulus,* and *Citadel,* which filed for bankruptcy in late 2009.

RADIO QUIZ

1. How many radio stations are in the US?

2. How many radios per person in the US?

3. In an average week, how many out of 10 listen to the radio?

4. How long do people listen each week?

5. What percentage of people does radio reach within an hour of their making a decision to buy a product?

(Answers are at the end of the chapter)

How AM & FM Work

Two bands are used in the U.S. for radio, AM (amplitude modulation) and FM (frequency modulation).

When comparing one radio station to another, listeners usually ask the wattage of each station. But the antenna height is just as important for an FM radio station as the wattage. Dial position plays a critical role in how far an AM station's signal goes out, along with its ground system (copper wiring placed in the ground around towers to help conduct the signal). And the lower the dial position of an AM station, the farther the signal will reach. If you are broadcasting on the AM dial, you are better off transmitting at only 5,000 watts down at 700 MHz than 50,000 watts at 1500 MHZ.

An FM signal is line of sight and an AM transmitter puts out waves. The higher the FM antenna, the farther the signal goes out. If I held a flashlight over a map, it would create a circle. I could put a stronger bulb into the flashlight, but that would only intensify the area already covered by the light. The only way to increase the area is to raise the flashlight higher above the map. FM works the same way. The height of the antenna determines how far a signal goes out, while the wattage determines the intensity of the signal. As the signal follows the curve of the earth, it begins to dissipate. Because of its nature, FM signals can be blocked by obstructions like buildings or hills.

On the other hand, AM radio stations send out waves that bounce around. They fare better in large cities where structures like large buildings get in the way of the radio signals. The signal, combined with an audience's desire to know traffic and weather when they hop in the car for their commute, is why news/talk AM stations can command high ratings. In recent Arbitron ratings books, WGN-AM in Chicago has earned the #1 position,

WSB-AM in Atlanta has shown up at #2, and KFI-AM in Los Angeles has taken the #3 spot.

The sun also interferes with AM signals. When it goes down, AM signals begin bouncing off the ionosphere. This "skywave" effect has led the FCC to impose stricter rules on AM nighttime broadcasting to avoid interference between stations.

Radio's Reach

Radio is…

- **Personal**

  The voice on the radio is a friend. Announcers should avoid talking to "everybody out there" because few people in the audience are listening in a group and they certainly aren't all together. Most people are alone, at home, in the car or at work. The radio station is a companion that joins each listener as he or she goes about the day. It fires the imagination so the listener is contributing to the experience rather than passively taking it all in. When a listener met her favorite DJ, her face fell with disappointment when she saw his average build. "I thought you'd be six feet, four and 250 pounds!" Radio gave her the opportunity to imagine the person she wanted to know as her friend.

- **Mobile**

  Radio steps into people's worlds right where they live, while getting ready for work or driving to school. It goes to the beach and works well in a mobile society.

- **Inexpensive**

  Advertisers find it inexpensive and flexible. Commercials can take hours and days to put together when video is involved. Radio spots can be produced in as little as five minutes.

The voice on the radio is a friend.

Radio's Challenge

Radio reaches more than 236 million people 12 and older in a typical week, according to 2009 figures from Arbitron. That's 92.5% of teens and older. When you consider only the 12- to 17-year-olds from that group of 236 million, the percentage is still 90%.

But now that broadcasters are competing with iPods and other digital technology, they must consider what will motivate listeners to keep tuning in. The most compelling reasons are new music and a desire to be plugged in to the local community.

A Jupiter Research study found radio is still the top choice for learning about new music. Even 63% of online users put it at number one, followed by recommendations from friends at 26% and then retail stores, TV music videos, TV shows and online radio. Broadcasters can encourage listeners to discover the latest music trends by emphasizing the hottest new singles.

A second option for broadcasters is to get in front of local events and discussions in the community. If listeners can find out about hot topics and nearby gatherings from radio stations, they're more likely to return.

The first option (focusing on new music) may compete with the second (local information) forcing radio stations to choose one or the other.

Music stations have cut back on frequent DJ banter because ratings from the new people meter suggest it's a listener turn off. The biggest radio moneymaker in the country, pop-formatted KIIS-FM, dropped afternoon traffic reports when a new Top 40 station received higher ratings without traffic updates. As carmakers add even more navigation systems and Internet access equipment to vehicles, it will become more difficult in coming years for radio to compete with what drivers have at their fingertips — information they control.

A Jupiter Research study found radio is still the top choice for learning about new music.

Another route for traditional radio is appealing to those who consider themselves socially or politically disenfranchised. Talk radio has worked this format well by positioning itself as the voice of those who are on the outside of the mainstream media looking for a voice to express their views. According to Arbitron, News/Talk/Information (N/T/I) ranked as the number one format in Fall 2008.

Noncommercial Radio

Only noncommercial educational radio stations (NCEs) are allowed to broadcast at the lower end of the FM dial between 88.1 and 91.9. NCEs account for about 19% of all radio stations licensed in the U.S.

A significant number of noncommercial broadcasters offer religious programming. But within the category of noncommercial broadcast there is a subcategory known as "public broadcasting." It encompasses those broadcasters who meet the minimum operating requirements established by the Corporation for Public Broadcasting to qualify for federal funding. CPB funds 800 radio stations so they can air programming from NPR and its competitor PRI (Public Radio International).

> Radio stations seeking a Community Service Grant from CPB must:
> Put a significant signal over the city of license.
> Have at least five full-time employees.
> Provide at least 18 hours of programming a day.
> Receive at least $100,000 from other sources besides the federal government.

Federal funding accounts for less than one-fifth of revenues for public radio stations. Noncommercial stations have to look elsewhere for financial support. Although NCEs cannot broadcast advertising, they can offer underwriting opportunities which identify the businesses and individuals who give gifts to keep the station in operation. These sponsors can be identified in these underwriting announcements by name and the location, slogan, and other basic info. Here's what cannot be included in underwriting announcements on noncommercial radio stations:

> A call to action ("Go eat at Joe's").

Superlative description or qualitative claim about the company or its products and services ("Joe's serves fantastic food").

Comparison statements about its products in relation to other companies ("They offer the best service in the city").

Price or value information ("The early bird special is only six dollars").

Other revenue sources for public stations may include selling ads in a membership guide or spring and fall pledge drives.

Radio's Power

Radio can be a powerful medium.

An FM station in Alabama has a daily feature where listeners can e-mail three song requests and someone's picks are played each day. Here's what one caller had to say:

> "Hello, my name is _____ and I was going to make a comment. Around 4 o'clock this evening, I don't know what you call it when someone e-mails three songs that they want to hear. Those three songs really ministered to me because around that time I was on my way downtown to look for my daughter. My daughter is in the street and when that song came out about a prodigal son (crying) that ministered to me so much. And I thank y'all for… your radio station. God bless you. Bye bye."

When the microphone is open, the DJ never knows who may be listening and what he or she may be going through at that moment. A life can be changed by just a friendly voice or information provided in a news report that empowers someone to make life changes or step out of an abusive situation. Even when announcers do not directly address someone's particular situation, they are able to have an impact because listeners tend to apply what they hear to their own concerns.

A life can be changed by just a friendly voice…that empowers someone to make life changes or step out of an abusive situation.

Radio & Music Trends

RADIO TREND: SLOW RECOVERY

Even if your radio station pulls high ratings, you still have to sell the air time to make money. The top-earning station in the country during 2008 was Clear Channel's KIIS-FM in Los Angeles which brought in more than $66 million. Notice that three of the top 10 are AM radio stations. In parenthesis you see the format of the station (CHR stands for Contemporary Hits Radio).

Top Radio Earners

1. KIIS-FM (CHR) Los Angeles $66.3 million
2. KROQ-FM (ALT) Los Angeles   56.1
3. KFI-AM (News-Talk) Los Angeles 54.4
4. WLTW-FM (Lite AC) New York   52.6
5. WINS-AM (News) New York   51.8

6. WTOP-FM (News) DC	51.7
7. WHTZ-FM (CHR) New York	49.6
8. WCBS-AM (News) New York	46.7
9. KPWR-FM (Rhymc/CHR) Los Angeles	46.3
10. KOST-FM (AC) Los Angeles	45.7

Source: BIA Financial Network

Radio's audience is declining and growing older, leading to greater use of cost-cutting measures such as computer automation systems. Radio is no longer the "hot place to be" in media.

RBIA Kelsey says ad revenues were about $13.7 billion in 2009 and predicts a 1.5% increase in 2010. That doesn't come close to offsetting the 18.4% drop in 2008-2009.

Station revenue in the top 50 markets dropped in 2009 about 9%. The fall was 6.6% for stations in markets smaller than the top 50. That difference may indicate that broadcasters in smaller markets are better positioned to survive because there's less competition for ad dollars. We'll discuss where that money may be going in the chapter on advertising.

This situation appears to be turning around for radio. The veteran newspaper editor and entrepreneur known as the *Newsosaur*, Alan Mutter, says ad spending on radio rose 6% in the first half of 2010. *Barclays Capital* analysts predict radio revenue will move ahead at least 2.2% by the end of 2010, revising an earlier estimate of a 4.0% decline. For 2011, Barclays predicts another drop of 0.8%.

Radio's audience is declining and growing older.

Despite recent falling revenue, the vast majority of media buyers offer an optimistic outlook. They believe terrestrial radio is not threatened by new media, according to a poll by *Media Life*. Services like *Pandora* and internet radio will take away some listeners, but buyers say the appeal is limited. New media has already had its impact on radio because those are going to switch over have already done so.

At the lower end of the FM dial, *National Public Radio* is doing well, thanks to multiple revenue streams. The radio service hit a record of nearly 34 million listeners every week during the first part of 2010.

Google tried to revolutionize an old-fashioned business by stepping into selling radio ads in 2006. Following its successful model for selling ad links to Internet searches, the online titan shook up traditional media by auctioning off radio ads to buyers. But *Google* dropped its efforts in 2009 because stations wouldn't turn airtime over to a computer algorithm (code that tells the computer, step-by-step, how to achieve a certain goal) that set prices — prices far lower than their own rates. It didn't help that big advertisers steered clear of the auction model.

Google scuttled a similar newspaper effort because it never found a way to measure listener response similar to knowing how often users click on the company's online ads. Its venture into TV ad sales is still going forward.

RADIO TREND: DIGITAL RADIO

The term analog comes from audio recording. It is the old way of processing sound for radio and television. The new way is digital. While the on-off digital process cannot repeat sounds in the way that analog media can because of the gaps left in the recording, the human ear cannot tell the difference because the digital sampling is done at very small intervals.

U.S. broadcast television stations moved from analog to digital transmission in 2009. While the FCC hasn't set a timetable for radio to move to digital broadcasting, the technology is available and many stations are already offering digital signals.

Digital radio (or HD radio) is superior to analog FM (what you now hear when you turn on your radio) because FM frequencies require a line-of-site path between the transmitter and the receiver. Hisses, pops, static, and fading occurs because FM signals are reflected from obstructions such as buildings or from people as they move around the room where your radio receiver is located.

HD radio differs by using digital technology that minimizes reception problems and offers freedom from such interference. HD radio allows existing FM channels to play additional content on *multicast channels* (channels that allow for more than one signal to be sent to receivers). Digital technology also allows stations to squeeze in additional services, thanks to compression technology, allowing a simple broadcaster to offer more than one format. For example, in the Washington, DC area your FM radio will pick up WAMU at 88.5. The American University radio station offers programming from National Public Radio on the main channel and three separate digital radio signals. Channel 1 at 88.5 is a duplicate of the analogue signal. Channel 2 plays Bluegrass Country. WAMU-3 broadcasts different programming from a Baltimore radio station along with NPR and the BBC World Service.

An analog FM signal fades gradually as the distance from the transmitter increases. The signal also becomes noisier, with more interference. With a purely digital signal, there will be either perfect sound or no sound. The signal will not fade, pop, click or hiss in the coverage area, but as the signal drops below a threshold level, the signal disappears completely. Another difference between FM and HD is when you first try to pick up a signal that is a digital signal can take up to five seconds to capture, leaving the listener with several seconds of silence before the station can be heard.

More than 1,700 HD radio channels now cover more than 83% of the country. While the first wave of HD radios were pricey, as much as $500, some models now sell for less than $100.

Many people mistakenly believe that in order to listen to HD radio, they must pay an extra monthly fee as listeners do for satellite radio. If you buy an HD radio device, you'll pay only for that piece of equipment because the service itself is free, like regular radio.

There's also an HD radio feature called *iTunes tagging*. It lets listeners hit a "tag" button on their radio when they hear a song they enjoy. iTunes will list the tagged songs after syncing with the iPod for previewing and purchase.

RADIO TREND: WEB RADIO

Besides digital radio, there is Web radio, or Internet broadcasting. Edison Media Research says online listening is growing. More than 42 million people each week listen to radio streamed over the Internet.

Can a fan just start playing music online, creating his own Internet radio station? No, an account must be set up with Sound Exchange. This performance rights organization collects payments from Internet music broadcasters on behalf of copyright owners.

Radio is lagging behind other media in revenue from the Internet. About 2.4% of radio's income is from online, while TV gets 3.4% and newspapers 7%. There's competition as well from the Web-only radio stations. About 24 million of the 42 million people who listen to Internet radio tuned in to Web-only radio.

Crowdsourcing radio is the idea behind Internet radio services such as Pandora. Users are allowed to create personal radio stations, approving some songs while banishing other tunes from their playlist. It's no surprise that *terrestrial radio* is trying the same concept. If Google created a radio station, what would it be like? That's the thinking behind KITS radio. The San Francisco alternative rock station is putting control in the hands of listeners for one evening a week. The audience decides whether songs get played on Sunday nights during the *Jelli Radio* program. Online votes pick what hits the airwaves. Some songs get yanked in mid-spin. The online voting experience is designed like a video game. Virtual bombs can be dropped on a song while animated rockets can shoot a song up the playlist.

Online radio will grow by double-digits in the next few years, according to SNL Kagan and BIA. Radio news department are slow to utilize the Internet, perhaps because of staffing. The typical radio station has a one person news staff, no Facebook page, and no Twitter account. A survey by the Poynter Institute found that while most radio news departments have a website dedicated to news, very few include news audio or video.

RADIO TREND: SHOCK JOCKS

Some DJs and radio talk show hosts focus on stirring up audiences with outrageous or off-color statements.

New York's *Opie & Anthony* show held a yearly contest awarding participants points for having sex in public places. Couples were trailed by a comedian or member of the show. The observer would call the program to report the location. The contest was sponsored by the makers of Samuel Adams beer.

The contest got national attention when Brian Florence and Loretta Harper from Virginia were arrested for having sex in St. Patrick's Cathedral. During the segment, the spotter can be heard lying to police and cathedral security guards, claiming they were looking for a bathroom. Intense media outrage encouraged by the Catholic League led to the firing of hosts Gregg "Opie" Hughes and Anthony Cumia. The Catholic League also threatened to get the New York radio station's license revoked. *Opie & Anthony* broadcast for one more week, but were ordered not to directly address the incident for legal reasons. But they did, by calling it "the peanut butter and jelly incident." Infinity (owner of the radio station) fired the hosts and canceled their show. However, the company continued to pay the duo to stay off the air for the balance of their contract. The Catholic League immediately dropped its bid to revoke WNEW's license, but the station never recovered its ratings, although it switched formats several times and even changed its call letters.

Here's what happened to everyone involved.

Brian Florence died of a heart attack the next year. A month later, Loretta Harper pleaded guilty to disorderly conduct and was sentenced to seven days of community service. The FCC fined Infinity $357,000, the maximum amount allowed by law and the second-largest indecency fine in American radio history. Infinity refused to pay the fine. The company is now CBS Radio.

What happened to *Opie & Anthony*? In April of 2006, CBS radio issued a press release that announced the return of *Opie & Anthony*. It quoted a CBS radio exec as saying:

> "*Opie & Anthony* have proven their determination to succeed in this business, and have a relationship with their audience that is second to none in the industry. It's great to have *O&A* among that stable again. Loyal listeners of *O&A* have grown accustomed to a show that's real and entertaining. As we move forward, we do so with confidence that this new enterprise will continue in that same spirit."

On April 4, 2007, Don Imus was fired for calling some of the Rutgers University women's basketball players "nappy-headed hos" during his radio program. The talk radio show host has always gotten to the edge of what was acceptable on radio. In 1969, he was fired for saying "hell" on the air.

Would you have fired him over the Rutgers comment? Imus was back on the air with another radio network by December. While radio shows like Imus' and *Opie & Anthony* steer toward outrageous comments, keep in mind that half-way around the world, some radio broadcasters are putting their lives on the line. One of Iraq's top radio stations was attacked by terrorists in May of 2007. Dozens of heavily armed gunmen stormed an independent radio station in Baghdad. A guard was shot and killed, equipment was destroyed and the station was knocked off the air. When the radio staff called the Iraqi army for help, they were told it was too dangerous and they wouldn't sacrifice soldiers on behalf of the journalists. After an hour-long gun battle, the staff was able to hold off the insurgents, protecting women and children in the news room. The radio station's director told CNN he hoped the Al Qaeda attackers were watching and they should know "they have destroyed only walls and some computers and maybe a mixer, but they definitely didn't destroy our will."

Imagine going to work knowing you might be attacked, having guns stacked around just in case, and working for a boss who tells terrorists to, in effect, bring it on?

College radio provides a great opportunity to get experience at a real radio station. After learning how to "do radio" in a college setting, five years later students may be helping broadcasters in Iraq or some other remote part of the world where radio announcers put their lives on the line.

MUSIC TREND: COMPRESSION

Despite all the technical advances in the last decade, quality has taken a step back when it comes to music. The tunes to which most people listen are compressed, trading fidelity for portability, smaller file size and loudness. Rather than listening to music in the living room on high-fidelity speakers, fans experience recorded music on *iPods* while exercising, cooking dinner or other activities. The songs are usually saved on the digital devices in a compressed format, eliminating some of the range of frequencies in order to add more songs to the device and cut down on download times.

Radio has pushed toward compression as well. Radio management has urged engineers to create loudness for stations so the signal jumps out at listeners scanning the dial despite the loss of high and low frequencies. Rock, pop and country stations create listener fatigue this way. Classical music stations will not provide as loud a signal as other formats because these stations avoid excessive compression to allow for a greater range of sounds. Ironically, this creates a situation where classical stations offer greater variety, as least when it comes to the range of sounds offered, than modern music stations, which offer a narrow range of sounds to listeners.

For Next Time

What's your favorite television show? Are there any shows whose popularity you fail to understand?

ANSWERS TO RADIO QUIZ

1. There are more than 13,500 broadcast stations in the U.S.

2. There are more than two radios for every person in the U.S.

3. Radio reaches more than 9 out of 10 Americans age 12 and older each week, a higher penetration than television, magazines, newspapers or the Internet. Nearly 95% of college graduates aged 25-54 tune to radio each week.

4. The average person spends 3 hours and 18 minutes listening to the radio in an average week.

5. Radio reaches 57% of customers within an hour of making their purchase decisions.

SEVEN
Television and Cable

Television Timeline

1939 The first true public demonstration of TV in the form of regularly scheduled broadcasts on NBC.

1946 During a time when the door to broadcasting is virtually closed to women, Pauline Fredrick becomes a political reporter for ABC news and the first woman to pick up a Peabody Award for excellence in broadcasting in 1954.

1948 A 10-inch TV set sells for $100. If you are poor, you buy it on the installment plan.

A survey of New Yorkers shows two-thirds of fathers purchased their first TV sets to see the baseball World Series.

Both NBC and CBS launch evening newscasts.

TV stations begin showing up across the country, enough to cause interference with one another. The FCC, based in Washington, sees the conflict taking place near their offices. TV stations in Baltimore interfere with stations in Washington, DC. The agency stops the approval process and freezes new TV applications. The temporary fix lasts four years, until 1952. The time lag gives television stations already on the air more time to establish themselves before facing more competition.

1949 About 1.3 million TV sets are being used in the U.S., most of them on the east coast. A set with a 16-inch picture tube costs $695 (half the price of a new car). Every TV station in the country is losing money but none as much as NBC. The fledgling TV network is bleeding at a rate of $13,000 a day (more than $100,000 in today's money).

Photo courtesy Flickr. John Atherton
Used under Creative Commons
license.

American television turns a technological corner late in the year when eight stations on the East Coast and seven Midwestern stations are connected through cable. The public can now see network TV programs live.

Not everyone is happy to see the new technology moving into homes. *The New York Times* writes, "When it offers a daily diet of Western pictures and vaudeville by the hour, television often seems destined to entertain the child into a state of mental paralysis." The *American Academy of Pediatrics* recommends parents limit children's use of TV. Numerous studies show a correlation between slower cognitive development and behavioral problems with television viewing.

Not everyone agrees.

A paper published in the *Quarterly Journal of Economics* in 2008 suggests that the advent of television in the 1950's had a positive effect on children's cognitive ability, particularly those growing up in homes where English wasn't the primary language.

The New York Times writes, "When it offers a daily diet of Western pictures and vaudeville by the hour, television often seems destined to entertain the child into a state of mental paralysis." The *American Academy of Pediatrics* recommends parents limit children's use of TV. Numerous studies have shown there is a correlation between slower cognitive development and behavioral problems with television viewing.

1950   Half the TV sets in the U.S. are in New York City, the first TV remote control is introduced, and *Nielsen* begins compiling ratings for television nationally.

1951   Only one in eight households has a TV. Owning a TV set is still a status symbol. Some people are confined to watching it flicker in store display windows.

Photo courtesy Library of Congress.

TV gets its first national hit. Talent scouts scour the country for contestants who can sing or demonstrate other abilities. Does this sound familiar? The CBS show, *Arthur Godfrey's Talent Scouts*, is the *American Idol* of its day. Many of today's TV concept shows are re-works of old ones.

Singer Diahann Carroll appears on the *Godfrey* show during the fall. Very few blacks appear on TV at the time. The makeup artist is unsure how to effectively use makeup on a black person, so Diahann herself puts it on. In 1968, she becomes the first black actress with her own TV series, the NBC show *Julia*.

This year another program debuts that changes the face of television production: *I Love Lucy*. Lucille Ball and her husband Desi Arnaz insist that CBS allow them to record the show on film in Hollywood instead of the standard practice of broadcasting from New York. As a result, weekly series can now be produced quickly and inexpensively, and the TV industry exits New York, pushing away from a theatrical look into a more "flashy" presentation. *I Love Lucy* was the first TV show to record on film, part of what made reruns possible. Ball and Arnaz use three simultaneously running cameras, making for a greater variety of shots.

1953   Lucille Ball has a baby. The birth is written into the *I Love Lucy* show. More than two-thirds of all households with TV sets watch the show.

1954   All the networks air 36 days of an investigation by Senator Joseph McCarthy into potential communist sympathizers in the Army and Hollywood. The incident becomes known as the *Red Scare*.

In the early days of TV, the emphasis was sports and entertainment. Television newscasts were essentially radio on TV, newscasters reading scripts into a camera. The McCarthy hearings help viewers think of TV as a way to connect to news events.

1956   NBC picks a bird as the network symbol. The nickname *The Peacock Network* sticks. It's a creation of the network's Director of Design.

1957   Television news reports from Little Rock, Arkansas bring the force integration conflict into the living rooms of Americans all over the U.S.

1959   More than 20 network TV quiz shows populate the airwaves. The public discovers popular TV shows like *The $64,000 Question* are "fixed" by advertisers and producers. The quiz show scandals led to a congressional investigation and change the way the networks do business.

Women become local news anchors for the first time.

1960   Nine out of ten U.S. households have a television set. Nearly 70 million people watch Nixon and Kennedy during the first televised presidential debate. When the candidates arrive, Nixon asks Kennedy if he is going to wear makeup. Kennedy suggests makeup isn't manly, so Nixon does not wear any. But Kennedy does. TV viewers say John F. Kennedy wins, while radio listeners gave the edge to Nixon. People watching the debate on TV think Nixon looks sickly and pale.

1961   FCC chairman (Newton Minow) declares TV has become a "vast wasteland." The #1 TV show of the decade? *The Beverly Hillbillies*.

1967   Color TV sets outsell black-and-white sets.

Graphic video on TV network news shows American soldiers dying in Vietnam. Some say the Vietnam War is lost in the living room as opinion polls show Americans begin to believe the conflict is not winnable.

1968   Journalists begin shooting with video in the field instead of using film, thanks to portable video-recording equipment developed in Europe.

1969   TV is broadcast from the moon, allowing millions to see Neil Armstrong's historic walk.

1971   Congress passes a law preventing TV stations from running cigarette ads. The government generally stays away from issuing rules about programming, but makes an exception in the interest of public health.

1972   *Home Box Office* (*HBO*) begins programming. Only a handful of homes can see it, but later, *HBO* owner *Time Warner* begins distributing the movie channel by satellite. Many experts say people will not pay for television, something they are used to getting for free. *HBO* grows and is joined by a host of other satellite-delivered pay networks.

1973   The major TV networks air the *Watergate* hearings. A record number of hours are devoted to the Congressional investigation. The scandal leads to the resignation of President Nixon , sending several of his aids to prison. Scandals begin getting "gate" tagged to them.

1976   Videocassette recorders (VCRs) are now common in most homes.

1977   The *VHS format* is introduced to the market to compete against Sony's *Betamax* tape. Despite *Betamax*'s better quality, consumers usually pick the cheaper VHS system. Within three years, VHS outsells Betamax by a two-to-one margin. A superior technology does not always win the day. The video outlets that drive Betamax from the market are almost exclusively pornographic.

1979   *ESPN* hits the air.

1980   Ted Turner starts the first television network devoted to news. The *Cable News Network* (CNN) is first seen in only about three million homes. The budget for the 24 hour news operation is about one-third the size of what each of the big three networks devote to their news operations. Before Turner's attempt to make money with a news format, the television networks considered providing news an obligation in the public interest.

1983   The CBS network airs the final episode of the TV series *M*A*S*H*. It is the most watched TV episode ever. Ratings begin falling for the big networks afterward, as new cable channels begin developing original programming.

1987   Rupert Murdoch's *FOX* network arrives. This fourth network joins the big three: *ABC*, *NBC* and *CBS*.

1991   An amateur videotape of Rodney King being beaten by Los Angeles police leads to riots in the city, showing the potential power of citizen journalism.

1994   *Direct Broadcast Satellite* (DBS) becomes available to the public and soon satellite dishes sprout in yards, providing programming from *DirecTV* and, two years later, from *Dish Network*.

Mid-   The *AP* begins pumping money into photo and video journalism products for
1990s   sale to broadcasters.

1996   *DVDs* (Direct Video Discs) go on sale in the U.S.

1999   Digital Video Recorders (*DVRs*), *TiVo* and *Replay Network* debut. Audiences begin to *time shift*, that is, watch programs after the original broadcast time.

2003   Nearly half (45%) of all Americans turn to *cable news* first for information on the Gulf War with Iraq.

2009   Congress mandates that TV stations convert from analogue transmissions to digital. The original switchover date is February 17, 2009, but many consumers report trouble changing over. The government isn't on top of processing the requests for converter box coupons, so the FCC gives stations until June 12th to make the transition.

2009   TV viewing hits an all-time high of 141 hours per month in the second quarter, according to *Nielsen*.

2010   The Super Bowl features a close game between the New Orleans Saints and the Indianapolis Colts. The Saints victory sets a record in total households by posting an audience of 51.7 million, breaking the previous record held by the *M.A.S.H.* finale, which had 50.2 million homes.

Television & Cable Today

Network news divisions have historically been family jewels for their parent corporations, lending prestige and an aura of public service as well as a shield against government intrusion. But now the audience for network television is eroding. In the mid-1970s, more than nine out of ten homes would be tuned to *NBC*, *CBS* or *ABC*. Now, those networks (along with *FOX*) barely attract half of television's viewers, thanks to the surge of cable.

While the TV news networks only pulled about 22 million viewers in 2009, down from about 50 million in 1980, according to *The New York Times*, the network newscasts still amass an audience that dwarfs any show on a cable news channel.

Besides the shift toward cable, Internet sites are gaining eyeballs. And yet, despite losing viewers, and newspapers' reputation as the medium for in-depth reporting, television is still the first source for news for most Americans, according to the *2009 State of the First Amendment* national survey conducted by the *First Amendment Center*. About half (49%) of those surveyed said they learn about and follow major news stories from TV, followed by the Internet (15%), radio (13%) and newspapers (10%). Television, particularly the national networks, dominate next-day stories as well.

...despite losing viewers and newspapers' reputation as the medium for in-depth reporting, television is still the first source for news for most Americans...

FOX's average prime-time audience increased 10% in 2009 to 2.2 million. *CNN* averaged 917,000 in prime time compared to 822,00 for *MSNBC*. Over any given 24-hour period in 2009, the average *FOX* audience was 1.2 million while *CNN* came in second with an average of 614,000.

Despite all the preparation in network TV news, sometimes what goes on the air isn't planned. In the movie *Naked Gun*, the star's microphone is left on when he goes to the bathroom. It's one of those problems with wireless mics. It happened for real during a *CNN* broadcast. Kyra Phillips introduced a speech by president Bush and then left the anchor desk to powder her nose. Everything she said in the bathroom could be heard over the air including comments about her sister-in-law.. Taking the technical problem in stride, she later appeared on *Late Night with David Letterman*, offering these Top Ten Kyra Phillips Excuses:

10. "Still haven't mastered complicated On/Off switch."
9. "Larry King told me he does this all the time."
8. "How was I supposed to know we had a reporter embedded in the bathroom?"
7. "I honestly never knew this sort of thing was frowned upon."
6. "Couldn't resist chance to win $10,000 on 'America's Funniest Home Videos.' "

5. "I was set up by those bastards at FOX News."
4. "Oh, like YOU'VE never gone to the bathroom and had it broadcast on national television!"
3. "I just wanted that hunky Lou Dobbs to notice me."
2. "OK, so I was drunk and couldn't think straight."
1. "You have to admit, it made the speech a lot more interesting."

It was rumored the person handling audio that day was fired. TV news people will tell you the director could have been blamed just as easily. Regardless, within a few days, *CNN* engineers changed the way wireless mics were set up so that a tone would be heard whenever the anchor was not at the news desk. A lesson to anyone in TV and radio — always assume cameras and mics are on — that someone may be listening or watching.

There's no single route to an anchoring job. Some take classes in Journalism school while some find a way around it. *CNN* anchor Anderson Cooper says he decided to go into broadcasting, despite any formal training in journalism, because he was always interested in television news. After being denied entry-level positions, Cooper says, "I came up with my own plan. I figured if no one would give me a chance, I'd have to take a chance." He had a friend create a fake press pass and he went to war zones with a hand-held camera. Cooper says, "If I went to the dangerous places, I figured there wouldn't be much competition."

CNN anchor Carol Costello offers this advice on getting a job as a reporter or anchor:

> "There is so much you need to know in the world of broadcasting that doesn't include how to edit a piece, doesn't include how to run a camera. I wish I had known that when I was a youngster in school because I only concentrated on the things that involved television directly. I wish I had paid more attention to my political science classes, my history classes.

> "Don't get discouraged. If you want it badly enough, you will get it. And don't allow anyone to put you in a box because they think you can't do it. You know what you can do. And if you have a confidence in that you will be able to do it. Or you will find a way around the traditional ways."

Malcolm Gladwell, author of *Blink* and *Outliers*, told *TIME* magazine that young journalists should study something besides just journalism. Gladwell said, "If I was studying today, I would go get a master's in statistics, and maybe do a bunch of accounting courses and then write from that perspective. I think that's the way to survive."

Network Bias

People with particular political views tend to have friends with the same views.

Because *CNN* and *FOX News* have so much time to fill, there isn't a lot of time to sit around and plot ways to bring a political enemy down. Setting aside the commentary portions of their broadcasts, if there is bias, it is likely to show up in the selection of stories or in the guest selections and particularly in stories related to politics. People with particular political views tend to have friends with the same views. If you consume coverage that supports those opinions, you are more likely to believe the topics your friends and your media cover are more important, and what America is interested in discussing.

The physical placement of a story in a newspaper or the time slot for a TV news story can reflect biased coverage. Unintended bias can show up in the people a journalist decides to interview and the selection of story assignments by an editor.

The TV News Adventure

For those who are bored sitting in front of a computer from nine-to-five, TV reporting is a job that gets you out. You walk right past those people who'll be sitting at computers all day. And you never know what's going to happen when you hit the streets.

WORKING AT A TV NEWS NETWORK

Should you be hired by *CNN* as a writer, here's an idea of what to expect. Producers pick stories, find video for the stories and arrange the order of scripts. Writers write the stories, of course. Copy editors check stories for accuracy (and probably take apart your writing). The anchor reads the story (stumbling over the cute sentence you were so proud of writing or laughing during the serious story you wrote for them). There will be many rules not used by local TV news outlets. For instance, you are not supposed to use the "F" word. Not the obscenity. The word *foreign* is avoided (except in titles) to prevent an "us" and "them" feel about the network. The goal is a more world-based rather than U.S.-based newscast.

A 24-hour news network never stops, which means you'll end up working weekends and most holidays (you may have to win a lottery to be off Thanksgiving or Christmas week). You could be placed on the early morning shift — coming in at 2 AM for the shows that run from 6 AM to 9 AM and not get off work until 10 AM. When you first arrive, you'll "read in" — that is, catch up on the latest news and then attend a "show meeting" where team members pitch story ideas and go over what live reports will be included along with other production elements to be created. As a writer, you will typically put together 20-30 stories each day. Once you have your story assignments, you'll probably start with the easiest ones, or at least those that aren't likely to change much.

Besides putting stories together, writers have the responsibility to add other elements: computer codes for video, graphics, listening to SOTs (Sound on Tape, a piece of an interview). You're expected to know such rules as how to abbreviate members of congress as "reps" but not senators, know how to format the information that identifies a speaker and gives the person's title and usually is shown at the bottom of the TV screen (sometimes called fonts, supers, or CGs). Local news aims at one or two shows a day but network news never ends. Writers have the responsibility of updating stories as new information comes in: *Two are dead. Now it's five. Seven. Correction, it's six.* The work is fluid and you have to be willing to work in that kind of environment. For some people, it is energizing. For others, it's just stressful.

TV reporting… gets you out. You walk right past those people who'll be sitting at computers all day.

The Entertainment Giants

When we talk about broadcast television, we are really talking about one part of five enter-tainment giants that use their control to cross-promote the various parts of their businesses.

All the major and most of the minor broadcast networks are controlled by five companies.

> *Viacom* (MTV, BET and VH1)
> *Time Warner* (HBO, CNN)
> *Comcast* (NBC, Telemundo)
> *News Corp* (FOX)
> *Disney* (ABC, ESPN)

(As of this writing, *Comcast* has agreed to purchase a controlling interest in *NBC Universal*'s broadcast network, cable channels and movie studios, pending approval from federal regulators.)

Television Trends

TELEVISION TREND: DIGITAL TV

Only about one-in-ten American hopes had HDTV in 2004. The percentage jumped to half in 2009. The research firm Forrester predicts that by 2014 nearly three-out-four households will have at least one high-definition television.

Local American television stations spent nearly $10 billion to go digital. What do they get for the investment? Among other things, the opportunity to broadcast something other than their main programming on what are sometimes called *side channels* or *subchannels*. Most of the 1,700 TV stations in the U.S. are using these subchannels to send different programming to the public. But only about one out of ten households can actually receive these signals. Cable and satellite companies aren't motivated to carry the broadcasts because the programming is untested and the material may compete with what they already are showing.

MAKEUP

Digital TV is changing the way anchors and reporters use makeup.

The two critical items have always been base makeup and powder. Base is used to smooth out your skin and cover blemishes. The powder is to cut down on your shine. Television lights can put out a lot of heat. The make-up artists may add to your eyebrows if they aren't strong for definition.

Now, there's digital TV which shows greater detail. HD shows every flaw, wrinkle, or blemish in vivid detail and with traditional makeup, you can see brush strokes.

If you are not sure what you need, go to a MAC counter and ask a consultant to advise you. MAC Cosmetics Director of Make-up Artistry Gregory Arlt says HD gives more information than a camera can handle, so "you have to treat the make-up as a tight non-retouched beauty photo." Make up artists have learned to apply HD cosmetics by airbrush which applies the makeup to the surface in a dot pattern and replicates the pixels that HD uses.

I'm especially appreciative of the make up artists at CNN who noticed a new blemish on my forehead and suggested I get it checked by a doctor. I said I would, but didn't until they kept nagging me. Finally, one day when I was in the make-up chair, I told them I didn't know who to see about it. They gave me the name of a dermatologist that other CNN anchors regularly visited. I made an appointment. The look on his face when he inspected the spot told me I was fortunate to have professionals checking me daily. After surgery, he said we caught the melanoma just in time.

One more tip: If you're going to act like an anchor, you'll want to look like one as well. *TVNewsCloset.com* can help. It's basically an online consignment shop where anchors and reporters can buy and sell on-air clothing at affordable prices.

One way TV stations hope to get around the distribution problem is to make the material available on your cell phone. A group called the *Open Mobile Video Coalition* has come up with a standard that will let TV stations use a sliver of their new digital frequencies for broadcasts to wireless devices. The group says at least 70 stations have agreed to use the standard. Broadcasters hope viewers will ask cable operators and satellite providers to carry the channels on their systems. Consumers no longer want to be chained to a box in their homes.

Another bit of fallout from the shift away from analog to digital TV signals. There will be open, unregulated spectra between the digital channels. These spots are called "white spaces." Cellphone carriers like Verizon and AT&T paid a combined $19 billion for some of these freed-up airwaves. The FCC is expected to allow more of the spectrum to go toward providing Internet services like Wi-Fi. These frequencies are lower, and can pass through objects easier and go farther than traditional Wi-Fi. This could add many rural homes to the digital grid.

TELEVISION TREND: NONLINEAR TV (or Consumption on Demand)

Viewers used to say, "I've got to get home from work to watch my show." But now, we watch when we are ready. This is *nonlinear TV*, or *consumption on demand*. No longer held hostage to a broadcaster's schedule, the balance of power is tipped in favor of the audience who watch whenever it suits them.

An Austin, Texas Internet news site tweaked the nose of its TV competition in an ad that told viewers to either wait around until 5 PM for local TV news or get reports right now from the Internet. The promo shows what looks to be a pompous TV reporter standing around, picking his teeth, waiting for the TV news broadcast to start. The next scene is the Internet journalists rushing around a newsroom with a sense of urgency.

Someone in his 60's saw the promo and wrote:

> "That must be good for all the people that don't have a job and can sit around and watch the news all day. Most working people don't care about getting the news that fast. The Internet will get a small share of the news audience."

This ad plays directly to the thinking of young people who expect instant everything. If you look at the numbers, youth are migrating in this direction. The "working people" referred to is really an older generation.

Once upon a time TV news was broadcast at 5 or 6 PM and viewed following a nine-to-five work day. That's not what those who grew up using the Internet are doing. They get pieces of news on the go or from programs like *The Daily Show* and *Stephen Colbert*. Anchors used to be paid well because they offered a familiar face, but that's no longer so important.

The change from watching "when TV folk tell me to watch" to the TIVO-type thinking of "watching when I'm ready" and if it's not ready "I will move on to something else" is here.

TELEVISION TREND: THE INTERNET

Americans spend more time watching television than they do surfing the Web, writing email, watching DVDs, playing computer games, reading newspapers and talking on mobile phones put together, according to a study by the *Council for Research Excellence*. Television is not going away. But it's no longer the only star in the sky.

The president of a television station in a medium-sized market is quoted as saying, "I don't consider myself a broadcaster anymore. We are local content creators."

"There are no TV journalists anymore. There are video journalists," says *MSNBC.com*'s Charlie Tillinghast. The Internet has pushed TV reporters and shooters away from thinking only of their chosen medium. TV news video is now being prepared for both TV and online consumption.

Reporters can go live with breaking news by pushing video to *YouTube*, *Facebook* or *Twitter* through applications like *Qik*, *Kyte* and *Flixwagon*. This allows users to automatically post links to live video streams. *TubeMogul* will upload your video to more than a dozen sites at the same time, and *Uttterli* allows a quick audio report to be recorded by mobile phone and uploaded to a website.

The successful combination of TV and the Internet hinges on whether viewers will be willing to watch television broadcasts online. The average 2009 viewer watches 151 hours of TV each month but only three hours of video online, according to Nielsen. Online viewing is small but rapidly growing. A 2008 study shows that nearly one-fifth of American households watch TV broadcasts online. That's double the viewership from just two years ago.

Rather than turn computers into TVs, it may work the other way around. North American consumers will buy 6 million TV sets with Internet capability, representing 14% of all TV sales in 2009. *ABI Research* says by 2014 the number will rise to 45 million, representing 69% of sales.

Companies are now racing to build marketplaces for TV programs that act much like *iPhone* apps, able to interact with social-networking services, play games, call up movies and other Web content—all using a remote control. Microsoft, Apple, Yahoo and TiVo are in the game. What is missing is the equivalent of a Windows system for the living room, a widely accepted way to write programs that appear and act the same on most TVs. But many companies are trying. Google hopes to provide this missing piece. Using the search engine's *Android* platform and the *Google Chrome* Web browser, *Google TV* aims to seamlessly integrate traditional TV with DVR and the Web. Viewers will be able to watch shows from TV providers, interact with social media, play games, call up movies or the Web — all using the same smart phone acting as a remote control. The technology will make it as easy for TV viewers to use Twitter or Flickr as it is to change the channel.

Research suggests sheer laziness is slowing the migration to the Internet and working in favor of broadcast and cable TV networks. Many programs are no more than a few mouse clicks away, yet it is too much trouble for viewers who simply want to turn off their brains for a period of time and "veg." Plus, television watching has a social aspect to it. People like to be "in the loop," watching shows seen by others. Even viewers who can play back shows at any time will typically watch live TV most of the time.

A social aspect to TV viewing must also be considered. English researcher Sarah Pearson found that in British homes more than eight out of ten shows were viewed at the time of broadcast. Most families compromise, starting with "let's see what's on," then move to a DVR if nothing satisfies, and lastly, try on-demand video. The most effective Internet-TV combination may be one that allows Internet side tasks that do not distract other viewers.

New technology has not replaced watching major events, but seems to help them attract larger audiences. At the turn of the century, the most popular show was *Who Wants to be a Millionaire* with more than 28 million viewers. The #100 rated show pulled 30% of that figure. Nine years later, *American Idol* was the top show with an audience of more than 25 million. The #100 rated show only got 20% of that audience. The big event shows are drawing similar-sized audiences to those of a decade ago while the also-rans are falling farther back. Watching major events as they happen gives viewers a shared experience as well as something to talk about on social occasions.

Whether the PC absorbs TV programming or TVs become Internet-ready, what we know today as two separate devices will eventually merge into one. The public already treats television receivers as dual-purpose items, offering passive TV viewing and active gaming.

TV stations' online advertising makes up less than 5% of their revenue. Borrell Associates predicts a 21% increase by the end of 2010 to nearly $1.4 billion, a 13% increase in 2011, and 7% in 2012.

Most of the 762 TV stations originating local news at the end of 2009 see the Internet as a vital part of their future. Yet a *RTNDA/Hofstra University* study shows only one in five TV newsrooms maintain a Facebook page. Only a little more than a third of TV newsrooms are using Twitter. While TV station websites are increasingly adding audio and video to their sites, many have dropped streaming of their entire newscasts. About half of all TV news directors don't even keep up with how many people visit their website, although a little more than a third of TV websites are profitable. The Media Audit found the audience for major daily newspapers beat local TV sites in size in 73 of 95 markets.

TV Everywhere

TV Everywhere is what the industry calls sites made available only to paying cable and satellite subscribers. It will allow paying cable television subscribers to view shows online for no extra charge. Prove you subscribe to pay television and you can watch all the channels that you have paid for on any device. Motivating the change is the pay TV industry's fear that it will find itself in the same position as newspapers: offering a product fewer people are willing to pay for and no clear revenue from the Internet. Just as mobile phones have replaced many customers' land lines, on-demand Internet video is whittling away at that 90% figure of U.S. households subscribing to some form of pay TV. The increase in Internet-enabled TV sets and devices like slates should boost the trend in Internet video viewing even further. *eMarketer* estimates that by 2014, 77% of U.S. Internet users will be watching online video at least once a month.

Football fans can now watch the Super Bowl (in some cities) on cell phones, netbooks and other mobile devices. TV broadcasters are using some of the analogue broadcast spectrum (given up in the move to digital) to send broadcasts directly to specially equipped mobile devices.

We've seen TV programs like *News Hour* become available for free on *YouTube* while the old media vision of entertainment video on the Web can be seen in free sites like *Hulu.com*. More than 40 million people visit the site each month. *Hulu* ranked second only to *YouTube* in overall streams in April of 2010 according to both ComScore and Nielsen.

The broadcasters that control *Hulu*, ABC, FOX and NBC offer some 1,700 shows and movies for free for viewing a few commercials. Watch for movie studios to soon launch *Epix*, their own version of *Hulu*. The site creates a social TV opportunity by allowing *Facebook* friends to sign in and watch shows together.

But paid subscriptions may be around the corner for *Hulu* because *Business Week* says it lost an estimated $33 million in 2009. The new arrangement could be similar to a *Comcast* cable model called *On Demand Online* which lets subscribers see shows online by entering a password. Lurking in the wings is Apple which plans to offer television subscriptions over the Internet to its 100 million-plus *iTunes* subscribers.

Most industry experts believe it will be easier to charge for entertainment than for news. Shows like *The Office* and *NCIS* are unique. No substitutes are being created by anyone else. When it comes to news, you can get the same information from many sources. General-interest news sites requiring payment are competing with alternative versions of the same stories from free news sites.

TELEVISION TREND: CITIZEN JOURNALISM

FOX, CNN, and other news networks have been trying to figure out what to do about all the video on the Internet that's taking attention away from their broadcasts. Any time something happens these days, video, photos, and texting are on the scene.

The positive side of citizen journalism is that we get lots of on-the-spot video and pictures. When an airplane went down in the Hudson River in January 2009, the first picture of the accident out of New York came to the public from Twitter. CNN started adding viewer-submitted video and pictures into the news cycle. CNN calls their version of photos and videos sent by viewers *iReports*. The typical iReport traffic is somewhere between 200,000 and 400,000 page views each day.

But it can go the other way as well. Citizen journalism could lead to fake news stories getting broadcast by accident. In the fall of 2008, CNN's user-submitted site included an iReport that claimed Apple CEO Steve Jobs had suffered a heart attack. Apple's stock tumbled more than 10% before the false story was removed from the site. Investors lost money because of the false report. The UK's *DailyMail*, Britain's second biggest newspaper and most popular website, reported an iPhone recall mistakenly based on a tweet from a notorious Steve Jobs pretender. This is why some professionals in the industry believe this shift toward the average person coming up with news will bounce in the other direction once legitimate news organizations get burned a few times and lose credibility.

Here's a note from a TV news producer who wrestled with her job when management discovered what was available through the Internet.

> "A manager bounced into our show meeting last week, all brimming with the latest brainstorm he'd just had. Management's newest "vision" seems to become the Internet of cable TV; they're trying to out-*YouTube* (which they're obsessed about, by the way) *YouTube*. So he has decided that for our upcoming coverage, we should bag the political analysts and go for "citizen reporting," which is to say: find one eloquent, glib person in each state, an average Joe or Josephine, preferably in their late 20's or 30's, who has a webcam and let them sound off on the daily events in the campaign."

> "What about folks who don't have a webcam?" "We'll have a contest, says he: we'll give away one free webcam in each state."

> "Uh, how are you going to vet these people?" "What do you mean," he asks? This is big time hardball politics, playing for all the marbles." "How're you gonna make sure one of your 'citizen reporters' isn't a shill for the GOP or Dems, or for a particular candidate? How're you gonna make sure a campaign doesn't get to them and woo them to spin for them? In short, how're you gonna be a responsible gatekeeper?" This was his direct quote: "That's old school! What matters now is 'real people' saying what's 'really going on', without any filters."

What do you think? Is this a good idea? The producer wrestled with this unsettling conclusion:

> "I swear, I wanted to turn my face to the wall and die. For the very first time in my career, I am ashamed at being part of this. My personal and professional standards have fallen so low, I'm willing to go along with it, just for a decent paycheck. I am a whore, a Judas Iscariot who has betrayed what I believe for the thirty pieces of silver that come in the form of six-weeks of vacation and a nice benefits package."

Is this an example of the demise of true journalism or a disgruntled employee who won't get on board with the wave of the future?

If individuals can hunt and gather on their own, what they will need is someone to help them process the information and make it usable. Citizen journalism may put the pros in a

"For the first time in my career, I am ashamed at being a part of this."

position where they spend less time going out to get the news and more time playing gate-keepers, shuffling through the stacks of digital suggestions flowing their way from average citizens.

Google's YouTube Direct is an attempt to bring media outlets and citizen journalists together. Media organizations are able to use the service in order to gather and review submissions based on their own criteria.

TELEVISION TREND: INFO-TAINMENT

Public Radio International CEO Alisa Miller presented a study at a 2008 TED conference showing a map based on the number of seconds that American network and cable news organizations dedicated to news stories by country during the month of February 2007. The more stories involving a country, the larger the land mass. She told the audience,

> "This was a month when North Korea agreed to dismantle its nuclear facilities and there was massive flooding in Indonesia. And in Paris, the IPCC released its study confirming man's impact on global warming. The U.S. accounted for 79 percent of total news coverage. The combined coverage of Russia, China and India, for example, reached just one percent. (One) story eclipsed every country except Iraq, and received 10 times the coverage of the IPCC report."

That story was the death of Anna Nicole Smith.

Putting news and comedy together is a related info-tainment trend. Comedian Stephen Colbert conducted a memorable interview with Georgia Representative Lynn Westmoreland in 2006. The Congressman was co-sponsoring a bill that would require Congress to display the Ten Commandments.

> Colbert asks, "What are the Ten Commandments?"
> Westmoreland: What are all of them?
> Colbert: Yes.
> LW: You want me to name them all?
> Colbert: Yes.
> Westmoreland: Uhhh. Ummmm. Don't murder. Don't lie. Don't steal. (Colbert is counting them on his fingers).
> Westmoreland: Ummmmm. I can't name them all.

The blur between news and entertainment, not only in the stories but in the newscasters themselves can be seen in a 2009 *TIME* Magazine online poll. Readers were asked to name the "most trusted newscaster." Here are the results:

> Comedy Central's Jon Stewart – 44%
> NBC's Brian Williams – 29%
> ABC's Charles Gibson – 19%
> CBS' Katie Couric – 7%

A comedian delivering satirical news is dubbed the "most trusted" newsman by a wide margin.

TELEVISION TREND: 3-D TV

In a 1955 episode of Jackie Gleason's *The Honeymooners*, Ralph tells his wife that he is not going to buy a new TV set because "I'm waiting for 3-D." Ralph, your day has come. Manufacturers now have a 3-D set on the market. Although the initial high price could keep Ralph on the couch, Sony and other TV makers are placing big bets that it will catch on. They need new innovations to keep the cash register ringing. Of course, the move to 3-D could be a fad. Watching football players run through the living room might be thrilling, but it's hard to say how many people would like to watch *The View* in 3-D. A viewer must wear special glasses, and while technology that allows 3-D without glasses is on the horizon, it might force viewers to sit in a particular spot or have other drawbacks. You'll only be able to use the glasses made for your particular TV brand. These glasses may improve the viewing experience, but they won't help with checking email or the other things people like to do while watching shows. Plus, some people do have abnormal depth perception. They cannot see in 3-D at all because of a minor eye muscle imbalance. The experience only gives them a headache. Sales in the first part of 2010 have been disappointing, but the typical consumer may be waiting for the initial price to come down.

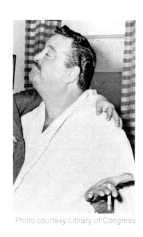

Photo courtesy Library of Congress

TELEVISION TREND: INTERACTIVE CABLE & TV

Interactive Cable and TV make possible video-on-demand and something called one-click shopping. In other words, you see a product, you click on some icon located on the screen and you can automatically order it. There's program interactivity where you can make predictions about upcoming plays while watching a football game, pick a camera angle, play along with show contestants, learn more about the actor on screen, etc. Interactive ads let viewers vote in a poll or use their remote controls to request more information about a product. Set-top boxes can send specific commercials to specific households or neighborhoods based on income, ethnicity or other demographics. Interactive ads allow advertisers to give a household with children a commercial about a macaroni and cheese product. Apple is working on net-connected televisions. The table set device could be used as a portable TV or for reading digital books.

Change is in the wind, but management guru Peter Drucker advises leaders not to try to force it to flow a certain way. No one can *manage* change. We can only be prepared to respond to change.

TELEVISION TREND: RECOVERY

Falling television revenue in recent years is partly due to the economy, partly due to the move of news to the Internet.

Nearly two-thirds of big advertisers, surveyed in 2008, said TV advertising had become less effective than the previous two years. Viewers objected to the number of ads during commercial breaks, leading to the increasing number of devices that allow viewers to circumvent TV ads altogether.

Local TV news audiences fell by an average of nearly 6% in 2009 while overall revenue dropped more than 22% from the previous year, according to *BIA Advisory Services*. The media research firm predicts revenue will reverse course and increase slightly each year through 2013. Alan Mutter, a veteran newspaper editor and entrepreneur known as the *Newsosaur,* says there's evidence to back that up. He says ad spending on TV rose 10.5% in the first half of 2010.

While the average amount of the broadcast day dedicated to news rose from 4.1 hours in 2008 to 4.6 hours in 2009, according to *The Project for Excellence in Journalism,* about 200 stations have turned over their local news coverage to another television station. KDNL in St. Louis and WYOU in Scranton, Pennsylvania have dropped their newscasts entirely. *The Project* also found TV audiences have fallen off about 1 million per year for the past 25 years, while at the same time the U.S. population has grown an average of 2.8 million a year. Local TV news shed some 1,200 jobs in 2008, and 450 jobs in 2009. *Media Bistro* puts the local TV job loss at 19% in 2009 and 8% at TV networks. The exception was cable TV news, which remained steady.

But it's not all bad news for local TV.

The same research from *The Project for Excellence in Journalism* has shown that by 2012, local TV stations could generate an additional $1.1 billion if they deliver news, information and entertainment to cell phones and other portable devices. Those joining the television news industry should be aware that they may soon be delivering news on portable devices.

The music industry's financial formula was upended when listeners found it worthwhile to cherry-pick from albums and buy just a single song or two. By contrast, TV viewers want to watch whole episodes of the Fox series, *House,* not just one or two scenes.

Despite inroads by Web advertising, TV remains the number one ad medium in the U.S. *The Wall Street Journal* says the TV industry made $69.4 billion in 2008. The cable TV business is on firmer ground than broadcasters because their business model remains very profitable. Cable programming channels producing content are not dependent on mass audiences because their revenue streams come from more than one source — cable systems and advertisers

For Next Time

What's the difference between an avid player and someone who spends too much time in front of the video game console? How can you tell if someone is a video game addict, or is there such a thing?

Video Games Timeline

1931   *Baffle Ball* is the first mass-produced arcade game.

1961   MIT student Steve Russell creates what is considered the first interactive computer game. What made *Spacewar!* interactive? Its use of toggle switches.

1972   *Atari* incorporates and releases the company's first arcade machine, called *Pong*. Set up in a Sunnyvale, California bar, the machine shuts down within days because the coin box is stuffed full of quarters.

1972   *Magnavox* sells the first home video game system, a TV console system called *Odyssey*.

1978   An arcade game created in Japan invades America. This game is called *Space Invaders*.

1980   *Namco* releases *PacMan* and it becomes an instant classic and all-time bestseller.

1981   *Nintendo* releases *Donkey Kong*. The game, designed by Shigeru Miyamoto, features a protagonist who saves his girlfriend from a gorilla. Nintendo's American employees name the mustachioed character Mario, after their office landlord.

1983   Atari goes from grossing $2 billion a year to losing more than $500 million in one year, thanks in part to a game about *ET: The Extra-Terrestrial*. The company hoped to capitalize on the surprise hit at the movies by rushing the product into the market. With only six weeks of development, the game involved *E.T.* finding pieces of a telephone in order to "phone home." Many places *E.T.* could search were completely empty. Sales were terrible and company revenue plunged.

1984   Warner sells *Atari*. Other major companies, including Mattel, leave the industry because they are suffering heavy losses.

1985   A Russian programmer creates *Tetris*.

   A Japanese programmer creates a cheat sequence to make a Nintendo game easier to test. The *Konami Code* is now built into many games. If the game is paused during the title screen and a particular sequence is entered (up, up, down, down, left, right, left, right, B, A, start) the user begins the game fully stocked with weapons. This information leaks out, allowing many average players to more easily win the game. For a while, you could type this sequence into ESPN.com and the page would fill up with rainbows and unicorns. The same sequence would fill Google Reader with ninjas.

1989   Nintendo invents the *GameBoy* hand-held system.

1993   Id Software releases *Doom*, offering a nearly three-dimensional perspective in first-person shooter games.

1995   Sony begins selling *PlayStation* in the U.S., a year after introducing it in Japan.

1997   *Grand Theft Auto* spawns a billion-dollar franchise and public controversy over violence and sex in video games.

2000   Will Wright designs a game he calls *The Sims*, in which players create virtual worlds and fill them with virtual inhabitants. The franchise goes on to sell more than 100 million copies worldwide.

2001   Microsoft challenges the console market with its *Xbox* system.

2002   Microsoft launches *Xbox Live*, an online gaming service connected to its console.

2006   Nintendo launches the *Wii* console. It allows players to move their characters by waving controllers in the air.

2007   Annual video game sales surpass those of the *music industry* for the first time.

2008   People spend more on video games than on *DVDs*. Video games own 53% of the packaged home entertainment market in 2008.

2008   In the final weeks before the November 4 general election, Barack Obama makes U.S. political history by placing the first presidential *campaign ads* in online video games.

2009   *Call of Duty: Modern Warfare 2* becomes the biggest entertainment launch ever when total revenue from first day U.S. and U.K. sales reaches $310 million.

2010   The Cub Scouts offer a pin for video gaming. Cub Scouts are required to demonstrate an understanding of the video game rating system, create a schedule that balances gaming and school work, and learn to play a new video game.

...video game consoles are close to being a 5th TV network.

Video Games Today

Many video games are simple shooter or arcade-style contests, while more sophisticated titles create new worlds where character experiences follow Hollywood-type plots, and well-known actors offer voice-overs. The U.S. Army makes use of video games for officer training. The games mimic real-life combat situations where competent high pressure decision-making is critical.

A report issued by *Nielsen PreView* called *The Video Game Handbook* says console game usage (gaming systems which are connected to a user's TV) accounted for 64 billion minutes in December of 2008. Only four other networks (CBS, ABC, FOX and NBC) got more viewing time. In other words, video game consoles are close to becoming a 5th TV network. Private equity firm *Veronis Suhler Stevenson* predicts that by 2013, the video game market will nearly reach the size of the shrinking newspaper industry.

But video games sales have slumped, according to the research firm *NPD Group*. U.S. video game sales including hardware, software and accessories, fell about 8% to $19.66 billion in 2009 and 11% in the first half of 2010. The revenue fall off can partiality be credited to the rise of new technologies such smartphone apps and social network titles. Bootlegged copies also eat into sales. A blog tracking filesharing called *Torrent Freak* reports the 2009 bestseller *Call of Duty: Modern Warfare 2* was illegally downloaded more than 4 million times that year alone compared with 290,000 retail purchases.

Despite sluggish sales, the industry still serves as a bellwether for technology. Because the video game culture is less stifled by legacy products and stodgy thinking, it can more easily suggest where media can take us.

VIDEO GAMER QUIZ

1. What percentage of Americans play video games?
2. Guess the age of the average gamer.
3. How many are over the age of 50?
4. How many are female?
5. The average gamer spends how many hours a week playing?
6. Adult gamers have been playing an average of how many years?
7. What percentage of adults play video games with their children?

(Answers are at the end of the chapter)

GAMING INDUSTRY QUIZ

1. Game console sales are the province of three companies. Name them.
2. What percentage of all games introduced to the market fail?
3. Advertisers are attracted to online games because players tend to stay with a gaming website longer than with other sites. What's the industry term for this effect?
4. Are U.S. video game sales up or down in the last couple of years?

(Answers are at the end of the chapter)

Video Games and Social Violence

Does playing video games stifle your skills at social interaction?

• In 1999, *Doom* fans 18-year-old Eric Harris and 17-year-old Dylan Klebold killed 12 students, a teacher, and wounded 23 others at Columbine High School in Colorado before killing themselves. The teens' "addiction" to video games was prominently noted in the news media. The Columbine shooters had even created a custom *Doom* to represent the shooting of their classmates.

• In 1998, 13-year-old Mitchell Johnson and 11-year-old Andrew Golden of Jonesboro, Arkansas, frequent players of the shooting game *GoldenEye 007*, set off fire alarms at their middle school and then shot at students and teachers as they fled the building. They killed four students and a teacher.

A few days after the Arkansas shootings, NBC's *Today Show* featured a debate moderated by Matt Lauer over violence in the media and its influence on children. Here are two quotes from the show:

Kathy McCoy, a child therapist with the *California School of Psychology*:

> "I think the greatest influence on children is what they see and experience at home and in their own communities. Certainly television is a factor, among many other things, but your average 11, 12, 13 year old is not going to watch a violent film and then go out and act on it. Kids who act violently usually show significant signs of trouble along the way. You don't go from being an average kid to being a mass murderer without showing signs of trouble."

Offering another perspective was Robert Peters, president of *Morality in Media*:

Every time a new media sweeps the nation, there are those who decry it as a tool of evil.

> "I don't disagree for a moment that children, for the most part, are more affected by what happens in their homes and communities; that's why most of them don't go out and do this. But in instances when it does happen, where are the ideas coming from? Are they coming from dad, mom, the church, the school? Or are they coming from a computer game or a rap music video or a brutal Hollywood film? That's the issue. The question is not whether parents normally have more influence over their children; the question is whether in a disturbing number of cases kids, for whatever reason, that are not getting that proper home upbringing, are being influenced by popular culture to commit crimes?"

Pause for Discussion: A Question of Violence

Whose opinion do you most agree with and why? Are video games a healthy escape for children? Just a reflection of society?

Consider this quote:

> "Is this to become a chief arm of education? Will the classroom be abolished and the child of the future stuffed with facts as he sits at home or even as he walks about the streets with his portable set in his pocket?" (From *Century Magazine*, June 1924, p. 149)

Here's another:

> "Its potential for lowering the speech standard of the country is almost incalculable. The fact that it is likely to be (used) by the less discriminating portion of the public operates to increase its evil effects." (From *Commonweal Magazine*, April 10, 1929, p. 653)

One more:

"Constant brutality, viciousness, and unsocial acts result in hardness, intense selfishness, even mercilessness, proportionate to the amount of exposure and its play on the native temperament of the child." (From *New Republic Magazine*, November 1, 1954, p. 12)

Guess which medium these quotes are talking about? The first quote is about radio in 1924, the second is about sound movies in 1929, and last warns about TV in 1954. Each time a new medium sweeps the nation, there are those who decry it as a tool of evil. Is the influence of video games different from previously-disparaged media?

Here's another perspective on whether playing video games has a negative effect on players.

The son of an Ohio pastor says he killed his mother and shot his father because they refused to let him play *Halo 3*. Daniel Petric claimed to be addicted to video games. The judge who sentenced him to 23 years in prison said, "I feel confident that if there weren't such things as violent video games, I wouldn't know (this young man)."

What do you think about the judge's comment?

The *Campaign for a Commercial-Free Childhood* claims *Grand Theft Auto 3* "portrays the brutal murder of women, minorities, the elderly, and police officers," while the *American Academy of Pediatrics* warns video games can contribute to "physical and mental-health problems."

In 2007, *The American Medical Association* turned down a request to make video game addiction a formal psychiatric disorder. Declaring it a formal disorder would have opened up millions in insurance money for those afflicted and created awareness for the topic. Reactions to the *AMA* decision were mixed.

A review of 130 studies by researchers at Iowa State University "strongly" suggested playing violent video games increases aggressive behavior. Researchers at Iowa State University reviewed data on more than 130,000 gamers, ranging in age from elementary school to college in the U.S., Europe and Japan. A professor at Texas A&M took issue with the findings, saying the analysis contained many flaws which "overestimated the influence" of violent video games on aggression.

A 2009 study showed that using the classic computer game *Tetris*, where players piece together colored puzzle pieces as they fall from the top of the screen, can enlarge the brain.

In this study, two dozen adolescents played for a half-hour every day for three months. Brain scans showed that some regions of the cerebral cortex had added new cells, growing as much as a half-millimeter thicker. The researchers are not sure whether the growth helps users do other tasks besides play *Tetris*.

Video game performance can be predicted by measuring the volume of specific parts of the brain. A University of Pittsburgh psychologist reported in January, 2010, that these areas determine a person's ability to refine motor skills, learn, strategize and adapt to new situations. The larger these parts of the brain, the better the person succeeds at gaming.

University of Oklahoma Medical School researcher Paul Lynch studied the effect of video games on 600 middle schoolers and found kids who play video games tend to have lower

Regardless of which position you decide to take on the media's impact, don't blindly go through your day never considering the larger questions about whether you are making a positive or negative impact on the world around you.

GPAs and see the world as more hostile and aggressive. Only 4% of those who played no violent video games got into fights over the course of a year, but of those exposed to long hours of violent video games, that figure rose to 38%.

In another study, reported in the November 2008 issue of the journal *Pediatrics*, children who were exposed to more video game violence became more aggressive over time than their peers who had less exposure. This held true even when researchers took into account the aggressiveness of the children at the beginning of the study.

While a number of studies show a correlation between violent video games and teenage behavior, actually proving the games cause violence is very difficult. It's the difference between causation and coincidence.

Hamburgers & Car Crashes

Most people who die in car crashes have eaten a hamburger less than a week before the tragic event that cuts their lives short. Does this mean eating hamburgers causes traffic accidents? Not at all. A connection between the two events has to be established before you can unfurl and plant the "cause and effect" flag. Otherwise, you may fall into the *causal fallacy*.

That's why when it comes to issues such as medical advice there needs to be numerous studies suggesting the same conclusions. Studies with mixed results suggest there could be other causes at work besides the one we are investigating.

Consider this: Rich people may live longer because they have access to better health care. Do they live longer because they are rich? Well, sort of. That's what gives them access to the better health care.

The whole cause-and-effect connection can become confusing when events happen around the same time frame. We have a natural desire to tie them together with a big bow. Remember the saying about trouble coming in three's? When we begin looking for groups of three, we tend to remember those times when our hypothesis was confirmed. We think it's true because we don't notice, or simply discount, situations when life didn't fit with our theory.

Halo Thinking

A member of the team that created one of the best-selling video games was questioned as to whether he believed making violent video games like *Halo* created more violence or had no effect on users. Was he indirectly helping to emotionally damage kids by encouraging them to act aggressively? He looked puzzled and said, "I never thought about that." It had never occurred to him to think beyond his current project and consider the ultimate impact of his product. Was he contributing to society by offering a catharsis for gamers or was he throwing fuel on the fire just by performing the duties of his job?

Regardless of which position you take on the media's impact, don't blindly go through your day never considering the larger questions about whether you are making a positive or negative impact on the world around you. Your responsibility is to define and put flesh on your views while studying the process of news gathering. Then, when you enter into the professional ranks you can make your own decisions rather than simply falling into the viewpoints of others around you. News develops so fast you won't have time to convene a committee and explore the philosophical implications as you go along. Stir your natural curiosity and look outside your box now.

As a journalist, you'll be in a position to decide whether you believe the media are society's mirror or whether they drive the social conversation. This will impact questions like: Will we encourage copycat crimes by running this story? Are we in a position to encourage positive social change by telling about a local hero or uncovering some injustice or inequity?

A critical component of responsible journalism is letting your natural curiosity drive your passion to learn and analyze information. Pursue and develop that gut-level journalistic instinct.

Another Offense

Maybe you don't see addiction as a problem. But some people object to games on other grounds.

Leaders of an Anglican cathedral threatened to sue Sony for creating what they called a "sick" game. The cathedral served as a backdrop for a bloody shootout in the *PlayStation 3* game *Resistance: The Fall of Man.*

Do you think an apology is in order?

Sony did apologize to the *Church of England* for the violent computer game. Tony Blair (Prime Minister at the time) told lawmakers that companies like *Sony* should focus on their wider social responsibilities, not just profit. The church was particularly concerned because *Manchester Cathedral* has a history of gang-related gun violence. But in its letter, Sony said it did not accept "that there is any connection between contemporary issues in 21st century Manchester and the work of science fiction in which a fictitious 1950s Britain is under attack by aliens."

Top U.S. Sellers 2008 (in millions of units)

1. *Wii Play* w/ remote   5.28
2. *Mario Kart Wii* w/ wheel   5.00
3. *Wii Fit* w/ balance board   4.53
4. *Super Smash Bros. Brawl*   4.17
5. *Grand Theft Auto IV*   3.29

Source: *NPD Group*

Video Game Trends

VIDEO GAME TREND: CONVERGENCE

The Internet is changing the way games are made and distributed. After a tough couple of economic years, companies are exploring new areas of delivering content digitally, through

Facebook and the iPad. The iPad could impact home console games if gamers find a reason to swap their console for the iPad, but they may be content with their current setup.

The development of smaller, faster, more powerful microprocessors is blurring the distinction between game consoles, personal computers and PDAs. At the same time, players are increasingly willing to play games on different platforms.

Cloud Computing makes it possible to have feature-rich gaming by tapping into resources over the Web, regardless of where you play or what kind of machine you use.

Virgin Gaming, BringIt.com, and *Gaaxy4Gamers.com* give players the chance to test their skills to make money online. Legal in 39 states, video games are considered games of skill rather than chance, so these companies avoid terms like "gambling" and "betting." Observers say they expect similar offerings on portable devices.

VIDEO GAME TREND: HYPERCOMMERCIALISM

Advertisers have come to think of games as much like magazines: Specific titles that attract very specific audiences. Different titles draw different demographics. *Mortal Kombat* and *Grand Theft Auto* pull in a different crowd than *Spiderman.*

Getting to the buyers you want to reach is critical for advertisers, so we're going to continue to see money moving toward in-game advertising. A research firm projects it will grow 18.5% from 2008 to 2013. Paid interactive television is expected to increase 38.7% during that same time period.

VIDEO GAME TREND: ADVERGAMES

Advergames are video games produced expressly as brand commercials. The auto industry, for instance, makes use of CD-ROM advergames. The *John Deere* game (find it at boldgames.com) encourages players to manage their own successful farm.

PepsiCo International and Microsoft teamed to create an advergaming campaign tied to the World Cup in 2010. Users move from *Zero* to *Hero* through five interactive games using instant messaging, e-mail and social networks involving Microsoft properties, like Windows Live Messenger and Xbox.com.

Microsoft created a game for PepsiCo tied to the 2010 World Cup in South Africa. Users manipulated avatars by utilizing instant messaging, e-mail, and social networks.

VIDEO GAME TREND: ADVOCACY GAMES

Advocacy games are produced by companies or organizations wanting to get their noncommercial messages out to the public. In *Swine Fighter,* for instance, players are called upon to fight swine flu illness. In doing so, they learn about how to prevent the sickness and how to treat it. Created by two online-game developers in their mid-20's, it offers helpful everyday actions suggested by the *CDC* that can help combat swine flu and give users the chance to donate to the *Red Cross.*

And the city health office in London, Ontario, created an online sex ed game called *Sex Squad*. A cast of superheroes (such as Captain Condom) answer sex knowledge questions and receive protection with correct answers but a wrong answer gets a player squirted with sperm. You can find a link to the game at *healthunit.com*. These are examples of advancing a cause in a game environment.

VIDEO GAME TREND: INTERACTIVE GAMES

It's not just for kids anymore or even young adults. Seniors are getting in on the act. Playing game systems like Wii are a great way to get up and get some exercise (though a recent study suggests the health benefits are overrated). Because of the Wii effect, 25% of Americans over 50 now occasionally play video games, according to *The Wall Street Journal*.

A freshman class at New York University is devoted to the study of *Guitar Hero*. The class explores questions like, "Why are video games like *Guitar Hero* so popular?"

VIDEO GAME TREND: ONLINE SOCIAL GAMES

The availability of so many free games on the iPhone and ad-supported websites force video game companies to invest more to chase consumers.

An unauthorized version of *Scrabble* that ran on *Facebook* boasted some two million registered users before legal threats shut it down. Playfish's *Restaurant City* has 15 million monthly active users. The *iPhone* game *Doodle Jump* is bringing gaming to the masses by allowing the user to interact with other players.

About three million gamers have downloaded *Microsoft's 1 vs. 100*, a live quiz show for the gaming community. A studio host tosses out trivia questions for players who try to accumulate *Microsoft Points*, which can be used to buy certain items. A games-on-demand service called *OnLive* promises to allow users to play any PC or console game on any computer or TV without the need for a console at all.

The consulting firm PricewaterhouseCoopers sees indie games as an evolving part of the online games market, which is set to grow from an estimated $8 billion globally in 2008 to more than $14 billion in 2012.

The ability for *Xbox* users to access *Facebook* and *Twitter* is an indication console gaming is becoming more social. *Uncharted 2* allows you to tweet your progress from inside the game.

ANSWERS VIDEO GAME QUIZ

1. *The Wall Street Journal* says 200 million Americans play videogames. A fourth (24%) are between the ages of 2 and 12 while a fifth (20%) are between 25 and 34. Americans, as a whole, spend more time playing video games than they do watching the CW television network. That's why video games have been called the real "5th Network" behind ABC, CBS, FOX and NBC.

2. The average gamer is 30 years old.

3. 19% of players are over 50. About one out of five.

4. In 2001, IDC research estimated less than 12% of game players were female. They now account for about 40% of the overall market in 2009, according to financial firm *Wedbush Morgan*.

5. The average gamer spends 6.8 hours per week playing.

6. Adult gamers have been playing an average of 12 years.

7. 80% of adults play with their children.

ANSWERS TO THE GAMING INDUSTRY QUIZ

1. Game console sales are the province of three companies: *Microsoft* (Xbox), Japan's *Nintendo* (Wii), and *Sony* (Playstation)

2. It may surprise you to know that 50% of all games introduced to the market fail.

3. Advertisers are attracted to online games because they are "sticky." That is, players tend to stick with game sites longer than with other websites.

4. The video game industry generated nearly $19 billion in U.S. revenue in 2007. It rose to more than $21 billion in 2008. But in 2009, the supposed recession-proof industry fell by 12% through October 3 from the same period a year before, according to *NPD Game*.

For Next Time

Find a website (or two) that you think would help a journalist, and come prepared to share it. And it can't be popular sites everyone knows, like Google.

The Internet

Internet Timeline

Mid-1880's   Englishman Charles Babbage creates designs for a rudimentary computer that makes algebraic computations using stored memory and punch cards.

1943   The British develop *Colossus* during World War II to break the German secret code. It is the first electronic digital computer, reducing information to a binary code made up of the digits 1 and 0. The term *bit* is a shortening of binary digit. *Bytes* is the more commonly used term, with one byte equaling 8 bits.

1946   The U.S. military creates ENIAC (Electronic Numerical Integrator And Computer), the first general-purpose electronic computer (using binary 1's and 0's).

1952   The first use of computers for news analysis. CBS television uses UNIVAC, the first commercial computer produced in the U.S. to accurately predict the outcome of the presidential election. Defying pollster expectations, UNIVAC proclaims Dwight Eisenhower will beat Adlai Stevenson in a landslide, which is exactly what happens.

1960   *IBM* dominates the commercial computer industry, which is described as "IBM and the 7 Dwarfs." IBM has a 70% market share of mainframe computers until the PC emerges.

A crucial part of the story of the Internet is the development of personal computers. IBM and other companies' mainframes and minicomputers employ terminals. These stations are where users work, and they connect to larger, centralized machines. The Internet becomes the province of the people who work in these settings.

Computers using big, hot, energy-draining and fragile vacuum tubes are considered first-generation computer hardware; transistors and diodes the second; integrated circuits the third; and microprocessors the fourth. Microprocessors are built on many thousands or millions of semiconductors.

When these semiconductors, or *chips,* become the essential information processor in computers, manufacturers find it possible to build small, affordable personal computers (PCs).

1964   AT&T introduces the *Picturephone* at the World's Fair. *The Wall Street Journal* describes it as a "huge flop."

1965   Intel co-founder Gordon Moore proposes the principle that computing power should double every two years without increasing in cost. The idea is later dubbed *Moore's Law* and used in the semiconductor industry to guide long-term planning. The hypothesis is based on trends and does not have a proof that it will hold true indefinitely.

1968   Defense Department employee Robert Taylor and MIT scientist Joseph Licklider publish *The Computer as a Communication Device,* one of the earliest papers envisioning the potential of a computer network. Taylor supervised computer research projects and foresaw the possibility of teams communicating instantly through a linked network. Despite his vision, Taylor never profited personally from the commercial boom of the Internet.

Although many people were involved, Licklider is considered by many to be the best person for the title *Father of the Internet.* Another candidate is Vint Cerf who helped develop the networking protocols on which the Internet and most commercial networks run (the way computers talk to each other). Cerf told *Esquire* magazine one of his disappointments with the Internet is the prominence of pornography but, "I've come to learn that pornographers are almost always the first ones to adopt new technology. If there is a new way of distributing their product, they'll find it."

Later in 1968, the so-called *Mother of All Demos* takes place at a San Francisco computer conference. A *Stanford University* research team introduces the mouse (made of wood), email, hypertext, and video conferencing.

1969   The first message is sent over the network that would eventually become the Web. *UCLA* computer science professor Leonard Kleinrock connects his school's computer to one at *Stanford Research Institute.* He plans to type in l-o-g (as in "log in") but after Kleinrock types two letters, the system crashes. He later says it was, in a way, "very prophetic" to send only "L-O" as if sending a Biblical angelic message, "Look and behold!"

The World Wide Web is only part of the Internet, just one car riding on the Internet's highway of data. The Web is a method of accessing the information built on top of the Internet using the Internet language, called HTTP (Hypertext transfer protocol) and Web browsers. The Web is the most commonly used channel on the Internet but it is not the only one. Other ways of tapping into the Internet include e-mail, instant messaging, telnet, SSH, FTP (file transfer), and many others. Now, new Internet channels are emerging, such as smart phone apps. The Internet remains the underlying connection.

1974   The government restricts its ability to collect and distribute information about citizens with passage of the *1974 Federal Privacy Act*.

1975   Bill Gates and Paul Allen start *Microsoft*.

As a college freshman in 1975, Bill Gates sees a magazine story about a small, low-powered computer, the *MITS Altair 8800*, that can be built from a kit and used to play a simple game. Sensing that the future of computing is in these personal computers, and that the power of the computers would reside not in their size but in the software that runs them, Gates drops out of *Harvard*. With his friend Paul Allen, Gates founds *Microsoft* and licenses their operating system (the software that tells the computer how to work) to MITS.

The same year, Melinda French becomes valedictorian of her graduating high school class and wants to attend *Notre Dame*, but as *Fortune* magazine tells the story, that's not where she ended up:

> "Notre Dame did not get her. When she and her dad visited, she recalls, officials at the university told them that 'computers are a fad' and that they were shrinking the computer science department."

Notre Dame turns down the woman who would go on to marry Bill Gates. She now chairs the Gates Foundation, which is expected to distribute $100 billion in philanthropic contributions in their lifetime. The lesson here: Simply because someone teaches at a prominent university doesn't mean he is really "in the know" or aware of where society, or even his own industry, is going.

1976   Steve Jobs and Stephen Wozniak launch *Apple Computer, Inc*. At nearly the same time that Gates establishes *Microsoft*, Jobs and Wozniak, also college drop-outs, perfect the *Apple II*: a low-cost, easy-to-use microcomputer designed specifically for personal rather than business use. It is an immediate hit.

Ronald Wayne is the little-known third founder of Apple. He worked with Steve Jobs at Atari and drew up the partnership agreement giving each Steve 45%. Wayne got 10% so he could play tiebreaker if there was a disagreement between Jobs and Wozniak. But Wayne backed out after only a couple of weeks. He had lost money in a previous business venture and didn't want the stress of running the new company that he feared would put him in an early grave. Wayne got a check for $1500 for his share of the new company. The stake would be worth about $23 billion today.

Steve Jobs believes we are now in the midst of a third age of computing: the age of the *digital lifestyle*. The first era was the *age of productivity* (1980 to 1994), and the second was the *age of the Internet* (1994 to 2000).

1983   FBI agents track down the world's first high-profile computer hackers. The *414 gang* had infiltrated a bank's computers, and worse, at the Los Alamos National Laboratory in New Mexico, where nuclear weapons are kept. The criminal masterminds turn out to be bored teenagers who name themselves after the area code of Milwaukee, where they live. The teens avoid jail time, mainly because laws against computer trespassing do not exist. Their congressional testimony helps encourage the U.S. Congress to change the situation.

1989   Tim Berners-Lee proposes a global hypertext project to be known as the World Wide Web. This work begins in October 1990 and debuts on the Internet in 1991.

1991   The first text message ("Merry Christmas") is sent over a mobile device. Why are users allowed only 160 characters? In the 1980s, a man named Friedhelm Hillebrand wrote the SMS or short message service protocol. He sat down one day and wrote out a bunch of sentences by hand, counting the number of characters in each. He found the average was about 160.

1993   The National Center for Supercomputing Applications at the University of Illinois at Urbana-Champaign creates a browser called *Mosaic*. It allows easy navigation around the World Wide Web, helping to bring the Web out of the laboratory of scientists and into the hands of the average user. The browser eventually becomes *Netscape*.

Computer engineer Ray Tomlinson invents e-mail. The *Guinness Book of World Records* says the first message is QWERTYUIOP — the keys positioned on the third row of the keyboard.

1994   A site called *Jerry and David's Guide to the World Wide Web* is renamed *Yahoo!*

1995   Jeff Bezos launches online book retailer *Amazon* from his garage in Bellevue, Washington. His parents sink a substantial portion of their life savings into the effort. "We weren't betting on the Internet," his mother would later say. "We were betting on Jeff." By the end of the decade, Jeff's parents are billionaires.

Ward Cunningham releases the first wiki to the public, calling it *WikiWikiWeb*. *WikiWiki* is Hawaiian for quick. It is designed to allow computer programmers to share information with each other.

1996   Congress passes a law forbidding the online transmission of any image that "appears to be of a minor engaging in sexually explicit conduct." It's called the *Child Pornography Prevention Act of 1996*.

Microsoft introduces a browser called *Internet Explorer* to compete with *Netscape Navigator*.

1997   Two *Stanford University* students almost call their search engine the Whatbox, but decide the name is too similar to Wetbox which sounds to them like a porn site. They choose instead to register the domain name *Google.com*, a play on the word *googol*, a mathematical term for the number 1 followed by 100 zeros. In little more than a decade, users will make 2.5 billion *Google* searches every day. In the *Harvard Business Review*, Thomas H. Davenport describes *Google's* presence on the internet as "informational kudzu." *Google* becomes the front door to the online world for many people, creating an environment where the way to make money in the media world is with OPC — other people's content. That's why some observers consider the company a "digital vampire." Instead of focusing on taste and elegance like *Apple*, the company is driven by engineering concerns about functionality. This is why Ken Auletta, author of *Googled: The End of the World as We Know It*, describes *Microsoft* as a company led by "cold businessmen" while *Google* is led by "cold engineers."

1998 Congress passes the *Digital Millennium Copyright Act*. Among other things, it allows "fair use" to be applied to the Internet. Read more about fair use in the media law chapter.

2002 *Wikipedia* is introduced. The wiki system allows anyone to contribute to the online encyclopedia.

2002 The Supreme Court rules the *Child Pornography Prevention Act of 1996* unconstitutional because it's considered unnecessary (due to previous laws) and overly-broad.

2003 The Supreme Court upholds the *Children's Internet Protection Act*, ruling that Congress has the power to require libraries to install filters. Figuring how to protect children online is an ongoing battle.

2004 Harvard student Mark Zuckerberg starts *Facebook* for his fellow students after nearly getting kicked out of school for creating a photo rating site. *PayPal* co-founder Peter Thiel helps the site get off the ground with an investment of half a million dollars. Two years later, he opens the site to anyone thirteen or older.

2005 The first video is uploaded to *YouTube*. The 19-second clip shows co-founder Jawed Karim at the San Diego Zoo.

2006 Social networking site *Twitter* begins offering tweets of 140 characters in length (with 20 characters reserved for names). The first man-made tweet is "inviting coworkers."

2008 The *Apple App* store opens. In little more than a year, customers will download more than 2 billion programs. More than 100,000 applications are now available.

For the first time, more Americans tell pollsters they get their news from the Internet instead of from print. Television remains the leading outlet. *FOX* is number one on TV, drawing many more viewers than *CNN* and *MSNBC*, but *FOX* lags far behind both online. *CNN.com* is number one online with a monthly average of 1.7 billion visitors — half a billion views more than its nearest competitor, *MSNBC.com*. *CNN* started early, making its Internet debut in 1995. On election day 2008, *CNN.com* records 282 million page views. That's up from 100 million page views on election day in 2000, according to *Pew Research*.

2009 U.S. Internet advertising grows into a $23.4 billion business, according to *The Wall Street Journal*. Online advertising growth is projected to fall to 8.9% after increasing 17.5% the previous year.

2010   The Internet passes newspapers to becomes the third most popular news platform, according to the Pew Research Center. That puts it just behind local and national television outlets. Most online news surfers rely on just a handful of sites. 57% get news from just two to five websites. 37% have participated in the news-making process or reacted to news by commenting on stories and giving feedback.

The Internet Today

The phrase "surfing the Web" perfectly captures the carefree, often serendipitous experience we get on the Internet. You'll find a little bit of everything. Communications scholar Fred Williams once said, "Going on the Internet is like going through someone's trash." Yet, we experience withdrawals when our glowing digital devices are pried from our hands. Computers have become our way of connecting with many people in our lives; now a need, not just a want, and the need is growing.

This was apparently true for a 19-year-old Florida man who swiped a laptop from a Starbucks customer's lap in an outlet mall. Why did he steal it? Because the owner would not let him use it to check his *Facebook* account. So, he grabbed the customer's laptop and ran out of the coffee shop. Two people in the parking lot tackled the man and held him until a mall security guard arrived.

More than 230 million Americans have high speed access and digital cable service... and 228 million used a mobile phone.

More than 230 million Americans have high speed access (broadband) and digital cable service, and 228 million used a mobile phone as of May, 2009, according to *Nielsen*.

While some 90% of American households use pay TV services such as cable and satellite, the *Yankee Group* says a shift in consumer thinking will lead one in eight of them to replace these services with Internet video during 2010. Market research firm *eMarketer* says about one out of three adult U.S. Internet users are willing to watch full-length TV shows online. That's up from about one in four in 2008.

The Revolution

It took more than 70 years for the telephone to show up in most homes. For electricity, it was more than half a century. Television made it into the majority of American living rooms in about 30 years. The Internet needed only a decade and in half that time *Facebook* was able to reach 300 million users.

To some observers, the rise of the Internet is a tale of economic destruction. Like a neutron bomb that kills people but leaves buildings standing, the Internet has shifted white-collar work overseas and eliminated the economic basis of industries like newspaper publishing. The ranks of those dispossessed by the Web continue to swell. News is losing some of its authority, clarity and coherence.

Others see the Internet as a shift in a new direction, forcing those clinging to their old ways to exit their comfort zones. The media have particularly been affected because of the nature of the Internet.

Thomas Jefferson once said, "Every generation needs a new revolution." The Internet may be this generation's upheaval. Are we watching the destruction of journalism or are we seeing its forced reinvention? No matter how we view the change, it is no longer possible for anyone to keep a lid on the freer flow of news and information.

Old media companies are often trapped in what Clayton Christensen calls the *Innovator's Dilemma* (he wrote a book by that title). As successful companies become large, they fight off new innovations and business models by becoming defensive rather than proactive. They are too invested in the legacy media. Here's one remarkable example: In 1996, Gannett, *The Washington Post* and *The New York Times* were invited to join New Century Network to sell ads on the Web. They rejected the offer because they couldn't imagine Web-focused companies taking away classified ads and other business from them. *Craigslist* now publishes about 40 million classified ads each month while newspaper revenue from classified ads has fallen from $20 billion in 2000 to $10 billion in 2008, according to the Associated Press. It makes sense to hedge until your legacy product is no longer profitable. But hedge too long and you miss making a profitable and timely transition to the new media form and may be left behind.

This scenario plays out in the lives of individuals as it does in the lives of companies. Leonard Kleinrock (the man credited with giving birth to the Internet by sending the first message) came up with the term *Feature Shock* as a way to describe why we are sometimes slow to adopt new technology. The UCLA computer science professor says at first we are overwhelmed by the power of the new devices and software. We have paid for all the extra muscle and feel guilty if we fail to use all of it. We invest time and energy trying to learn all our options and eventually give up, assuming the next version of the product will probably just add more frustration to our lives with additions we'll never use. We become invested in what we already use and resistant to new possibilities, even if they promise to be much better than the originals. *Feature shock* slows down the rate at which new applications and features are accepted once the public grows accustomed to old ones. Why fix something that isn't broken?

We become invested in what we already use and resistant to new possibilities...

Consider the layout of the computer keyboard, based on a design created in the 1800's. Frequently used letters were placed farther apart to force the typist to slow down, preventing keys from jamming. The need for this design ended a century ago. Placing the often-used keys closer together would speed up typing, but the old technology is still in use today because of the work effort required to retrain everyone used to the old system.

Open-Source

In 1991, Finnish university student Linus Torvalds wrote a *kernel* (the core of an operating system which, when combined with the right drivers manages a computer's essential resources). He combined his creation (the lower middle part of the system) with parts borrowed from GNU tools to make a complete system. Enthusiastic programmers debugged and expanded Torvald's effort until it became known as the *Linux* operating system. The collaborative style of work and free content used in the project is now commonly referred to as *open source*. *Linux* now plays a prominent role in our digital experience, showing what open source can accomplish.

Open source advocates promote the free sharing of programs and software, allowing others the opportunity to change and develop the underlying code. Others advocate what might be described as a *walled garden*.

Two companies that symbolize these competing views are Apple and Google. Locked in a steel cage death match, the two are at war and the battlefield is mobile devices. Apple offers a beautiful but controlled experience, while Google gives users efficiency in an open field. Google freely gives away its smartphone operating system (*Android*) while Apple insists on keeping software and hardware under tight control, vetting all applications that run on the iPhone through the iTunes App Store. Apple wants to move computing to a curated environment while Google believes that the operating system should be a background player. Apple favors the orderliness of an autocracy over Google's messy freedom of a more open system.

An even better example of open source is Wikipedia. Google picks and chooses which areas it is willing to be open, but anyone is free to reuse Wikipedia entries however he or she chooses, as long as the same open ethic is followed and credit to given to Wikipedia. This applies to publishers and companies that have built businesses around the site's content. Richard Stallman, an activist for the free software movement, believes that for software to qualify as open source, it is not necessary for it be inexpensive and, once purchased, the user should be free to do with it whatever she pleases. Wikipedia doesn't meet this stringent requirement because the content is controlled by a policing agency.

A related issue of concern to Stallman and other supporters of a free Internet is network neutrality. Should an Internet service provider be allowed to charge more for using a larger chunk of bandwidth (such as sites like *YouTube*) or charge more based on the system, content or application of the user? Supporters of network neutrality insist there should be no discrimination among the types of content flowing through the Internet. The FCC has attempted to require companies to give Web users equal access to all content, even if some of that content is clogging the network.

The Web Tomorrow

The Web's future might depend on whether it is slowly splitting into walled gardens of content or whether standards will eventually unify the parts that are separating. Some are calling this the *Splinternet* (though technically, it is the Web and not the Internet that is splitting). Compatible formats have allowed users to have the same experience regardless of browser or computer. Now, depending on whether one uses an iPhone, Android, tablets or Web TV, the experience will vary. Each device has its own formatting and ad network. At the same time, chunks of interesting experiences are now hidden behind passwords (think Facebook). If this fragmentation is temporary, the Web standards will emerge to unify our experiences to some degree. If we are forced to live in separate gardens of content, then everyone from journalists to advertisers will need the flexibility to adapt to working in a variety of interactive worlds.

Internet Trends

INTERNET TREND: INTERACTIVITY

Web 1.0 refers to the part of the Internet with constraints and barriers to users. The term *Web 2.0* refers to websites that get at least some of their value from the actions of users. For instance, the contributions of users makes *Wikipedia* what it is. The audience is contributing sweat equity. The next step, *Web 3.0*, is also known as the *semantic Web*. It creates "smart data" and links it together in more productive ways. For example, a Web page could cover the topic of "house boats" and the semantic Web will know whether the page is about house boats for sale, for rent, to visit, the history of house boats, a guidebook or how to repair one. Web 3.0 will only pull together those websites we are interested in visiting.

Some media outlets have failed to grasp the fundamental shift in how consumers are interacting with news content. It's a mistake to think of a company's website as an extension of the base product and therefore less significant than the mother ship. Consider this: *Forbes* magazine reaches 4.5 million people, but Forbes.com has some 20 million unique visitors.

Many of us don't want to visit a news site where we passively consume information. We want to post comments and add our own pictures as citizen journalists. We want to chat with friends, and share the stories and videos with others. We want to follow links and arrange the information in ways that suit us. The unique combination of our coming together, this *collaborative publishing*, is the power behind *YouTube* and *Craigslist*.

A newspaper is something we read, but the Web is something we do. Since the Web has become interactive, users now expect their news experience to be similar. For journalists, this means the news experience is no longer a lecture, it is a conversation.

Media mogul Barry Diller, the man who started the *FOX* network before Rupert Murdock bought him out, told *Business Week*:

> "I thought nothing would interrupt the story, and people want to sit there and watch passively, and that is the storytelling experience. (Now) I don't think passivity is going out the window, but it will shrink in significance, thanks to interactive tools that enable people to 'manipulate' forms of content."

The three-minute pop song came about because manufacturers once could only fit a few minutes of music on vinyl 45s, so it's hardly unheard of for technology to shape content.

The Living Stories project is a recent attempt to personalize the news. A joint effort between *Google*, *The Washington Post* and *The New York Times*, users can easily navigate through a news topic by viewing a timeline of coverage on the story. The experiment essentially rigs Google's search results to favor continued, serious reporting.

INTERNET TREND: CONVERGENCE

Convergence is the erosion of traditional distinctions among media. This combining and coordinating of various media together has allowed Internet users to follow stories as they develop in real time.

It's a mistake to think of a company's website as an extension of the base product and therefore less significant than the mother ship.

Before long, an iPhone-like device will be pointed at the nearest screen to play video that may come from the device's memory, an Internet download or from an over-the-air signal. We may move seamlessly between our phones, TVs and computers. The content will stay the same but the platform will shift. This liquidity is changing the way we discover the significant events in the world around us. The convergence of media is forcing news organizations to rethink how to cover stories. If you work at a newspaper with an active website and discover a great story, do you put it up on the website before it appears in the paper, allowing your website to scoop your print publication?

Information about the China quake and the Burma cyclone disasters of 2008 came at first — not from professional journalists — but photos and videos posted on the Internet by nonprofessionals. Iranian election protesters gathered public opinion by tweeting their messages, tagging them with the topic and allowing others with similar interests to discover the posts.

When a story comes in to a convergence environment, the journalist asks:

> "What makes the most sense to best cover the story?"
> "Which medium can get the information out in the most effective way?"
> "Is it likely to have photos?"
> "Does the story lend itself to graphics?"
> "Can it wait to be printed in the newspaper?"
> "Is it breaking news?"
> "What method makes the most sense to best cover this story?"

Some observers warn that the Web itself is actually fragmenting. We no longer have compatible formats that allow us to see pretty much the same thing regardless of the device in use. Much is hidden behind a login and password. Facebook apps only work in the realm of Facebook, hidden away from the prying eyes of search engines like Google. The fear is that we face a splintering of the Web as a unified system — a *Splinternet*. If so, marketers will have to reach audiences living in many different interactive worlds ruled by Apple, Facebook, and Google platforms. Others believe such fragmentation is temporary and that standards, helped by natural selection, will emerge and technologies flexible enough to deliver in these differing formats will emerge.

Animated and Automated News

A newcomer to the media landscape is animated depiction of events that no journalist actually witnessed — and that may not have even occurred. This may be the future of journalism from the tabloid division. Leading the way is *Next Media*, based in Hong Kong. The company uses programmers, designers, animators and actors to create robotic-looking video avatars illustrating events from news sources. This new journalistic art form leans on imagination to fill in the gaps, creating what many critics would consider a significant ethics gap.

On the automated side, computer algorithms are being used to create news stories. A sports site, StatSheet.com, is producing automated game summaries with help from engineers at

Northwestern University. The goal is to eventually create algorithms to cover local stories. (There is more on this effort in the chapter on Writing News).

Pause for Discussion: Created by Computers

Should websites indicate whether a story has a human or computer creator? How does copyright fit into the equation, given that the computers will borrow from previously written material? Is this a positive development that will allow news sites to cover more stories by helping them to cope with information overload, or will it simply be used by number crunchers to replace real journalists with bland repetition?

INTERNET TREND: HACKER JOURNALISM

The word hacker has a different meaning to the public than it does to techies. During the mid-80's, when teenagers were caught breaking into computers, hacker became associated with thievery and illegal surveillance. But the word originally referred to those skilled at hacking away at lines of computer code. They wanted to understand how parts of computer programs worked, together and separately. They saw themselves as motivated by a desire to build, not destroy. A few in the community of hackers used their knowledge to break live systems.

In today's culture, these brainiacs are more likely to be referred to as geeks. In the early days of computing, many of these whiz kids encouraged anyone to copy and improve any piece of code. Others, like Bill Gates, treated software as intellectual property — illegal if used without permission. This is the divide discussed in the earlier section in this chapter on Open Source.

Hacker journalism (or *data journalism*) combines a bit of coding with the reporting. Old media already understand that photography tells a story in a different way than a newspaper article, and video tells a story in yet another way. Hacker journalism brings a new dimension to story-telling. It involves journalists who are also programmers, regularly using computer databases and search engines to assist with reporting. These programmer/journalists help develop the technology to dig up facts and build sites and apps around events, or to complement coverage. Many engineers share a common interest with journalists in that both often want to change the world by what they do.

Many engineers share a common interest with journalists in that both often want to change the world by what they do.

Adrian Holovaty is an example of someone in this hybrid role combining an interest with storytelling. He's a journalism school graduate who joined *Google Maps* with Chicago police department crime data in 2005. *ChicagoCrime.org* won awards and Holovaty extended the idea to come up with community-focused *EveryBlock*. The site gathers news, information on crime, property and business licenses, and makes the data searchable by address, ZIP code and neighborhood. The site also aggregates reviews of local businesses from *Yelp*, combines photos from *Flickr* and listings from *Craigslist*. These sites are part of a push toward *Hyperlocal News*.

One way to step into hacker journalism is learning API (*Application Programming Interface*) programming, which lets two different Web services connect and share information. This is how *Google* makes its maps available for use on your own web pages. Journalists can use API to mix the data with other information sources to allow users to compare data in new ways.

A new media outlet making waves with its splashy style of hacker journalism is *Wikileaks. org*. This investigative journalism site released a video in 2010 showing an American helicopter three years earlier killing two journalists on the ground, along with ten others. The tapes are classified, but Wikileaks got copies and posted them online. In the Summer of 2010, the whistleblower site released a document called the *Afghan War Diary*. The collection of classified battlefield reports revealed a remarkable view from the ground of the war's progress.

Funded privately, the site pays a small staff and stores online articles in Sweden, where journalists are not required to reveal sources. The staff has a string of high profile posts, including hundreds of thousands of pager messages from New York City on the morning of September 11, 2001. Is this a new form of hard-hitting journalism or simple sensationalism designed to work around law and ethical concerns?

A journalist in today's digital age needs to be literate in the practical applications of software, hardware, and network technology.

Without a fundamental understanding of how the Web works, how its building blocks fit together, how do you know "what is possible?" A journalist in today's digital age needs to be literate in the practical applications of software, hardware, and network technology. This does not mean being able to build a newsroom's content management system or create the next Google. It does mean being able to hold an intelligent conversation about it to help bridge the gap between a journalist's vision and a programmer's execution. A journalist should learn programming concepts for the same reason that an engineer or scientist learns how to write: It makes him better at the job.

Journalists should be able to look at the world with a coder's point of view by grasping the underpinnings of programming and interactivity. Plus, journalists who can produce quality work and program as well are a hot commodity in today's newsrooms.

INTERNET TREND: RISE OF THE APPS

The Internet is no longer just a collection of Web pages, but also a collection of applications. The bite-sized software programs can be loaded onto smart phones or tapped into on the Web.

Juniper Research reports 2009 revenues from mobile apps at nearly $10 billion, and estimates that it will more than triple by 2015. Apple says it has already passed more than $1 billion in revenues and that its App Store now offers 225,000 apps which have collectively been downloaded 5 billion times. Independent Mobile store *GetJar* offers programs for a variety of handsets and claims 72,000 apps and 1 billion downloads. Like a downloadable song, most apps cost about $1.90 and most never become hits. Even many successful apps quickly fade into obscurity.

Among the most successful apps are T-Pain's *Auto-Tune* app, and *FarmVille*. There are 20 times more people playing *FarmVille* than actual farms in the U.S. App stores are not only offering games and novelties, but useful tools. Devices people can carry anywhere are able to perform computing that previously had to be done at a desk. Journalists can utilize those powerful apps, available on devices like *Blackberries* and *iPhones*.

A place to look for iPhone apps is *AppShopper.com*, the most comprehensive resource for tracking price drops, newly popular apps and updates. Video reviews of apps are available at *Appvee* or *148apps*. *Appouliscious* offers social network ratings, and *Chorus* is an app that will make recommendations based on the choices of your friends.

The market research firm Piper Jaffray projects that consumers will have paid $2.8 billion for mobile phone downloads in 2009. The $1 billion app market is expected to soar to $4 billion by 2012, according to *Business Week*. Social games are particularly hot. They make up $720 million of the app market now and are expected to move up to $2 billion by 2012.

Iceberg Reader lets iPhone users download any of 170 daily newspapers, and *NewsFuse* delivers news from a variety of sources. *Evernote* provides a handy way to write messages on your device that is accessible on the Web. A journalist covering an event can start writing her story using *Evernote* and later pull it up on a newsroom computer at *Evernote.com* to polish it off. *Evernote* can also record audio notes and store documents and photos. Issue voice commands with *Vlingo* to perform tasks like sending text messages and updating your *Facebook* status.

For the iPhone, there's *RadarScope*. TV meteorologists use it to see NEXRAD data (Next Generation Radar) and other weather information. This network of Doppler weather radars is operated by the National Weather Service. With *Photogene*, you can crop and adjust the color of photos. Having *Dropbox* installed on your iPhone means you can skip bringing paper documents to interviews related to assignments, even if you don't have a Wi-Fi or cellular connection. Use *Instapaper* to save a Web page so you can save articles off-line in text-only format. *FStream* will turn your phone into a police scanner. Use *Tweetdeck* or *Tweetie* to filter messages, and make columns of Tweeters to help keep up with important topics or a news competitor.

The Blackberry already comes with a *Voice Notes Recorder* and *Documents To Go*. A journalist covering a protest could add *UberTwitter* and use it to find out what people are tweeting nearby or to check a *hashtag* associated with the event. A hashtag is used to gather posts on a particular subject, making it easier to track conversations in the twitter timeline through search. Creating a hashtag is as simple as putting the # sign in front of a keyword or targeted group.

Google Voice can help a journalist avoid missing an important call from a source. A caller to your new Google phone number will ring all of your phones. Plus, conversations can be recorded, voice mail can be transcribed, and calls screened. You can even switch between phones in the middle of a conversation.

Watch for news media companies to experiment with creating their own social news gaming applications. NBC has released a game that lets users gain points for spreading news about shows or getting friends to watch it. Similar concepts could be applied to news content.

Devices people can carry anywhere are able to perform computing that previously had to be done at a desk.

A filmmaker working with *Compassion International* survived the January, 2010 Haiti earthquake with the help of his iPhone apps. Dan Wooley was trapped under the rubble at his hotel for 65 hours before rescuers found him. He used information from an app he had downloaded to look up treatment of excessive bleeding and compound fracture. He ripped his shirt in stripes for a tourniquet for a cut in his leg and a sock to stop the bleeding from his head wound. Wooley set his phone's alarm to go offer every 20 minutes so he wouldn't fall asleep and go into shock.

INTERNET TREND: CLOUD COMPUTING

Cloud computing is another name for information that exists on the Web instead of your computer. Your information sits on servers, so you can access it from anywhere. If your computer dies, your documents continue to live on the Web and you simply switch devices to access them. Cloud computing means the space you take up storing information isn't in-house, but "out there" on the Web. For companies, this means tapping into raw computing power, storage, and software applications from large data centers over the Internet.

Using the cloud allows businesses to avoid building their own data centers and buying servers and disks. Customers pay only for the computing resources they need, whenever they need them. There are no dedicated computers and none of the hardware is dedicated to a single use as are servers in data centers.

Web-based e-mail such as *Google's Gmail* is an example of simple cloud computing. Data sits on central computers that users don't own or control. Cloud-computing technology is utilized by *YouTube*, *Skype*, and *Twitter*. This trend is even evident in the U.S. intelligence community. The *Defense Information Systems Agency, National Geospatial Intelligence Agency, National Security Agency* and even the *Central Intelligence Agency* have all publicly announced their intent to use cloud computing in one form or another.

An *internal* cloud is a cloud that sits behind a corporate firewall. Some companies fear their data, scattered over the Web, won't be secure. This is the downside of Web computing. Errors can cut off access. Accounts maintained on centralized computing services and delivered over the Internet (a.k.a. the cloud) are subject to hacking. In August of 2009, the risky nature of cloud computing was exposed by a Gmail outage lasting more than an hour.

For Next Time

How can journalist use social media in her work?

Social Media

Americans now spend more of their online time with social media than with any other activity. Gaming and email are their second and third favorite online activities, according to research by the *Nielsen Company*. Social networking brings together words and coded speech with technology in an experience-focused and event-driven collision. In effect, we now carry the press in our pockets.

On its most basic level, social networking is simply an online community. Flash Mobs got their start through social networking. Each year in March, several thousand people show up simultaneously at Union Square in New York to pummel each other with pillows. The yearly ritual of flying feathers is organized through a Facebook page.

Connect your Facebook account with social news sites like *Digg*, and your existing friends become a filter for the most interesting web links. Google's new *Social Search* lets users add their social networking profiles to a Google account so they can mine their friends' search results.

One of the new entries is *Foursquare*, a location-based social network that lets users play a game by "checking in" at various places by logging their location through the website. Whoever logs in the most at a particular location is deemed the "mayor." There are more than two million Foursquare users, and the service is growing after getting tied into Facebook and Twitter. Businesses see revenue potential in this and other geo-tagging apps through rewarding repeat customers, offering specials and digital coupons, while journalists see the service as a potential new source of information for reporters.

Social networking is having an impact on careers as well. Hollywood studios are concerned about leaks and embarrassing posts. Lawyers are inserting anti-social-networking clauses into the contracts of stars, according to the *Hollywood Reporter*.

Whatever you put online during your college career may follow you into the workplace.

University of Florida researchers reviewed the Facebook pages of the school's medical students. They found photos of students dressed as pimps, cross-dressers, and

Whatever you put online during your college career may follow you into the workplace.

one wearing a lab coat labeled Kevorkian Medical Clinic. Others included photos of students drinking and grabbing breasts and crotches.

An Illinois obstetrician had his son unfriend (or defriend) him on Facebook after the doctor wrote on the 25-year-old's wall, "I can see what you are blowing your money on, so don't come whining to me about money." The senior had posted photos of himself taken at bars, restaurants, movies and concerts.

Frustrated students can post screen views of outrageous antics by their so-called helicopter parents at myparentsjoinedfacebook.com. Examples include the mother who told her daughter to stop drinking soft drinks to avoid cavities and the results of one stepfather's comments on a What "sex position fits you best?" quiz.

Rise of the Real-Time Web

Social-network sites are nearly real time and some (such as Twitter) are present tense, offering friction-free feedback.

News is becoming increasingly present tense. Television news is pushing toward reality TV as cable news channels focus on live talk and live coverage of breaking news events. Internet news is also becoming more real time with the availability of live streaming content.

Social network sites are nearly real-time, and some (such as Twitter) are present tense, offering friction-free feedback. The combination of tweeting, Facebook status updates and YouTube videos, along with similar services, are collectively referred to as the *Real-Time Web,* or instant Web. The name is a bit of a misnomer since not all of it happens in real time. The term refers more to the sense of immediacy each one carries. It's a sense of living in the now. Users like to snack, preferring an *amuse-bouche* (single bite) instead of a full meal. The 24/7 "anywhere and anyplace" real-time Web serves as a complaint desk that runs on social media steroids.

OneRiot.com is a Boulder, Colorado startup looking to make a dent in Google's search dominance by offering real-time searches. OneRiot and Project Ellerdale scour current news and posts on Twitter, Digg, and other social networking services.

How big is the Real-Time Web?

> Facebook—60 million updates daily.
> Twitter—50 million Tweets are posted every day.
> YouTube—24 hours of video is uploaded every minute (more than three years of content being uploaded daily). The site reached an all-time high of 14.6 billion video views in May 2010, according to ComScore.

Some observers expect pulsating real-time news streams to entirely replace static websites, at least for breaking news.

Lifelogging

Social networks are already creating a memory pathway of lives, as millions of people pour themselves into social networks. The next step for the data-obsessed could be lifelogging, documenting our lives in digital detail. Each of us is breaking the story of our lives.

The technology to do it is on its way. Most of us already carry a primitive lifelogging tool: a cell phone. As these devices add features like video cameras, email and GPS (global positioning technology), their potential to record our daily activities grows. Our cell phone provider knows where we go and how long we stay there.

Microsoft research scientist Gordon Bell says we're headed toward the day when electronic devices will be able to digitally capture our every moment. Technology will follow us, recording each person we meet, each walk around the block, each moment of disappointment and triumph. We'll be able to tap into a digital database at any time in order to see our exact location at a specific time. His book *Total Recall: How the E-Memory Revolution Will Change Everything* envisions easily finding our lost keys or discovering the name of a person we briefly bumped into on the street. We'll be able to analyze our routines and find ways to make our lives more productive.

Do we really want the ability to preserve all of our past?

When it comes to our past, we have selective amnesia. Like holding an antique hearing aid to our heads such as an ear trumpet (with a small opening at one end and a large opening on the other), we filter out parts of our past and preserve in our minds select memories. You can't retain it all, so the types of events you decide to recall reveals something about you. Many mothers say they don't recall the pain of childbirth, only the overwhelming feelings of bonding and holding their child for the first time during its initial moments of life. But what happens when there's no escaping the past? Instead of painful memories fading over time, we'll have the option of digitally replaying them vividly in our mind over and over again.

Pause for Discussion: Friending

Relationships need boundaries. So, what rules would you set down for parents who want to friend their kids? Should kids gain more freedom as they get older? Should parents let their kids know about whether they are monitoring their Facebook page? Would you ignore a friend request from a parent?

FACEBOOK CHALLENGE

Facebook is a significant influence in other parts of the world, as groups have begun using it to organize rallies and protests. A Facebook group backing the monk-led protests during 2007 in Myanmar attracted more than 100,000 members in less than 10 days. People around the world tried to harness the power of the Web to support the resistance movement. Media freedom is severely restricted in the reclusive Southeast Asian nation and few foreign journalists are permitted to operate there.

Let's see how much you know about social networking leader Facebook.

    1. The Facebook nation is about the size of:

       a. Brazil

b. The United States

c. Two Brazils

2. How much time on the website does the typical Facebook user spend compared to a regular user of *The New York Times'* website?

   a. twice as long

   b. 9 times longer

   c. 17 times longer

3. Mark Zuckerberg founded Facebook while he was a student at:

   a. Yale

   b. Harvard

   c. Princeton

4. Before coming up with Facebook, Zuckerberg first created something that nearly got him kicked out of school. The site let users rate photos and was called:

   a. Face-ter

   b. Face Party

   c. Facemash

5. How much of Facebook is owned by Microsoft?

   a. All of it

   b. 50%

   c. 1.6%

6. What percentage of Facebook users are outside the U.S.?

   a. 70%

   b. 40%

   c. 20%

7. What's the fastest-growing demographic on the site?

   a. Men over 40

   b. Women 55 and older

   c. Women in their 30s

8. What percentage of Facebook users are on the site each day?

   a. 25%

   b. 50%

   c. 75%

9. Facebook helped to make possible the largest live video event ever in the U.S. It was:

   a. Election Night

   b. Obama's Inauguration Day

c. The Super Bowl

10. How many "friends" does Facebook now claim?
    a. Over 100 million
    b. Over 200 million
    c. Over 500 million

11. How much money does Facebook expect to make by the end of 2010?
    a. $300 million
    b. $700 million
    c. $1 billion

12. The New Oxford American Dictionary selected this as its 2009 Word of the Year.
    a. Friend
    b. Unfriend
    c. Status Update

13. How many Facebook updates are posted each day?
    a. 10 million
    b. 30 million
    c. 60 million

14. What is the most popular Facebook page dedicated to honoring?
    a. Michael Jackson
    b. Homer Simpson
    c. Barack Obama

15. The average number of Facebook friends is:
    a. 30
    b. 70
    c. 130

(Answers are at the end of the chapter.)

Journalists Using Social Networking

Here's how social networking can help reporters.

When Ivan Oranksy was managing online editor of *Scientific American*, he friended a former coworker. Not long afterward, Oranksy noticed a status update referring to his friend having the worst month of his life and references to lawyers. That led to a *Scientific American* investigation that developed into three stories about the organization where his friend worked. Facebook can serve as a lead generator.

Social networks can also alert journalists through timely conversations about important issues in a community, or about a significant topic. They may help craft questions for interviews or reveal sources of articles. Fan pages can be used to reach a particular group.

But news stories cannot be based solely on information gathered through social media. Facts have to be verified. Just like Wikipedia, these sites can serve as a jumping off point but not as sources.

In addition to journalists using social networking to advance stories, there's the issue of whether journalists should be posting and tweeting themselves. Today's blogging and twittering journalist has led *The Washington Post* to require its reporters to give up some of the personal privileges enjoyed by private citizens. The paper has decided to treat its journalists' online social networking as the equivalent of what appears beneath their bylines in the printed newspaper. *Post* contributor Howard Kurtz jokingly wrote, "Under new WP guidelines on tweeting, I will now hold forth only on the weather and dessert recipes." In a subsequent Twitter posting, Kurtz told followers, "Actually, I always assumed you shouldn't tweet anything you wouldn't say in print or on the air."

Should journalists put their thoughts on Twitter and Facebook? And if so, should news organizations restrict their postings to avoid controversial political and social views?

An understanding of social networking could be the door through which journalism students find a spot on a news team.

An understanding of social networking could be the door through which journalism students find a spot on a news team. The social media director's job is to create conversational communities by tweeting, blogging, and friend finding throughout the day. SMDs help other members of a news organization learn to build new audiences and interact with them. The goal is promotion of the media brand and sometimes delivering breaking news.

Social media come and go quickly because users are not loyal to a brand. They are loyal to what they want. So, they'll go wherever this is provided for them. The traditional press is unfamiliar with this mindset since media companies have been built on the idea that brands become familiar, dependable sources to people, a positive symbol in their lives of responsibility, intelligence, etc. Reading *The New York Times* is a rite of passage, something adults do. This viewpoint is offered by Bill Kovach and Tom Rosenstiel in their book, *The Elements of Journalism*. "Rather than selling customers content, newspeople are building a relationship with their audience… Providing this service creates a bond with the public." This type of bonding is fading and lost on younger media consumers. One platform is easily tossed aside for another. The source is not important. This means journalists have to accept a new relationship with consumers. The rules have changed and fluidity is a now a critical part of survival.

Feel the Tweet

The average American teen sends 2,272 texts every month. That's nearly 80 a day. Most are frivolous. Some text messages are a matter of life and death.

Boulder, Colorado police say a teenager was forced into the passenger side of his car by five men in October 2009. He managed to send a one-word text message to his father: Kidnapped. Police quickly found and arrested the men. The victim was unharmed.

The popularity of texting is perhaps most clearly seen in Twitter. This social networking set up is microblogging or group IM (instant messaging). Like the status updates on Facebook, twittering explains what I'm doing right now in just a few words.

Twitter is having an impact on U.S. politics. More than 30 of the nation's governors use microblogging site for everything from emergency announcements about the weather to what they had for lunch, according to *USA Today*. The success of President Obama's election campaign in using online media convinced many campaign professionals that there is real potential in social media.

Here's what *Business Week* has to say about Twitter's origins:

In late January of 2001, in the depths of the dot-com crash, a San Francisco startup called Pyra Labs ran out of money. Its staff departed. The co-founder of the company, a young Nebraskan named Evan Williams, decided to make a go of it alone. He scraped together $40,000 in new funding and moved Pyra's servers into his apartment. This permitted the company's 100,000 registered customers (and counting) to keep using Pyra's service, Blogger, to publish their online journals, or blogs. A year later, Blogger had 700,000 subscribers. By 2003, Williams was able to sell his business to Google for a lucrative pile of pre-IPO stock. Three years later he and his partners launched yet another tool for global publishing, the micro-blogging phenomenon, Twitter.

A vibrating cell phone receiving a text message in someone's pocket reminded one of Evan's team members of a twitch. Looking up twitch in the dictionary led to a nearby word, twitter.

It's what birds do when they converge. Co-founder Biz Stone is quoted by *USA Today* as saying, "The sound they make is technically defined as a trivial chirp. How perfect... hear a trivial chirp on your phone, look down and it's your friend." He told comedian Stephen Colbert it's the "messaging system we didn't know we needed until we had it."

Ten, 20, or 1000 people may be signed in to receive your tweets. This immediately comes in handy at conferences and conventions, where you can tell folks, "There are free hot dogs at booth 12 on the display floor. But just for the next 10 minutes. Come and get 'em."

Imagine you are on the West Coast when the *American Idol* results show is broadcast on the East Coast. You could wait until the show airs on the West Coast, or you could find out who was voted off by doing a Twitter search. The info will be out there in seconds after the announcement telling who was voted off the show.

Here's a more serious application. A website offering background checks called *Been-Verified.com*, needed to create a logo design. By twittering about it, the company received more than 150 proposals and wound up paying a fraction of the price they would have had to pay a typical designer.

The service received a legitimacy boost in 2008 when Barack Obama announced Joe Biden as his vice presidential nominee through Twitter. Later that year, news of a terrorist attack in Mumbai, India, first reached the world through Twitter.

In April 2008, a UC-Berkeley journalism student was covering a rally in Egypt when he was arrested. Fearing he and his translator would simply disappear, he managed to send the word "arrested'" on his Twitter feed. Help was soon on the way.

In January 2009, a Twitter picture brought us the first image of the US Airways flight piloted by Sully Sullenberger that made an emergency landing on the Hudson River.

Demi Moore received a Twitter message in April 2009 from a woman threatening to kill herself. Moore used Twitter to rally her fans to the woman's aid. In response to the outpouring, she changed her mind. In that same month, anti-Communist activities in Moldova used Twitter to create massive protests against the government.

When Iran's election results set off a firestorm of protests in June 2009, the Iranian government shut down websites and closed newspapers. Demonstrators used Twitter and other social media to get the word out. The communications revolution suggests global implications for repressive governments using firewalls and filters in an attempt to control how the Internet is used by their citizens.

In response to the situation in Iran, the satirical news site *The Onion* offered a fake article supposedly quoting Twitter's founder as saying Iranian protesters missed the point of his creation.

> "I couldn't believe they'd ruined something so beautiful, simple, and absolutely pointless… Twitter was intended to be a way for vacant, self-absorbed egotists to share their most banal and idiotic thoughts with anyone pathetic enough to read them."

Third party developers invented apps that let an unborn baby tweet when it kicks and a plant tweet when it needs water. Twitter search allows users to see what trends are taking place and TwitterVision offers a sampling of real time tweets.

The Twitter mission for journalists is primarily about passing along important, often breaking news...

The *Twitter* mission for journalists is primarily about passing along important, often breaking news that assumes shared values in the Twitter community. A self-described news junkie offers instructions for building what he calls a *Twitter Mood Box* at instructables.com. The device searches for tweets using words indicating a particular mood and displays the overall emotional reaction by lighting up a box with a particular color (red for anger, yellow for happy, etc.).

TWITTER QUIZ

1. How many characters are twitterers allowed to use per tweet?
2. How many visitors does Twitter have each month?

3. How long does the typical tweeter spend tweeting each day?

4. When did the site debut?

5. How many tweets are posted each day?

6. How many followers does the average Twitter user have?

7. What percentage of Twitter users have no followers?

(Answers are at the end of the chapter)

Twitter finally declared itself profitable for the first time at the end of 2009 because search deals with Google and Microsoft made the company about $25 million. Other high buzz Internet sites face the same predicament: How to make money. For instance, YouTube lost nearly half a billion dollars in 2009, according to *Slate.com*. A few years ago, wrestling had bigger audiences than some prime-time TV shows, yet wrestling never monetized well because most advertisers didn't want to be associated with the content. Environment did matter and that fact will probably work against YouTube in favor of professionally produced video. A slow spot for monetizing social media is its slow mobile adoption. A study by the *Pew Internet & American Life Project* found one out of ten American adult Internet users have activated smart phone or wireless laptop to access a social network.

Twitter still lacks credibility as a news source. Nearly half of those surveyed by the First Amendment Center said they didn't know enough about the service to have any opinion of its significance. Of those who did have an opinion, only 3% said Twitter is a "very reliable source of news." One-in-five (21%) say its information is "not reliable at all."

Despite concerns over the format used by Twitter, brevity does not take away the power of story telling. Ernest Hemingway is said to have created the shortest short story ever written after betting friends $10 during a New York lunch that he could write a captivating tale with a beginning, middle, and end in only six words. His companions agreed that he won the bet when they read what he scribbled on a napkin. "For Sale. Baby shoes. Never worn."

...brevity does not take away the power of story telling.

ANSWERS TO THE FACEBOOK CHALLENGE

1. There are more than 400 million Facebook users. If Facebook were a country, it would have a population more than twice as large as Brazil's.

2. Facebook's typical user is on the site for an average of 169 minutes per month — 17 times longer than *The New York Times* website holds a reader, who hangs around for only 10 minutes a month, according to comScore.

3. Mark Zuckerberg founded Facebook while he was a student at Harvard.

4. Zuckerberg was depressed from a girlfriend's rejection when the geeky underclassman hacked his way into the servers of some of the school's dorms. He created a site that showed the head shots of students and asked viewers to vote on which in each pairing was "hotter." Zuckerberg called it Facemash.

He was brought before the school's administrative board to answer questions about how he gathered the Facemash data. He was allowed to remain in school. Zuckerberg has said when he later started Facebook, his parents asked him not to make another site. Then all his Harvard classmates — as well as students from the rest of the Ivy League — joined, and he spent the remainder of his college money on servers. Zuckerberg never completed his degree.

5. In 2007, Microsoft invested $240 million for a 1.6% stake in the company. Through its *Windows Live* social network it is also a competitor of Facebook. But since taking a stake in the company, Microsoft has been working closely with the site to create links between Facebook and the Windows Live social network so that when members update their status message or upload photos on Facebook, that information appears on the Microsoft site too. Microsoft's new operating system OS7 has a slew of features similar to Facebook's playbook.

6. More than 70% of Facebook users are outside the U.S.

7. The fastest-growing demographic on Facebook is women 55 and older, up 175% since September 2008.

8. Half of Facebook users are on the site each day.

9. The largest live video event in the United States was Obama's Inauguration Day. You could log into CNN's streaming video (CNN.com Live) using your Facebook ID. You could watch the festivities while interacting with your friends through Facebook Connect. More than 27 million clicks made it the largest live video event ever. Marketers like Connect because they can interact with the Facebook community in a casual way. Connect funnels back what you do on those sites you log into through it.

   When retailers use the service, they are given a Facebook log-in window on their website. Connect users can tap their friend lists for input as they shop. Whenever they see an item they want to buy, they can send product details and a photo to Facebook friends, who may recommend the buy or something else. These comments from friends can show up months later. Facebook hopes shoppers eventually will turn to the social networking site rather than search engines such as Google.

10. If you connected with everyone on Facebook, you'd have more than 500 million friends. One out of every 22 people is now on Facebook. Zuckerberg has set a goal of having Facebook become the first social networking site with a billion members.

    Zuckerberg eventually wants to give users the ability to have a different Facebook personality for each Facebook friendship and turn Facebook into the planet's standardized communication (and marketing) platform. Your Facebook ID quite simply will be your gateway to the digital world. He says, "We think if you can build one worldwide platform where you can just type in anyone's name, find the person you're looking for, and communicate with them that's a really valuable system to be building."

11. Facebook is expected to generate more than half a billion dollars during 2009, though that's still small compared to Google and Yahoo. It has about 9% of the display-ad views during July 2009, up from about 7% in January, 2009, according to comScore.

12. *Oxford University Press* selected *unfriend* as its 2009 Word of the Year. It means to remove someone as a friend on a social networking website. Other finalists include netbook (a small laptop) and sexting (sending sexually explicit texts and pictures by cell phone). While some Facebook fans complained that defriend was preferable to unfriend, the publisher responded that the later was selected because it is more commonly used.

13. There are more than 60 million daily Facebook updates.

14. The most popular Facebook page is dedicated to Michael Jackson. The second most popular is Homer Simpson's page.

15. The average number of Facebook friends is 130.

ANSWERS TO THE TWITTER QUIZ

1. How many characters are twitterers allowed to use per tweet? 140 characters

2. How many visitors does Twitter have each month? 54 million

3. How long does the typical Tweeter spend tweeting each day? 30 minutes

4. When did the site debut? March 2006

5. How many tweets are posted each day? 50 million

6. How many followers does the average Twitter user have? In January 2009, the average Twitter user had 27 followers, down from 42 in August 2009.

7. What percentage of Twitter users have no followers? About 25% of Twitter users have no followers and about 40% have never sent a single Tweet, according to a study by RJMetrics. Seventy-five million people had signed up for a Twitter account by the end of 2009, the study said, but just 17% of them sent even a single Tweet in December 2009. Twitter has a high number of inactive accounts, but its frequent users are deeply committed.

Online Newsgathering

Remember 2004? At that time, there was no *Facebook* (as we know it today), *Twitter* or *YouTube*. *MySpace* had yet to become a significant player. In the short period of time that has passed since then, tools have emerged that journalists could have only dreamed of using previously. Bloggers and tweeters give reporters an instant cheat sheet through the power of the real-time Web. While you're digging for online information about reporting topics, someone could be *Googling* your name at same time. A Microsoft survey called *Online Reputation in a Connected World* found that 78% of recruiters use search engines to conduct background checks on candidates.

Reporters working for online news organizations have several advantages over traditional media. They:

- are free of scheduled broadcasts and press runs.
- can offer more depth than "on air" minutes or "in print" spaces allow.
- may link to source materials, related stories and more.
- can use multimedia when words aren't enough.
- are able to collaborate with viewers on stories.

On the Web you can get story ideas and conduct research. This does not make you a hacker journalist as described in the Internet chapter, but might stir enthusiasm for online newsgathering.

First: Some Internet terms worth knowing, and then specific sites that can empower you. Toss any confusing jargon or acronyms into a search engine, read for a moment and then keep going. Don't lose sight of the larger picture among the maze of available products and technology. The tools are important, but avoid fixating on them.

Internet Terms to Know

URL stands for *Uniform Resource Locator,* the official address of a site. Inside a *URL* domain is the Domain name, the site's unique address. Domain names are used in URLs to identify particular Web pages. For example, look at the following URL.

http://www.pcwebopedia.com

In this URL, the domain name is pcwebopedia.com.

Have you ever wondered how to find out who owns a site? Companies that sell websites, like *Go Daddy, WhoIs?,* or *Network Solutions,* allow you to look up a site owner. Look for their *who is* option.

Browsers are software programs used to download and view Web files. Examples are *Netscape, Firefox, Internet Explorer* and *Google's Chrome.* Developers have created plug-ins and add-ons which can perform helpful functions such as blocking pop-up ads. Websites and text display often vary among different browsers, as well as different *versions* of browsers.

A *cookie* is a chunk of code added to a computer's hard drive by a visited website. These cookies identify a computer and can be read by any of the thousands of websites also belonging to that network. This can happen without your knowledge, regardless of whether you've actually visited the websites. The software is most commonly referred to as spyware, i.e., code placed on a computer by a website without permission or notification. An example of a company dropping tracking cookies on computers to follow users from site to site is *Double Click* (owned by *Google*). The cookies report what commercial ads are viewed and which are clicked on. Not all cookies are malicious. Some simply identify the computer for a site so that a user will not be required to log on before each visit.

Spam is probably the most annoying Internet communication. These unsolicited commercial emails make up three of every four emails sent on the Internet. Yet spam email is just one way false information bombards us. Sometimes false information comes from friends and family in the form of Internet rumors.

For instance, *Procter & Gamble* was victimized by online stories falsely asserting that one of its cleaners could kill pets. *Starbucks* was falsely accused online of refusing to provide coffee to Marines serving in Iraq. Gotten any good ones lately? Check out urban legends and myths circulating the Internet on sites like *Snopes.com.*

Reliable News Sources

It is critical for a journalist in the digital age to discern truthful information from false or misleading information...

It is critical for a journalist in the digital age to discern truthful information from false or misleading information in the media. Quality brands (like *The New York Times* and the *BBC*) have earned their reputations over time as consistently reliable news sources. The bar is higher for obscure, unfamiliar sites, especially when they offer unusual news items. Check the site's "About Us" page for information about who operates it. Look for a date somewhere on the page to make sure the story is not outdated. Reliable sources want readers to know when the information is posted and will usually have the date clearly displayed near the "headline."

More clues can be found by conducting a Google search, using the query "link: website name." This will indicate what kind of other sites link to the one you are inspecting. Compare the information you get from a site with other sites you trust. Find out whether the site offers quality information on other topics besides the one you are investigating.

Online Newsgathering Sites and Tools

LINKS

Use AssignmentEditor.com to find links to information that reporters may need while working on a story. To find out if a newspaper in a particular city has more information on a developing news story in that city, try *ThePaperboy.com*.

ALMANACS

Suppose you are working on a car theft story. To find out in which cities crooks swipe the most cars, visit *Yahoo*'s online list of almanacs at Yahoo.com/Reference/Almanacs. Using one of the featured sites, *InfoPlease.com*, if you click on U.S. cities, then *Car Thefts by City* (in the right hand column), you'll find the information you need. *This Day in History* (in the left column) offers a look at what happened on a particular date. If a reporter is working on a story that will be due Friday of next week, he might click on this selection and discover that it's National Cheesecake Day next Friday. He could write a feature on the topic to be posted or printed on that day with plenty of time to beat the deadline.

Maybe a story needs a quote from an expert. Try *RefDesk.com*. There are many helpful links for journalists on the site. Scroll down to find *Help and Advice* in the right hand column. Click on *Ask the Experts* to find a list of people who can be quoted because they understand the issues.

LISTSERVS

A ListServ comes in handy if you're looking for someone who is familiar with a particular field and can provide more information than just a quote. The recipients respond with specific commentary about specific subjects and often go back and forth on multiple issues. It's like a group conversation between everyone that you can read or join. It's a great way to get advice from a wide group. Join a group focused on a particular subject and feel free to ask beginner questions. There's always someone, or a group, ready to help. A number of them are listed at *tile.net/lists*. This website is like a search engine for *listservs*. Click around and look for groups to join. A journalist can join a *listserv* while working on a particular story and leave when the article is completed.

Listservs are often moderated, which is kind of like having a copy editor. To get in, send an e-mail to the address indicated on Listserv. Drop out the same way. Creating an e-mail account just for getting these messages will prevent clogging up your personal e-mail address. Listservs sometimes generate lots of notes back and forth between users. It's amazing how much can be learned just by reading the answers to other people's questions. Users can e-mail a single person on the listserv, to strike up a private conversation, bypassing everyone else on the list.

NEWSGROUPS

Newsgroups are part of the Internet known as the *Usenet*. It's like a newsroom bulletin board. The info is often old, so it's not really "news." You'll find a little bit of everything at *Newsgroups.com*, *Cyberfiber.com* or *Groups.Google.com*. You can post requests for information and get answers to specific questions.

ALERTS

News organizations, like *FOX*, *CNN*, and of course *Google*, offer alerts about news stories in specific areas of interest like sports or celebrities. They will send notes to your e-mail account or mobile phone. This is why those headed into journalism may find themselves writing news for smart phones — very short blurbs, to draw people to websites for more on the story, or to entice them to watch cell phone video.

BLOGS

The number of TV and radio stations is limited, but the Net turns every user into a potential mass communicator. One way is through blogs. These "Web logs" began as personal online diaries and now there are many considered legitimate news sources. If you decide to start your own blog, you can take over an inactive blog instead of launching a new one. *Orble.com* lists abandoned blogs that can give you a head start on gaining an audience.

"One of the problems is newspapers fired so many journalists and turned them loose to start so many blogs. They should have executed them... But they foolishly let them out alive."

Start one by going to *Google* and clicking on blogs. Follow the instructions and you could be up and running in five minutes using the provided templates. *WordPress* and *Google's Blogger* offer the most popular quick and easy setups. Some in the news business consider blogs to be merely opinions and not legitimate journalism. Apple founder Steve Jobs has said he wants to avoid seeing American journalism descend into "a nation of bloggers." However, the quality of the information found on blogs has indisputably improved following recent newspaper layoffs. Alan Mutter, author of the *Reflections of a Newsosaur* blog, warned in a *New York Times* article, "One of the problems is newspapers fired so many journalists and turned them loose to start so many blogs. They should have executed them. They wouldn't have had competition. But they foolishly let them out alive."

Blogs have their own search engines. *Google* has one (*blogsearch.google.com*) and so does *Sphere.com*, *Icerocket.com*, and *Technorati.com*. These sites keep up with which in the blogger army are the most popular. In order to search several blog search engines at the same time, there's *Talkdigger.com*.

Blogging is becoming more lucrative for those who can amass a following. Despite the economic downturn, *Technorati* reports the average blogger salary in October 2009 was more than $42,000 — over $122,000 for full-time bloggers and nearly $15,000 for part-timers. A large portion of the income isn't from Internet ad revenues but speaking engagements, news assignments, and conferences.

Some journalists are experimenting with *blogozines*. These more elaborate blogs have the goal of keeping readers engaged for longer periods of time with richer layouts and more media options.

PODCASTS, MOBLOGS AND VLOGS

A *podcast* is sort of the verbal expression of a blog. The *New Oxford American Dictionary* picked podcast as its *2005 Word of the Year*. Some newspapers and other media outlets use podcasts to summarize the day's news. Podcast growth has stopped as streaming media has come on strong, offering quicker access and fewer clicks. People love live events.

A *Moblog* is a combination of a mobile phone and a blog. These blogs are produced through cell phones.

Vlogs are video blogs. Instead of text, you post video of yourself. An example is a quirky site *Rocketboom.com*. The deaf often make use of Vlogs because American Sign Language, not English, is typically their first language. They enjoy being able to see someone else sign to them. *JoeyBaer.com* is an example.

Some journalists are using inexpensive cameras (*Flip Cams* are one example) to post video. While not broadcast quality, it is good enough for the small screen of the Internet or mobile phones. Though simple to use, *PC World* declared flip video cameras dead upon the launch of the *iPhone 3G S*. This version of the *Apple smartphone* can shoot video about the same quality as a *Flip Cam*. Why carry multiple single-use devices when you only need one? Chips and sensors are becoming smaller and more advanced, quickly replacing and making obsolete single-serving devices like GPS units and cameras. With the latest advancements in image sensors, we're about to see the eradication of the pocket point-and-shoot camera and the video camera. *OmniVision* has a new chip that's based on image technology used in spy satellites for years, and which will give us mobile devices with visual quality equal to most high-end cameras on the market today. Images on mobile phones will soon compete with handheld cameras, and at some point the need for flash on digital cameras will be eliminated by new sensors. The only way for a specialized device to survive versatile competition is for it to perform much better than its rivals. Many smartphones now rival the *iPod* as music players, making the popular device another example of technology whose time may be coming to an end. Cameras and e-book readers may face the same dismal future.

FEED READERS

A feed reader is also known as an RSS feed or aggregator. Users download a small program that brings new postings to them, so they don't have to continually check for updates. One way to expand your reach is to search a topic on *Google* news, copy the address into a feed reader and watch the stories roll in whenever *Google* finds a new article on the subject. This is one of the most underutilized and powerful ways for journalists to research or remain informed on a subject.

This is one of the most underutilized and powerful ways for journalists to research or remain informed on a subject.

WIKIS

Wikipedia is an example of an online encyclopedia written by thousands of people. The pop culture concordance works on the principle of the *hive mind*. As seen through the efforts of insects (such as bees working together in a hive), something of value increases in relation to the number of people who contribute to it.

Have you ever tried to guess the number of jellybeans in a jar? Research shows combining the guesses of more people together results in a more accurate final answer. Sites like *Wikipedia* work on the same principle.

Notice that it is called WIKI-pedia. A *Wiki* is a collaboratively written document published online where team members can post information relating to a particular project. Someone posts an entry and other people can instantly see it. They add to it or edit it. It gets refined.

But be careful. Mistakes slip through. A Virginia teenager wrote his own obit on *Wikipedia*, describing his tragic death in a shot put accident. It stayed up for only a day before it was removed.

If you are a journalist, can you use *Wikipedia?*

Dr. Kevin A. Clauson of *Nova Southeastern University* conducted a study of what *Wikipedia* had to say about 80 drugs. He discovered most of the information was accurate. The problem was with what was missing. The online, free encyclopedia left out important details, such as telling readers that St. John's wort can interfere with the action of the HIV drug Prezista (darunavir).

For journalists, *Wikipedia* can be a jumping-off point for research. It can be used to recall the name of something on the tip of your tongue, but facts for a news story, especially medical research, should depend on a more reliable source.

> *For journalists, Wikipedia can be a jumping-off point to get research started… But facts for a news story, …should depend on a more reliable source.*

Another example of the *hive mind* is *Yahoo*'s answer site *Answers.Yahoo.com* or *ChaCha.com*. People post questions to the site and a team of real experts answer them. Some people warn the hive mind can be used for evil, as well as good, which can lead to mob rule. Jaron Lanier, author of *You Are Not a Gadget*, said a series of online postings in China incited throngs to hunt down accused adulterers in 2007. Whatis.com is another online encyclopedia offering "definitions for thousands of the most current IT-related words."

One of the most curious Wikis involving journalism is *Wikileaks*. The online service for whistle-blowers to leak government and corporate secrets got its start in 2007 when Australian hacker Julian Assange assembled some 800 volunteer coders, activists and lawyers from around the world to generate the site's content. The site drew attention around the world by surreptitiously obtaining video of a U.S. helicopter mowing down unarmed civilians in Iraq. It has published information on illegal financial dealings in Iceland and evidence of corruption in Kenya. Anyone can submit a document through Wikileaks' Swedish servers (where disclosing sources is a crime) and Belgium (where conversations with journalists obtained through wiretapping is not admissible in court). The site is designed to prevent any single government from removing or stopping publication of a document.

WIDGETS

Widgets are another type of tool the Internet provides for journalists. A *widget* is a portable, self-contained chunk of code that, once installed, will execute a function or add content to a page. In other words, a widget can display constantly updated snippets of information. They can stream audio, play games, monitor systems, and serve as clocks, calendars, timers, etc. You can find these little programs seamlessly integrated with social media sites like *Facebook. Yahoo* has a collection at widgets. yahoo.com

TAGS

A *tag* is simply a word used to describe a particular bookmark, like "boats" or "Super Bowl." Click on a "Super Bowl" tag and you'll get a list of items related to the big game. Sites that use tagging are helpful when reporting on particular topics. A site like *del.icio.us* heavily employs tags.

Tag clouds are a series of words grouped together and linked to items tagged with these selfsame words, the larger fonted words indicating which are the more popular.

METATAGS

Metatags are key words embedded in the code of a website. You can view these key words by clicking on *View*, then *Page Source*. This should open up a page showing the code underneath the Web page you are viewing. Do a search for the word *Meta* and that should locate the Metatags for the page. They help automated search engines by describing the main words with which to associate the page.

Websites show up higher in search engine rankings the greater the number of visitors and links to the site. Many search engine users don't realize that *Google* has set its search to pull more results from the area of the world in which the user is located. A search in England will produce different results than the same search in America. Just because a site is ranked highly by a search engine, doesn't mean it's the best result. Sometimes it only means the creators have been effective at design and promotion.

Google Searches & Features

Google controls about 65% of searches in the U.S. and 67% outside the country, according to *SmartMoney* magazine. Showing up as the first Google entry is an important means of driving traffic to a website. But many users don't maximize the *Google* experience.

Google's default search setting is AND. Typing *global warming* will produce items that contain those two words, *global* AND *warming*. But other search modifications are available. Use them to get to relevant information more quickly. For instance, quotation marks around the two words will search for the phrase *global warming*. *Global* OR *warming* will give you one or the other, but not a Web page using both. A MINUS sign right in front of warming will produce *global*, but NOT *warming*. You can also combine these modifiers. For a story about *bacteria* that survive in refrigerators, increase the chance of a successful result by using a search string like *bacteria and freeze* OR *ice*. That would tell the search engine to find documents containing the word bacteria plus the words freeze or, alternatively, the word bacteria and the word ice.

OTHER *GOOGLE* FEATURES...

CACHED

Under the results of any random *Google* search is the word *cached*. It comes in handy if a Web page link doesn't work. Click on it for a snapshot of what the search engine found when it crawled the page. If someone has taken down a website, you still may be able to get to part of the page using this method. Cache also refers to temporary storage on computers. It's a smart idea to regularly clear these temporary files to keep the system running effectively.

GOOGLE 411

Call *800-GOOG-411* for *Google* voice-recognition cell phone service. Call the number, speak a search term ("comedy clubs, Chicago" or "Domino's Pizza, Cleveland"), and *Google's* auto-voice reads off the closest eight matches. Speak the name and be connected automatically at no charge. The user never knows or cares about the actual phone number. Say "text message" at any time to have the address and phone number zapped to mobile phone.

GOOGLE SMS

Another *Google* tool is its SMS feature. Send a message to *GOOGL* (or 46645). In the body of the message, type the sort of information desired: weather report ("weather dallas"), stock quotes (twx), movie showtimes (type "Gone with the Wind 44120"), definitions ("define cyborg"), directions ("memphis tn to 60609"), unit conversions ("liters in 5 gallons"), currency conversions ("25 usd in euros"), and so on. Five seconds later, *Google* texts back the details.

GOOGLE ALERTS

Keep tabs on what the world is saying about you, your company or your interests. At *Google.com/alerts*, type a search phrase (such as your name), and specify what to monitor (blogs, Web pages, discussion groups and so on). When you are mentioned online, you'll find out about it in an e-mail alert. It's a personal clipping service at no charge.

GOOGLE SETS

At *labs.google.com/sets*, type in several items in a series (like "cleveland browns" and "dallas cowboys"); *Google* fleshes out the list with others like it (all the other football teams). This is a great help when something's on the tip of the tongue (a kind of fruit, president, car, holiday, currency) but you can only remember something similar to the item you want to recall.

SEARCH BOX SECRETS

Usually, whatever is typed into *Google's Search Box* is treated as a quest for Web pages. Certain kinds of information, however, get special consideration. For example, you can type in an equation (like "23*9/3.4+234"); press Enter to see the answer.

GOOGLE CONVERSIONS

Think of *Google* for conversions. For example, type "83 yards in inches," "500 euros in dollars," or "grams in 3.2 pounds"; then press Enter.

GOOGLE DICTIONARY

Google is also a dictionary (type "define:ersatz"), package tracker (type your UPS or FedEx tracking number), global Yellow Pages ("phonebook:home depot norwalk ct"), meteorologist ("weather san diego"), flight tracker ("AA 15"), stock ticker ("AAPL" or "MSFT"), and a movie-listings site (type "movies:10024," or whatever your ZIP code is).

GOOGLE FLU

There's a curious health search function offered at *Google.org/flutrends*. Whenever people get sick, they use *Google* to search for health information. By collating these searches, *Google* has created an early-warning system for flu outbreaks in your area, with color-coded graphs. *Google* says that its *Flu Trends* has recognized outbreaks two weeks sooner than the *Centers for Disease and Control Prevention*.

GOOGLE FAST FLIP

Google's Fast Flip project is an attempt to create an experience similar to leafing through a magazine. Pages of a magazine or website are loaded not as text, but as a series of photos of pages which are stored in Google's system to load nearly as quickly as a reader could leaf through a physical magazine. Rather than finding items of interest by linking to a title, *Fast Flip* is designed to offer a sense of the graphics.

The Wider Net

Using only search engines like *Google* and *Yahoo* to find information also means you could miss out on large chunks of the Internet. You can also use directory search engines and meta search engines.

Directory search sites are organized by human beings. Examples include:

> *Yahoo*'s directory at *dir.yahoo.com*
>
> The Librarians' Index at *lii.org*
>
> Academic Info at *academicinfo.net*
>
> *WolframAlpha* is vetted by 200 researchers using *Mathematica* (computational software created by Stephen Wolfram)

A meta search engine will allow you to cast a wider net. These include *Vivisimo.com, Metacrawler.com* and *Dogpile.com*.

If you want to read more on how search engines work, check out *SearchEngineWatch. com*.

PORTALS

Columbia University estimates 90% of the Internet's information is invisible to today's search engines. Most major government, university and public corporation sites must be entered and searched through a portal. Many of them provide access to other portals within, or point to other portals. A prime example is the U.S. Federal Government website *USA.gov*. This entry page and the internal search engine it provides opens millions of pages about state and federal government information and services. Most of this is not revealed by even the most clever search engine.

WAYBACKMACHINE

WaybackMachine or *The Internet Archive* is available at *Archive.org*. This resource stores different versions of a large number of Web pages and historic portal entry points going back to the mid-90s. For example, you can view pages showing staff changes at a company over the years, to see who moved up in rank and who moved on to other jobs. Comparing page evolution can reveal how someone's biography could have been edited over time.

A *Boston Globe* reporter used the archive as a resource when researching George W. Bush's biography. This allowed him to show how details of Bush's military record changed through the years on State Department websites. Type in a university website address and look at the Web page as it appeared a year ago, five years ago, 10 years ago.

Memento Web (*MementoWeb.org*) makes it easier to see an array of archived websites. Users plug in a date and then browse the World Wide Web as it was on that day. The effort is financed by a grant from the Library of Congress.

MASHUPS

A *mashup* is a combination of two or more data sites in a new way. *Twittervision* is an example of a *mashup*. It shows tweets and their source location on Google maps.

A similar site called *FlickrVision* combines *Google* maps with *Flickr* photos. It's just fun to watch and wonder, "Why was that photo taken?" Or "What an interesting-looking place." Need to take a break from studying? Visit *FlickrVision* and let your mind wander.

Other mashups combine *Google* maps with *Craigslist*, showing houses for sale in an area. One of these is *HousingMaps.com*.

ChicagoCrime.org (now *EveryBlock.com*), mentioned in the last chapter as an example of hacker journalism, combines crime data with *Google* maps. A mashup created by the World Health Organization provides the latest updates on diseases and outbreaks in the different regions of the world. Find it at *healthmap.org/en*.

Putting things together in new ways is one of the most obvious and creative aspects of the Internet.

CROWDSOURCING

Crowdsourcing is inviting the public to develop a new technology, carry out a design task, refine an algorithm, or help capture, systematize or analyze large amounts of data. Web 2.0 loves the wisdom of the crowds. An example of this is *Digg*. Readers submit and promote articles from other websites. *Digg* users vote for stories they like by giving them "diggs." *Digg* has influenced many other news sites to do the same thing.

iStockphoto is one site doing this. It has created a market for the work of amateur photographers, with about 22,000 contributions charging between one and five dollars for each image. This is nearly putting professional photographers who sell stock photos out of business.

By anonymously tracking users of *Google Maps* on their mobile phones, *Google* is crowdsourcing real-time traffic conditions that extend to busier side streets. To see it in action, pick a city in *Google Maps* and activate the traffic layer. Of course, this begs the question: Should a driver be looking at *Google Maps* on a phone in a moving car?

Should a driver be looking at Google Maps on a phone in a moving car?

Drew Curtis of Fark.com says this about crowdsourced news:

> "My local newspaper website tells me what the most popular stories of the day are but they might as well just replace that with every article they write about Kentucky basketball because it's the same list of stories. One day, UK Coach John Calipari cut down a tree in his front yard, it became the most popular article on their website. Does that mean it's also the most important? Absolutely not."

OhMyNews.com is crowdsourcing at the next level. The South Korean site supported by content from citizen journalists has more than 55,000 reporters producing up to 200 news articles a day. The site requires all citizen reporters to sign a legal document before submitting stories in which they promise to follow a code of ethics, absolving the site of any consequences should legal problems arise. They are forbidden from using a fake identity and must give their real names. The company verifies identities through a government-sponsored authentication process before it grants membership. Then, professional editors screen the submitted content. About 30% of the submitted material is rejected. The site also has a committee composed of citizen reporters and other outside watchers who monitor the site.

Is this the face of journalism in the future, where "professionals" who earn Journalism degrees spend their days sifting through the material submitted by local citizens rather than gathering stories?

A broader attempt at *crowdsourced* storytelling is getting a workout through sites like *the3six5* which tries to get 365 people — one for each day of the year — to write about something happening in the world that day and how it relates to them.

USER-GENERATED CONTENT

One problem with user-generated content like that gathered by *OhMyNews.com* is that someone might put up copyrighted material or obscene material, etc.

Three ways to deal with audience-generated content are:

> 1 – use journalists to check the content before it is published.

> 2 – trust the audience and publish unedited.

> 3 – find some technology to monitor content, such as identifying and deleting specific key words.

Here are some problems with each option:

> 1 - If you choose the first method, you need a large staff.

> 2 - Using the second option may cost you credibility.

> 3 - And the third does not always work because technology does not think but merely reacts. For instance, banning the word "sex" may cut out stories about same sex marriage and health information.

HYPERLOCAL

Localism.com is run by a real estate blogging network. It's a hyperlocal news site powered by real estate agents covering their own neighborhoods. The pitch is connectedness. "They are on the street every day, looking at houses and making friends in the community."

The Washington Post launched *LoudounExtra.com* to fanfare in 2007, as a virtual town square for one of the country's most affluent and fastest-growing counties. But a year later, the site designed to cover everything down to Little League games still hadn't found its audience or advertisers and the team of Internet geeks who put it together had left for other projects. The hyperlocal effort was based on the idea that while newspapers cannot compete with cable TV or the Internet when it comes to covering breaking news, they can dominate what happens in their backyards.

The saga of *LoudounExtra* hasn't deterred others from trying. In 2009, we saw the launch of many hyperlocal online news start-ups from *Texas Tribune* to the smaller *Oakland Local*.

Some observers believe what we see and call new media will not replace old media. Instead, they predict traditional media will change to absorb the best of new media.

Covering local news is not the same as hyperlocal. If you cover a city or a town, you're a local site. Hyperlocal is a subset of local, not the catch-all buzzword for all of it. Adding a garage sale map to a city news site does not make it hyperlocal.

EveryBlock's Adrian Holovaty doesn't describe his site as hyperlocal but *microlocal* because it gets all the way down to granular coverage like land use reports. Read more about *EveryBlock* in the previous chapter on the Internet.

CONNECTEDNESS

Think for a moment. How old is the Internet? It's less than 5000 days old.

Kevin Kelly, the founder of *Wired* magazine says the web is "like a black hole that is sucking everything into it," and eventually every item or artifact we make will have some sliver of the webness in it, some connectedness to "the machine." He predicts our current spectrum of media (TV, film, phones, blogs, radio, etc) will become one media platform because they are liquid and merging together.

Chapter One refers to Marshall McLuhan, the media critic who asked if a fish knows it is wet. He's also famous in media circles for saying machines are the extension of the human senses. We see through television. It extends our sight. McLuhan said machines are the extension of the human senses. Kelly says the situation is now reversed. Humans are the extended senses of the machine.

For Next Time

What is the aim of public relations? To positively manage a company's image or to manipulate and propagandize it to the public?

TWELVE
Public Relations

Public Relations Timeline

1800 BCE Tablets are discovered in what is now Iraq offering what we would call a public information bulletin. It provides farmers with information on sowing, irrigating, and harvesting their crops.

50 BCE Julius Caesar feeds Roman citizens reports of his achievements through the *Acta Diurna*, or *Daily Events*, to maintain morale and solidify his reputation and power.

1200 Genghis Khan sends advance men to tell stories of his exploits to frighten villagers.

1773 The Boston Tea Party attracts public attention.

1889 Westinghouse Electric establishes the first corporate public relations department.

1896 The modern national political campaign is born when the presidential candidates set up campaign headquarters in Chicago from which they issue news releases, position papers and pamphlets. The image of public relations begins to turn negative.

1906 The Publicity Bureau opens in Boston. It's the first publicity company and it works to help the railroads challenge federal regulations.

1914 John D. Rockefeller hires a former newspaper reporter to clean up his image and that of his company, Standard Oil. Ivy Lee helps transform Rockefeller's public image from robber baron to that of a kind employer and generous philanthropist. Lee is later considered the "father of public relations."

1917 President Woodrow Wilson selects a former newspaperman to lead a committee to promote U.S. involvement in World War I.

1930's President Franklin D. Roosevelt embarks on a sophisticated public relations campaign to win support for his radical New Deal policies.

1934   Ivy Lee is brought before Congress to defend himself against charges that he is a Nazi sympathizer. He dies before the issue is settled publicly. But the damage is done and in some people's minds PR becomes a dirty word.

1936   The group that eventually becomes the Public Relations Society of America (PRSA) is formed. The PRSA is the principal organization for today's public relations professionals.

1938   Congress passes the Foreign Agents Registration Act. It requires anyone engaging in U.S. political activity on behalf of a foreign power to register as an agent of that power with the Justice Department.

Public Relations Today

You may wonder what this chapter and the next are doing in a book about media. While public relations and advertising are not mass media themselves, they are important support industries for the media. They use the media and the media use them.

A shallow Hollywood couple gathers with their public relations advisors to create a pretend relationship to generate publicity. Is this really how it works? A popular *YouTube* short film directed by Dave Moldavon suggests it's just a typical day for the PR pros. Search his name in *YouTube* and you'll find a five and a half minute parody.

The *Public Relations Society of America* (PRSA) would disagree, offering this definition: *Public Relations helps an organization and its publics mutually adapt to each other.* "Publics" can refer to its consumers, regulators, employees, shareholders, activitists, and the media.

Brand credibility is usually associated with trust, transparency, authenticity, responsiveness and affirmation.

If you ever want to upset a PR professional, just say his or her industry falls under marketing. While distinct, the two professions are clearly complementary. Public relations is more focused on influencing reputation, and when combined with marketing and advertising, a brand is created. Brand credibility is usually associated with trust, transparency, authenticity, responsiveness and affirmation. Tony Cohen of *Fremantle Media* says once people fall in love with a brand, they want to interact with it in all sorts of ways.

PR is most directly about managing the public perception of a company. Let's more clearly distinguish it from some close cousins:

> *Marketing* is about brand image. PR isn't about selling, it's about reputation.
>
> *Advertising* is buying time in the media. PR deals with publicity.
>
> *Journalism* is about being objective and balanced. PR is about telling one side and telling it well.
>
> *Press agents* seek to put their client in the news in a positive light.

Public Relations overlaps these areas because there is common ground in the main areas of focus. These common interests include:

>   Research
>   Employee relations and communication
>   Issues Management
>   Crisis Management

A typical day for a PR specialist might include editing layouts, writing news releases or corporate newsletters, working on websites, monitoring media coverage, helping reporters get information, or navigating a publicity crisis for a company. The ability to move quickly, be creative, listen, multi-task and handle deadlines are essential skills for the public relations specialist.

The ability to move quickly, be creative, listen, multi-task and handle deadlines are essential skills for the public relations specialist.

A company's public relations division works with the media and community organizations, deals with multi-cultural relations, oversees a company's charities, and even helps the corporation deal with environmental issues. PR is also about greater opportunities to directly build relationships. Today's social web now allows public relations specialists greater opportunities to build relationships directly with consumers and stakeholders.

Journalists sometimes make the move into PR because both jobs requires similar skills. Former journalists are considered valuable in PR because they know how the news system works. They are attracted to the change because working in the grind of news can be difficult. Journalism means unusual hours and working holidays. Public relations is more of a 9-to-5 weekday life. Juggling the responsibilities of a family with the demands of journalism can make a dependable, regular schedule very attractive. But once you make the move to public relations, it can be difficult to go back into news since PR pushes you away from the objectivity many journalists aim to achieve.

FREE SITES

HelpAreporter.com and *PitchRate.com* are free PR sites. If you sign up on these sites and have expertise or a compelling personal story, a reporter or producer might contact you.

PUBLIC RELATIONS QUIZ

1. How many people work in the public relations industry?
2. How many public relations firms are there in the U.S.?
3. How much did American public relations firms make in 2005?
4. What percentage of the Public Relations Society of America are women?

(Answers are at the end of the chapter)

Job Comparison

Over the last decade, the number of journalists has fallen but the number of PR specialists has grown.

	Reporters and Correspondents:	Public Relations Specialists:
1998	52,380	98,240
2007	51,620	225,880

Source: U.S. Bureau of Labor Statistics

A *Media Bistro* report shows that public relations jobs had the highest growth rate in 2009, soaring 22% from the previous year. Marketing-related jobs rose 18% and online/new media jobs climbed 15%. TV jobs fell 19% and magazine publishing, advertising agency, graphic design, and art director positions were down 9%.

Government PR

After World War II, in an attempt to reduce government bureaucracy, some members of Congress pulled language out of the 1913 Appropriations Act that said designated funds were not to be used by a publicity expert unless specifically appropriated for that purpose. The provision doesn't actually prohibit government public relations, but is nevertheless often interpreted that way. That's why there are many in government who fall under the PR banner but do not use the name. They may be called press secretaries, information officers, public affairs specialists, or communication specialists.

Toxic Sludge is Good for You

Toxic Sludge is Good for You was written by critics of the PR industry in an attempt to expose the dark side of PR. The authors say PR specialists heard about the book and asked that "toxic sludge" be removed from the title. To the authors, it was ironic, since they see public relations as manipulation and propaganda.

Some companies try to steer clear of the negatives associated with PR by calling the department something else, like Public Information, Corporate Communications, The Communications Department, or Media Relations. Regardless of the label, these departments still fulfill PR's duties, such as representing a company at social functions, dealing with crises, and meeting with various publics.

Creating Brand You

Have you ever thought about becoming a PR person for yourself? Have you considered creating *brand you*? People often attempt to post alter egos on social networking sites, painting an edgier image of themselves through fashion and hobbies. Why not do it in real life?

Management guru Tom Peters says we should take charge of our image and become the CEO of *Me Inc.*, reinventing ourselves every few years while balancing a series of provocative, fascinating projects. Dan Schawbel, who calls himself a "personal branding guru" offers self-branding tips on his blog. Schawbel emphasizes the significance of social media and branding. For instance, he shares the story about using *Facebook* to gather information about a prospective employee. He found a group protesting her getting kicked out of a dormitory and decided to give the job to someone else.

"You have to take control of your brand," says Seth Godin, an author and entrepreneur who calls himself an agent of change. *Business Week* quotes him as saying, "Many of us are taught to do our best and then let the world decide how to judge us. I think it's better to do your best and decide how you want to be judged. And act that way."

Since a brand is not on a shelf but in the hearts of people, your own brand is the sum total of perceptions about your product (you) in the heads of your relevant audience.

Should you treat co-workers not just as colleagues but as your audience? Ready to put together a set of 8,000 *Facebook* friends and 3,200 *LinkedIn* connections?

Pause for Discussion: Taking Charge of Our Images

If the concept of branding bothers you, consider this: When you take a photo down from *Facebook* because your eyes appear crossed or your hair is out of place, are you branding yourself? Are you attempting to create a particular image of yourself for the public? And if you are, how far is too far? Is thinking of yourself as a brand inappropriate?

For Next Time

What are some memorable advertising slogans? Is it the slogans and images that make advertising work or is it the promoted products themselves that ultimately make an advertising campaign effective?

ANSWERS TO PUBLIC RELATIONS QUIZ

1. 350,000 people work in the public relations industry.
2. 7,000 public relations firms operate in the U.S., according to the 2006 U.S. Census.
3. American public relations firms made $3.7 billion in revenue during 2005.
4. 70% of the membership in the *Public Relations Society of America* are women.

> Since a brand is not on a shelf but in the hearts of people, your own brand is the sum total of perceptions about your product (you) in the heads of your relevant audience.

THIRTEEN
Advertising

Advertising Timeline

3000 BCE Babylonians hire barkers to shout out goods and prices at passersby.

15th Century Product-promoting advertising becomes widely circulated in Europe.

1625 The first newsbook containing ads is printed in England.

1704 The first newspaper advertisement appears in the *Boston News-Letter* seeking a buyer for an estate.

1869 Ads become more complex, creative, and expensive. F. *Wayland Ayer* opens in Camden, New Jersey, becoming the first "full service" advertising agency. There are more than 500 agencies today in the U.S.

Early 1900s Magazines get more support from ads than from readers who buy copies of the publication. The advertising industry establishes professional standards and regulates itself.

1914 The Federal Trade Commission (FTC) is established to monitor and regulate advertising.

1938 Under the *Wheeler-Lea Act*, The FTC is charged with overseeing advertising associated with products otherwise regulated by the Food and Drug Administration. Ads for prescription drugs are an exception and remain under the authority of the FDA.

1941 With 7,500 TV sets in New York City, NBC's WNBT begins telecasting. The first TV commercials feature a Bulova watch ticking for 60 seconds at the beginning and closing of each broadcast day.

WWII Health posters emerge as a way to educate the public. After the War, advertising made its way from radio to TV.

1946 *The Hucksters* by Frederic Wakeman becomes a bestseller. The next year it becomes a film starring Clark Gable as a war vet fighting for honesty in the ad game.

1954	The CBS television network becomes the largest advertising medium in the world.
1956	Videotape makes prerecorded commercials possible.
1957	Vance Packard's attack on advertising, *The Hidden Persuaders* becomes a bestseller. It tells how advertisers use psychological methods to tap into our unconscious desires in order to "persuade" us.
1958	The National Association of Broadcasters bans subliminal ads.
1963	*Confessions of an Advertising Man* by David Ogilvy becomes a classic handbook for modern advertising.
1964	NBC allows comparative advertising for the first time. CBS and ABC keep their bans in place until 1972.
1967	Mary Wells becomes the first woman to head a major advertising agency at *Wells, Rich, Greene.*
1969	New York's *WOR-TV* runs the first infomercial, a paid program that amounts to a really long commercial.
1971	Congress bans TV ads for cigarettes, costing broadcasters some $220 million in advertising.
1973	The Supreme Court restricts the power of the government to regulate commercial speech.
1976	The Supreme Court recognizes First Amendment protection for the advertising industry.
1991	Congress passes the *Telephone Consumer Protection Act of 1991*, laying out guidelines for telemarketer phone calls and allowing consumers to be removed from companies' call lists.
1992	The Food and Drug Administration Modernization Act mandates, among other things, FDA regulation of health claims for foods.
2008	Google's ad revenues equal that of CBS, ABC, FOX, NBC and the CW — combined.

Advertising Today

The AMC cable show *Mad Men* follows the fortunes and strategies of mid-20th-century advertising executives and their role in the industry's post-WW2 rise around Manhattan's Madison Avenue. The drama taps into the American nostalgia for the hedonistic glory days when ad giants ruled the media and swayed the masses.

The fashionable time machine transplants viewers back to a simpler, though far from innocent, time in the 1950s and 60s. *The New York Times* says the series offers consolation to a generation knocked around by "skyrocketing unemployment, plunging retirement savings and mounting home foreclosures."

Glimpses of information from the 2010 census suggest the days are gone when advertisers could aim at Mr. and Mrs. Average American. We no longer have a single broad demographic and there is no racial or ethnic majority in the ten largest cities. Yet media remains dependent on advertising income. More than 70% of commercial media revenue comes through ads.

The future audience at which advertisers will aim can be seen in a breakdown of age groups. White non-Hispanics will make up 80% of the population over the age of 65, but only 54% of Americans under 18, according to *Ad Age*. The publication suggests that the 2010 census will show the most prevalent American household is a married couple with no kids, followed closely by single-person homes, leaving marrieds with kids making up just over a fifth (22%) of all households.

Advertisers will have to find more creative ways to reach these audiences. *NEC Electronics* believes it has one. The company sells flat-panel monitors that display ads, the kind you commonly see in stores and airports. Unlike traditional ad-display monitors, however, NEC provides unique software and a camera embedded into the monitor to truly "target" its audience.

It can film people walking past, scan each face to roughly calculate the person's age and gender, then provide ads targeted to the person or more information to advertisers about who they can reach. Cable companies in Brooklyn, New York already personalize TV ads based on demographics.

> *...information from the 2010 census suggest the days are gone when advertisers could aim at Mr. and Mrs. Average American.*

Advertising Facts

- U.S. advertisers and marketers spend $500 billion a year.
- How many commercials or ads do we encounter each day? Hundreds? How about thousands? In his book, *Adland: Searching for the Meaning of Life on a Branded Planet*, James P. Othmer claims the average American is hit by as many as 20,000 ad "impressions" a day.
- The typical person in the U.S. will spend more than one year of his or her life watching television commercials.

The most effective medium for prompting ad recall is TV over both radio and online ads, according to a Canadian study released in January 2010. However, using biometric research that tracked its subjects' physical reactions, such as heart rate and skin sweat, researchers at *Innerscope* found each media type has its own strengths. Some appeal more to the mind, others to the emotions.

Display ads in magazines created to look like real articles are called *advertorials*. Advertorials often feature small-print disclaimers reading, "paid advertisement."

Advertisers spend lots of money trying to convince the public to do something and they go about it very scientifically. Pull back the curtain and take a look at some of the secrets of how they try to convince us.

The Agencies

Ad agencies typically operate in four areas. Agencies employ people to work in

Creative (copywriters and designers create content), Client Management (working directly with customers), Media Buyers (developing plans for purchase of time and space), and Research (collecting and analyzing data on consumers and their habits).

The Bureaus

The media have established their own advertising bureaus to help individual broadcasters and media operators market themselves. There is the *Radio Advertising Bureau* (*RAB*), the *Television Bureau of Advertising* (*TVB*), *Cable Advertising Bureau* (*CAB*), and the *Interactive Advertising Bureau* (*IAB*). They provide members with many resources to aid local marketing efforts. There is also *Promax*, a professional association of promotion and marketing executives.

KNOW YOUR ADVERTISERS

Provide the company associated with advertising slogans below:
1. Just do it
2. Milk's favorite cookie
3. The jeans that built America
4. Breakfast of champions
5. Melts in your mouth, not in your hand
6. Be all you can be
7. Mmm, mmm good
8. Soup That Eats Like a Meal
9. Like a good neighbor
10. The make-up of make-up artists
11. Diamonds are forever
    (picked best slogan of the last century by *Ad Age*)

(Answers are at the end of the chapter)

Can you sing one of the *Oscar Meyer Wiener* songs? "I wish I were an Oscar Mayer Wiener / That is what I'd truly like to be…" It's been going strong since 1963. School marching bands picked up the tune, and radio stations played it on the air. In the 1970s, it was replaced by "My bologna has a first name…" The *Mr. Clean Song* is an even older jingle. It ran from 1957-2008. And the *Chiquita Banana* song hit the airwaves before the end of World War II (1944). It was finally tucked away in 1999.

The Power of Advertising

Children as young as two years of age can recognize familiar brand names, packaging, logos, and characters, while associating them with products. Packaging alone sends strong signals. *Stanford University* researchers discovered kids rate food as tasting better if it's wrapped in *McDonald's*-branded paper as opposed to the same food wrapped in plain paper. An overwhelming number of the children even said vegetables and milk were tastier when wrapped in the *McDonald's* wrapping.

Dan Ariely's book *Predictably Irrational* says the taste battle between *Coke* and *Pepsi* offers some insight into the power of advertising associations. In the famous *Pepsi Challenge*, begun in 1975, *Pepsi* came out ahead in taste tests. But *Coke* declared itself the winner following its own taste tests. Ariely says the difference came in the ways the two companies evaluated their products. *Coke* based its conclusions on consumers' preferences when they could see what they were drinking. *Pepsi* ran its challenge using blind tasting. Neuroscientists settled the argument by using brain scans while conducting their own taste tests. The brain activation of the participants was different depending on whether the participant knew which drink was offered. The frontal area of the brain was more activated when the bright red can and swirling script of *Coke* was visible. *Pepsi* won the blind taste test, but the favorable brand image gave *Coke* an advantage because of the powerful association in the brain's pleasure center. Ariely writes, "This should be good news to any ad agency, of course, because it means that the myriad messages that have come down to consumers over the years are as much responsible for our love of *Coke* as the brown bubbly stuff itself."

> *Stanford University researchers discovered kids rate food as tasting better if it's wrapped in McDonald's-branded paper...*

Documentary film makers in France hoped to show the power of the media through a fake reality show called the *Game of Death*. They tricked 80 people into believing they were game contestants expected to administer electric shocks to other contestants (actually actors) who provided incorrect answers. As in the experiments of psychologist Stanley Milgram in the 1960s, nearly all the volunteers punished the contestant — until he appeared to die.

Pause for Discussion: The Game of Death

Is this a demonstration of the power of the media? An indication that most people will give blind obedience to the commands of an authority figure no matter how evil (as with the Nazi death camps)? Or is this an example really an example of contestants who are savvy enough about reality TV that they assume the producers will not allow anyone really die or be seriously injured? Did they simply play along in this make believe world for the camera?

Advertising Dilemmas

Tension between the advertising and editorial divisions of a news medium are common. Some veteran journalists treat sales as a necessary evil. At the other end, some in the news room are willing to cater to advertisers.

Pretend you're the editor of a college newspaper. You find these ads on your desk, waiting for approval. Decide whether to publish them.

1. Bob's Auto Center is offering a Super Bowl of a sale. Celebrate the big game with outrageous prices!

2. AIDS ALERT: My name is Janet Smith. I recently tested positive for the AIDS virus. If you have had sexual contact with me, please contact me or contact the health department ASAP.

3. Need attractive female models for a professional photography shoot. $40/hour.

4. Gay marriage is wrong! Giving homosexuals a right to this sacred bond undermines the traditional family instituted by God. There will be a meeting about this issue in front of the Student Union Thursday afternoon at 2 p.m. Please come and show your support!

5. Renter wanted for house located in traditional neighborhood. Great for empty-nesters. No utilities. #1500 a month.

(Discussion at the end of the chapter)

Advertising Terms

The *AIDA* approach – Attempts to persuade consumers based on shared values of beauty, kindness, prestige, family, love, success, etc. This strategy aims to: attract *Attention*, create *Interest*, stimulate *Desire*, promote *Action*.

Consumer Culture – A culture where personal worth and identity reside, not in ourselves, but in the products with which we surround ourselves.

Cyberadvertising – The convergence of print and broadcast with the web.

Demographic segmentation – Appealing to audiences by their personal and social characteristics such as race, gender, and economic level.

Psychographic segmentation – Appealing to consumer groups with similar lifestyles, attitudes, values and behavior patterns. Psychographics is a term coined in the 1960s to refer to a measurement of consumer psychology.

VALS – Classifying consumers according to "Values and Lifestyles." VALS is the best-known psychographic system. There are eight segments of consumers based on VALS: *Actualizers, Fulfilleds, Believers, Achievers, Strivers, Experiencers, Makers, Strugglers.*

If you'd like to find under what category you fall, take this test:

http://www.strategicbusinessinsights.com/vals/presurvey.shtml

Influence on Story Content

One common way advertising shapes content is through location of ads. Airline ads are moved away from stories about plane crashes. Cigarette ads rarely appear near articles on lung cancer. This happens in TV as well. Have you ever watched *CNN* at the airport? That channel is a special feed called *The Airport Network* that avoids airline stories. Travelers will never see a story about a plane going down on that channel. The commercial influence on publication is greater than ever. Financial pressure is challenging some of the fundamental tenets of newspapers. The wall between the advertising and editorial sides of the house isn't as high anymore. The shift in ad dollars to the Internet has left some news organizations searching for revenue in new ways and redrawing traditional boundaries.

During Spring 2009, what looked like a news article on the front page of the *Los Angeles Times* was actually an ad for a network TV show. The *Detroit Free Press* (owned by Gannett) published a series of articles later in the year about Medicare. The idea for the articles came not from a reporter or editor but from a health insurer (which bought advertising beside one of the articles). Does this approach compromise editorial content or simply make connections for marketing purposes?

Some marketers are skipping journalists entirely to produce content themselves. *Winning the Web* magazine is a free monthly print publication focused on emerging trends in online marketing, produced by only two full-time staffers. A new trend may emerge as companies, already producing blogs and Facebook pages, shift to produce media content themselves.

PR v. Advertising

If you have a product to sell, which promotional path will serve you better, advertising or public relations? Most people assume public relations ("free" publicity) is always better than advertising, but a study out of the *University of Miami* finds there's little difference between the two when it comes to product promotion.

The best choice may depend on the goals. Advertising focuses on generating sales while public relations may boost business visibility and credibility. The kind of product for sale may indicate which is more important. If you are pushing a high-end item, the opinions of experts and neutral third parties may drive purchasing decisions more than advertising. But with common, inexpensive items like soap or chips, unpaid media support may not help as much as direct advertising pitches.

Advertising Trends

ADVERTISING TREND: SLOW RECOVERY

Advertising is beginning to pick up again following the recent economic downturn.

Radio ad revenue fell a whopping 22% in 2009, according to the Pew Center, despite maintaining a stable audience. BIA/Kelsey says radio will recover in 2010 with significant growth in revenues from digital and mobile revenue streams Barclays expects radio market share will continue losing ad market share.

The Pew Center reports a 10% decline in newspaper circulation during 2009, with a 26% fall in newspaper ad revenue for both print and online. The total loss from 2006 to 2009 is 43%. Moody's expects newspaper's revenue drop to slow during the next few years and reach a relatively unchanged outlook in 2012.

Local TV news audiences fell by an average of nearly 6% in 2009, while overall ad revenue fell 22%. One estimate puts the job losses at more than 1,600 jobs or 6% of the editorial positions out there for TV. Network TV fell 8%. The exception was cable news which did not fall during 2009.

SNL Kagan says TV stations will climb 14.3% by the end of 2010 to $19.8 billion and radio will move up more than 6% in 2010 over the previous year. But TV news has a problem. The audience is mostly made up of seniors. For instance, the average FOX News viewer is 64, the typical CNN viewer is 62, and an MSNBC viewer is about 59 years old.

Among the fastest-growing areas of marketing and communications are paid product placement, with a compound annual growth rate from 2008 to 2013 of 17.6%; e-mail marketing and in-game advertisements (both 18.5%); mobile advertising outside of texting (33%); Internet and mobile home video downloads (34.4%); mobile advertising and content tied to broadcast television (35.5%); paid interactive television gaming (38.7%); and mobile gaming and advertising (46.2%).

Although the tech industry expects a fast disruption from mobile ads, the numbers are modest so far. Spending on mobile ads in the U.S. reached only $416 million in 2009, up from $320 million in 2008, according to *eMarketer*. That's a fraction of the more than $22 billion U.S. online ad market. The research firm now estimates that mobile ad spending will only reach $1.1 billion by 2012. *Juniper Research* is more optimistic, predicting that worldwide mobile ad spending will more than quadruple to $6 billion by 2014.

The key to the success of future media companies may be multiple revenue streams, especially for old media companies. Market research firm *Veronis Suhler* projects that by 2013, newspapers, magazines, and radio will be taking in 41% less in ad revenues than in 2006.

ADVERTISING TREND: INTERNET ADS

Online advertising fell about 5% in 2009, dropping for the first time since 2002, according to the Pew Center. *Outsell*, a consulting and research firm predicts what *Media Post* calls "one of the most important symbolic milestones in the history of online advertising." *Outsell* says total U.S. ad dollars will surpass what's spent on print in 2010 after having passed radio in 2008. A report from *ZenithOptimedia* says marketers spent more in 2009 on Internet advertising than in magazines.

Jesse Garrett, author of *The Elements of User Experience* says it is important for advertisers to learn to be in the Web and not on the Web. Garrett says not to think of the Web as a delivery channel for your product but your product, as part of the Web itself. The shift in thinking will open up to some of the new possibilities that come with ads on the Internet.

In November 2008, Brian Govern posted a satirical review of a T-shirt on Amazon. No one noticed for six months until *CollegeHumor.com* picked it up. More than

1,500 reviews lauded the *Mountain Men's Three Wolf Moon Short Sleeve Tee*. The joke made the T-shirt the #1 apparel item in the store for two months, showing the power of online feedback.

Marketers have begun to branch out from only advertising only with big companies like Yahoo and MTV, and hiring smaller, edgier sites to create branded entertainment shows for them like *Break.com* and *CollegeHumor.com*. These niche sites are increasingly compelling to advertisers because of their ability to attract a young demographic. At the same time, they have built up significant distribution networks that spread their clips across the Web.

One edgy Internet ad showed up as a *YouTube* video promoting *JC Penney*. The commercial featured two teenagers practicing quickly dressing and undressing, in case they were unexpectedly caught by their parents in a compromising situation. *JC Penney* wasn't happy with the risqué content, saying it never approved the ad. The company blamed the ad agency. The ad agency blamed a third-party vendor for creating it. Yet, the ad won a prestigious international advertising award at the *Cannes Film Festival*.

Besides video ads, the Internet offers display ads, banner ads (which run across the top of a page like a banner) and search. *ComScore* and *Starcom USA* say about 85% of display ad clicks are coming from roughly 8% of the online population. In other words, display ads reach less than 10% of Web surfers. Banner ads now come in a variety of sizes and often include video, animation or interactive quizzes. Media companies have traditionally charged advertisers for banner ads based on the cost of reaching a thousand audience members (referred to as CPM). But banner ads have proved disappointing and have been passed over in favor of other types of advertising. When an ad opens a new window, this may be an interstitial ad or superstitial ad. Interstitial ads immediately became unpopular because they cover the page the user wishes to see. Advertisers have switched to slightly less intrusive superstitials that cover most, but not all of the page. Superstitial ads are similar, but may crawl across a screen or appear in a corner.

Apple makes its money on hardware, Amazon by selling content, but Google makes its money through advertising. Google made 97% of its $22 billion dollars in revenue from online ads in 2008, according to *The Wall Street Journal*.

Apple is joining Google by adding an ad system to the software running the iPhone, iPad, and other mobile gadgets. The makers of apps in Apple's App Store will be able to include ads in their software through iAd.

During the first quarter of 2010, Internet advertising revenue grew 7.5% over 2009's first quarter earnings to $5.9 billion, according to the *Interactive Advertising Bureau* and *PricewaterhouseCoopers*.

Despite inroads by Web advertising, TV remains the number one ad medium in the U.S. *The Wall Street Journal* says the TV industry made $69.4 billion in 2008. Television particularly dominates political advertising. When political groups want to sway the uncommitted, they go to television. In 2009, 96% of political spending

Despite inroads by Web advertising, TV remains the number one ad medium in the U.S.

went to TV ads, according to *TNS Media Intelligence*. Political campaigns use the Web for raising money and pushing news to the already committed.

ADVERTISING TREND: MOBILE ADS

The mobile ad market is small, but promising. Our cell phone provider knows where we go and how long we stay there. The company can use this information for its own advertising purposes or to sell to another company. Marketers have been slow to buy mobile ads, largely because customers aren't visiting mobile websites in meaningful numbers and because the process is challenging. U.S. advertisers only spent $416 million on mobile ads in 2009 — a fraction of the online advertising market.

ADVERTISING TREND: REGULATION

The *Federal Trade Commission* has taken notice of the ad dollars flowing in the direction of the Internet. The FTC has ordered bloggers and others touting products online to disclose any cash or gifts received in exchange for supportive comments about products or services.

In an effort to ward off federal regulators, the advertising industry has agreed on a standard icon for online ads – a little "i". Click on it and you will be taken to a page explaining how the advertiser uses users' Web surfing history and demographic profile to send them certain ads. The Interactive Advertising Bureau has already started an online campaign to educate consumers about the effort.

ADVERTISING TREND: AUGMENTED REALITY

Point a camera phone at a building and up pops information identifying it as a museum, along with admission prices, video clips of the facility and other relevant information.

The camera recognizes objects and your phone automatically fills the screen with pertinent information. Built-in location tools tell your phone where you are standing and superimpose icons on the scene you are looking at through the phone. Imagine walking around a city and seeing it come to life as *Wikipedia* provides information about the sights you see with reviews of the restaurants that you walk past. An app can tell you what businesses are around you, like an on-demand Yellow Pages. Or aim a camera phone at the night sky and an overlaid star map tells which constellation is on the screen.

These applications are examples of *augmented reality,* which involves overlaying data on your physical environment. It can provide information about navigating a city or learning about services that are not visible at an address. It is a cutting-edge technology that merges virtual reality with real-world images. This blend of digital data with the physical world will make mobile phones even more powerful. Many programmers are developing smartphone applications that incorporate GPS, including *Yelp's* application for the iPhone called *Monocle*. It shows the location of businesses recognized by *Yelp*. Pan right or left and the "radar screen" pans with you.

The marketing world sees augmented reality as a means to push ads toward a young demographic. It has the potential of engaging consumers more deeply than other forms of social media. *ABI Research* says the augmented reality market is only $6 million now but will reach $350 million in 2014.

In one augmented reality marketing campaign, consumers print and cut out small square patterns and then place them in front of a webcam. When viewed on screen, each square becomes an animated character. Customers can create whatever real-world background or stage they choose for a video. The contestant who creates the video with the most hits wins prizes.

An augmented reality game created for an automobile company features animated hamsters. Players control on-screen action with a virtual magnet connected to his or her forehead. The question facing advertisers is whether this is a passing novelty that will wear off quickly.

Topps is offering baseball cards which cause a 3-D avatar of the player to appear when held in front of a webcam. Some *McDonald's* packaging includes animated figures from the film *Avatar* that come to life when scanned by a webcam.

ADVERTISING TREND: SOCIAL NETWORKING

A few years ago researchers at Yahoo discovered if someone clicked on an online ad, the people on his instant chat buddy list were as much as four times more likely to click on it themselves. Friends share interests so it makes sense that Internet advertisers would tilt toward opportunities to reach people who hang out together. A world-wide Nielsen survey of 25,000 consumers found they trust recommendations and consumer opinions posted online more than any other source. You are more likely to try a new restaurant or consider a political candidate if an expert or unbiased observer makes the recommendation. But the strongest influencers for the biggest decisions of your life are your small circle of intimates. This is one reason word-of-mouth or *buzz marketing* has become so important for advertisers.

That's the push behind *Facebook Connect*. When online shoppers are logged into *Facebook* and spot an item they want to buy, they can press a button to send a photo and product details to their friends' *Facebook* pages who can give it the nod or recommend something else. These comments may even appear months later when mutual friends are searching for similar information.

...Yahoo discovered if someone clicked on an online ad, the people on his instant chat buddy list were as much as four times more likely to click on it themselves.

Social networks pose a threat to *Google* search. Some day shoppers may choose *Facebook* rather than search engines such as *Google* to find products they are interested in buying.

ADVERTISING TREND: GUERILLA MARKETING

Small electronic devices designed to promote *Cartoon Network's* animated TV series *Aqua Teen Hunger Force* were planted in large cities during 2007. The battery-powered LED placards resembled images of one of the cartoon characters.

After two weeks, Boston city workers discovered some of the devices and, not being familiar with the show, reported the suspicious devices to police. City officials shut down a number of areas and roads, deploying bomb squad units throughout the city. They began blowing them up, just in case. The operation was halted after police found out what they were blowing up. Two young men were arrested for the stunt and after they appeared in court all they would talk about at their news conference was their hair. TV network anchors were appalled that the pair didn't take the charges seriously.

This was the face of *Cartoon Network* and *Turner Broadcasting* for several days. The company didn't comment, so TV news outlets, including *Time Warner's* own *CNN*, kept playing video of these two men. Eventually, the company offered an apology. The mistake was that company officials did not get out in front of the story and put their own face on it, something politicians have learned to do when the media digs up something embarrassing.

The *Aqua Teen Hunger Force* promotional campaign is an example of *Guerilla Marketing*, an unconventional system of promotions on a very low budget. Here's what happened to those involved: All charges against the two-man guerrilla marketing team behind the ads that set off a citywide bomb scare were dropped. The duo apologized to the court and performed 60 hours of community service, designing a mural for the *Spaulding Rehabilitation Hospital* in Boston. The general manager of the *Cartoon Network* resigned. *Turner Broadcasting* paid $1 million to reimburse the Coast Guard for its wasted time.

Guerrilla marketing online attempts to circumvent traditional media outlets by creating buzz or word-of-mouth (WOM) and getting discussion groups, email, videos, text messages, etc. to reference a product or campaign. It is also known as *viral marketing*.

Pause for Discussion: Getting the Word Out

Was this an effective promotional campaign? Most of the 9/11 hijackers boarded planes in Boston. So it comes as no surprise that the authorities reacted quickly and seemed overly sensitive. On the other hand, the promotion did not cause a stir in other cities where law enforcement recognized the characters and "got it." Is any publicity good publicity, or was this an embarrassing episode that damaged the company's image?

ADVERTISING TREND: PRODUCT PLACEMENT

Companies stopped paying TV networks on the basis of how many people watched shows in 2007 and instead began paying networks on the basis of how many people were watching the commercials. *Nielsen* found that in May 2009, one-third of all households owned ad-skipping DVRs. Networks are more desperate than ever to get viewers to watch their advertisers' commercials. The situation has led producers to think about putting the products into the programs themselves to make brand names highly visible to the audience. Advertisers like to call it *integration*.

The *NBC* show *30 Rock* has made fun of product placement in several episodes. In one episode, comedian Tina Fey lauds Verizon phones, then looks in the camera and asks, "Can we have our money now?"

But groups like *Free Press* are not laughing. The coalition of 50 organizations, ranging from consumer advocates to pediatricians, are waging war on product placements. They want the *FCC* to step in with federal rules forcing disclosure for what they consider stealth advertising.

In the first half of 2009, product placements in prime time TV rose 8% from the same period in the previous year, according to *Nielsen*. FOX's *American Idol* had 580 product placements alone. Some projections indicate that paid product placement will grow more than 17% between 2008 and 2013.

The technique has found its way into the music business as well. The research firm *PQ Media* says money spent on product placement in recorded music rose by 8% in 2009 over the previous year. Revenue from product placement in music videos is an estimated $15-20 million in 2009, more than double the revenue earned in 2000.

The practice has been around a long time. Steve McQueen drove a Ford Mustang GT in the 1968 film *Bullit*. In 1981, Paul Newman drank a Budweiser in the movie *Absence of Malice*.

Martin Lindstrom's book *Buyology*, calls into question many common beliefs about this type of marketing. He says brain scans indicate that product placement is overrated.

> "It works when Coke-bottle-shaped furniture is part of the set design on *American Idol*, for example, or when Reese's Pieces candy was used for bait in the movie *E.T.* However, when a product is not integrated, such as FedEx packages appearing in the background of *Casino Royale*, there is no measurable effect with regard to viewer recollection of brand."

An article in *Ad Age* magazine tells readers, "marketing experts say the jury is still out on the validity of the neuroscience on which the Lindstrom book depends."

This field of study has its own name: *neuromarketing*. The question is whether you can draw conclusions about behavior using brain-imaging data. If my brain lights up when I see a Coke can, does that justify a prediction about my future behavior? Is it a *correlation* or *causation*? In other words, do these things just happen to take place during the same time frame or can we say that one causes the other? Read more about correlation and causation in the section titled *Hamburgers & Car Crashes* in the Video Game chapter.

Despite uncertainties about the pop science of neuromarketing, Nielsen is investing in brain reading through the research firm *NeuroFocus*, which shows ads to consumers and looks for brain reactions.

Product placement is used in more than just entertainment shows. It's now showing up on news programs. Two cups of McDonald's iced coffee sit on the morning news desk of a TV station in a major market. While they appear frosty and tantalizing, they are fakes. These fixtures will probably remain secured to the anchor desk as long as the sponsorship agreement remains in place.

Are there limits to how far agencies will go to promote a product? A *PRWeek* survey found one in five marketers had purchased advertising in return for a news story about their company or product. One out of ten admitted having an informal agreement with a reporter or editor for favorable coverage in return for buying advertising. And one in 12 gave away gifts in exchange for coverage.

Subliminal Advertising

Comedian Steven Wright once said, "I saw a subliminal advertising executive, but only for a second."

Television networks banned subliminal advertising in 1958 after reports surfaced of movie audiences consuming more Coca-Cola and popcorn when exposed to fleeting images of "Drink Coca-Cola" and "Eat Popcorn." The images were reportedly flashed for three-thousandths of a second. That would be far too fast for conscious awareness. It turned out to be a hoax and subsequent research found that subliminal advertising is rarely effective. However, Lindstrom suggests in some cases it may have an impact because our guard is down.

A Canadian professor pushed the concept in a new direction in 1970 when he accused advertisers of planting magazine ads with hidden images of death, fear, and sex in advertisements.

For Next Time

Do the media mirror society or lead it? Are we being led by the media we consume or do they reflect who we are?

ANSWERS TO KNOW YOUR ADVERTISERS

1. Just do it (Nike)
2. Milk's favorite cookie (Oreo)
3. The jeans that built America (Lee)
4. Breakfast of champions (Wheaties)
5. Melts in your mouth, not in your hand (M&M candies)
6. Be all you can be (U.S. Army)

7. Mmm, mmm good (Campbell's)
8. Soup That Eats Like a Meal (Campbell's Chunky Soup)
9. Like a good neighbor (State Farm)
10. The make-up of make-up artists (Max Factor)
11. Diamonds are forever (DeBeers)

ANSWERS TO ADVERTISING DILEMMAS

There is no obligation for the newspaper to run any of these ads. The staff has a right to reject or require edits to any ad for any reason.

1. The term *Super Bowl* is a trademark owned by the National Football League and it is protected. The term cannot be used in any advertising or promotional announcements that are not sanctioned by the NFL. This prohibition includes sweepstakes and contests as well. Using *Super Bowl* sales in ads or referring to the newspaper or broadcast station as the Super Bowl Authority in promotional statements is strictly off-limits. These restrictions explain why you often hear it referred to as *The Big Game*.

2. AIDS. Is Janet a real person? Is it a joke? If the newspaper reveals she has AIDS, but she did not submit the ad, this could be an invasion of privacy. If she doesn't have AIDS and did not submit the ad, it could be defamatory. If it turns out she really wants this ad run in the paper, there are no legal reasons not to do so.

3. Models. Nothing overtly illegal. Perhaps the paper decides to require the ad include the phrase "adult models" and the name of the photographer or studio.

4. Same-sex marriage. The ad doesn't support unlawful activity or target anyone specifically. The editor can run it if she chooses though she should check to make sure the group actually submitted the ad. Many papers have an policy about running issue ads. The editor may add a disclaimer indicating this is not the paper's views.

5. House for Rent. There are Federal laws against discriminatory language in ads based of religion, ethnicity or disability. This would preclude phrases like "traditional neighborhood."

FOURTEEN
Media Theories

Activists say minority groups are portrayed in inappropriate ways by Hollywood. For instance, many Asian-Americans are cast as doctors or Kung Fu artists but seldom as romantic leads. Italians are often portrayed as gangsters. Are the activists right? Does the media promote stereotypes? Are the media wrong to play to these stereotypes? Are they influencing public opinion in a negative way or does it even matter?

Media theories offer various explanations of these types of issues. Here are five ways to show how different theories apply to you. The first three questions are true or false.

1. Most people are just looking out for themselves.
2. You can't be too careful in dealing with people.
3. Most people would take advantage of you if they got the chance.
4. How much television do you watch each week?
5. Draw the outline of a dime.

Hang on to your answers. Here is some background before we consider what the answers tell us.

Minimal Effect

The effect of mass communication on society is hotly debated. Is technology limited by the amount of power given to it by a culture? Or is it the other way round? Here are five arguments for the theory that the media have a *minimal impact* on culture. Following each argument is a *counterargument*, offering positions taken by those who say the media have a *major impact* on society.

ARGUMENT ONE: MAKE-BELIEVE

The media have limited or minimal effect because people understand it is only make-believe. They know it isn't real.

Counterargument:

Those who disagree will say, "News is not make-believe and we are supposed to take it seriously. Most film and television dramas (like the *CSI* television shows) are intentionally produced to seem real to viewers. And before children develop the ability to know any better, what they see is real to them."

ARGUMENT TWO: JUST ENTERTAINMENT

The media have limited or minimal effect because it's only entertainment.

Counterargument:

Even if the media content is only pretend or fiction, it is still an important way for us to learn and develop knowledge of ourselves and our world. Is it only entertainment? Consider the efforts of programs such as *Sesame Street*. Are educational shows like this pointless because they cannot impact children beyond entertainment?

ARGUMENT THREE: A MIRROR

The media have limited or minimal effect because the media are simply holding a mirror to society.

Counterargument:

But the media hold a selective mirror. The whole world, in all its vastness and complexity, cannot possibly be fully represented, so media practitioners make choices. For example, 14% of TV families are headed by a single father. Do you have any idea what the percentage is in the real world? Only 6%. And when was the last time you saw a car explode into balls of fire in an accident?

And when was the last time you saw a car explode into balls of fire in an accident?

ARGUMENT FOUR: REINFORCES

The media have limited or minimal effect because they only reinforce preexisting values and beliefs.

Counterargument:

The traditional socializing agents have lost much of their power to influence us in this complicated and fast-paced world. And reinforcing is not the same as having no effect whatsoever. If media can reinforce the good in our culture, media can just as easily reinforce the bad.

ARGUMENT FIVE: UNIMPORTANT

The media have limited or minimal effect because they are impacting the unimportant things in our lives, like fads and fashions.

Counterargument:

Fads and fashions are not unimportant to us. The media have helped make them central to our self-definition and happiness. Kids don't kill other kids for their $150 basketball shoes because their mothers told them that the shoes were cool. Plus, if the media influence only unimportant things in our lives, why are billions of dollars spent on media efforts to sway opinion about social issues such as universal health care, nuclear power, and global warming?

Whether you accept these arguments or counterarguments, all the ideas you've just read are based on one or more mass communication theories. There are more theories than those offered in this chapter, but these are of special interest to journalists.

If you had to vote, which side would you come down on? Do the media have a minimal effect or major impact?

Reality TV has taken some dark turns but none more sobering than the *Game of Death*. Documentary film makers in France tricked 80 people into believing they were contestants on a game show in which they administered electric shocks to contestants. Echoing the famed experiments of psychologist Stanley Milgram in the 1960s, participants were told to "electrocute" a fellow contestant — actually an actor — if he got answers wrong while the audience chanted "punishment." All but 16 of the volunteers punished the contestant until he appeared to die.

Pause for Discussion: The Game of Death

Is this a demonstration of the power of television? An indication that most people will submit to the commands of an authority figure no matter how evil (as with the Nazi death camps) in a fit of blind obedience? Or simply proof that contestants on what appears to be a reality TV show are savvy enough to assume the producers won't really let someone die, so they "play along" in a make-believe world of performance for the camera?

A Matter of Theory

Look over the answers to the four questions and drawing test offered earlier.

According to *cultivation analysis*, a person's response to the first three statements can be predicted by your answer to #4. The theory of cultivation analysis says the more people watch TV, the more likely they are to respond "true" to these unflattering comments about others.

Almost everyone draws the dime too small. Attitude-change theory says this is because we perceive the dime to be inconsequential; we see it as smaller than it really is. *Our perception guides our behavior.*

Our perception guides our behavior.

Media Violence

Does media violence lead to aggression? Here are three theories about the issue.

- *stimulation model* – there is a direct causal relationship between violent content and aggressive behavior.
- *aggressive cues model* – the way the media portray certain groups of people makes it more likely that some people will act violently toward them.
- *catharsis* – the idea that watching violence in the media smooths viewers' aggressive drive.

NBC news received a package in the mail in April 2007. The material inside had been mailed by the Virginia Tech shooter between his first and second shooting episodes. He killed 32 people at the campus before turning the gun on himself. The package included an 1800-word manifesto, photos, and 27 digitally-recorded videos of him talking. If you had been in charge that day at NBC, would you have shown the exclusive material, helping viewers better understand what happened? Or would you withhold the material from air, because the broadcast of those tapes would give him a national platform for his rants?

If you believe the media have a major impact on society, you could be concerned about copycats. If you believe the media have a minimal impact, you could be more concerned about getting as much information as possible out to the public.

A series of seemingly unrelated knife attacks on Chinese school children was blamed on "sensationalist reporting" by an official Chinese website. After a fifth attack during the Spring 2010, the government ordered most of the main news outlets to stop running follow-up stories on the attacks.

In a paper for *Stockholm University*, David Yanagizawa suggested the area covered by the broadcasts of a radio station in Africa had a significant impact on the 1994 Rwandan genocide. His research focused on villages within reach of the broadcast signal from radio station *RTLM*, which offered anti-Tutsi propaganda calling for violence against Tutsis. Violence in those villages was 65-77% higher than in the areas not reached by the radio station's signal.

Pause for Discussion: A Killer's Last Words

Imagine you are the one who gets the video in the mail from the Virginia Tech shooter. Do you play it? Why or why not? Let's turn to another issue: Drugs and alcohol. Does the portrayal of drugs and alcohol in the media increase consumption? The wealth of scientific evidence suggests a link between media portrayals of alcohol consumption and increased drinking and alcohol abuse among youth. Yet there is a good deal of research that discounts a direct causal relationship between media portrayals and real-world drinking.

For Next Time

The First Amendment guarantees free speech to U.S. citizens. Is there anything that's off-limits? What, if anything, goes on the list of banned speech in America?

Free Speech

Free Speech Timeline

1787 The U.S. Constitution is adopted by the Constitutional Convention, and the states ratify it the following year without a provision guaranteeing freedom of speech or freedom of the press.

1789 The First Continental Congress adopts and submits to the states for consideration, a list of 12 amendments intended to safeguard individual liberties to calm the fears of those who distrust the new central government. Ten of the amendments are ratified in 1791 and they become known as the Bill of Rights. The First Amendment explicitly states "Congress shall make no law… abridging the freedom of speech, or of the press."

1789 The *Alien and Sedition Acts* punish anyone who publishes "false, scandalous, or malicious writings against the government of the United States." An editor went to prison for accusing John Adams of corruption. Thomas Jefferson pardons everyone convicted under this act when he becomes president.

1798 The *Alien and Sedition Acts* prohibits spoken or written criticism of the U.S. government in response to a threat of war with France. Although the *Sedition Act* expires in 1801, Congress has passed other Sedition Acts since then during times of war.

1919 The Supreme Court upholds a 20-year sentence for three men, convicted of publishing and distributing leaflets urging workers in munitions factories to go on strike (*Abrams v. United States*). In another case (*Gilbert v. Minnesota*), the Court upheld the conviction of a speaker for publicly opposing involvement in World War I. Some 1,900 people are prosecuted for criticizing the government, the draft, or American involvement in the war. Some of these provisions are repealed following the war.

1931   The Supreme Court rules a Minnesota law allowing limits on the press is an unconstitutional violation of the First Amendment. State officials wanted to stop a scandal sheet from publishing. The High Court establishes the principle doctrine that with narrow exceptions, the government cannot censor or prohibit publication in advance, even if the communication could be punishable after publication.

1964   The *Berkeley Free Speech Movement* takes place in California. Mario Savio puts a face on the movement with his impassioned plea at the University of California, Berkeley.

In *New York Times v. Sullivan*, the U.S. Supreme Court rules the media must have acted with actual malice and displayed a reckless disregard for the truth for someone to have been libeled. The court hopes to prevent publishers from becoming so fearful of making a mistake that they hesitate to print anything controversial.

1969   *Tinker v. Des Moines Independent Community School District.* Tinker, her brother and another student in Des Moines, Iowa, decide to wear black armbands adorned with peace symbols to school in protest against the war. The courts uphold the right of public junior high and high school students to protest the Vietnam War. The Supreme Court declares students do not "shed their constitutional rights to freedom of speech or expression at the schoolhouse gate."

The *Tinker* ruling protected speech unless it could be demonstrated that a student's words or images could create a substantial disruption of school activities or invade the rights of others. Then it may be censored.

The Supreme Court has since recognized exceptions to *Tinker's* protections, such as when student speech is lewd and vulgar, or advocates illegal drug use.

1988   The Supreme Court rules in *Hazelwood School District v. Kuhmeier* that high school administrators can censor students' newspapers that are not "public forums" for student expression if officials can come up with a good reason for doing so. Some states have since passed laws overturning the *Hazelwood* standard for high schools.

1994   The 6th Circuit Court of Appeals ruled that students' First Amendment rights are violated when *Kentucky State University* administrators confiscate copies of the student yearbook. The vice president for student affairs doesn't like the theme, colors or story selections. The court says the *Hazelwood* ruling does not apply to colleges and university campuses.

2005   The 7th Circuit Court of Appeals rules in *Hosty v. Carter* that the *Hazelwood* standard can apply to public colleges. No other court decision agrees with that ruling so it only applies to states under that jurisdiction.

2008 The 3rd Circuit Court of Appeals upholds a judge's ruling that the *speech code* at *Temple University* is unconstitutional. It prohibits "generalized sexist remarks and behavior."

Three students at *Texas Southern University* are kicked out of school and arrested for helping to expose a financial mismanagement scandal that led to the firing of the university's president. They file a lawsuit, claiming the university retaliated against them for publicly criticizing the administration. Jurors decide the students' First Amendment rights were violated and award them $200,000.

EDUCATIONAL RECORDS TIMELINE

1974 Congress passes *FERPA* (or Family Educational Rights and Privacy Act) which is also known as the *Buckley Amendment*. The law requires federally funded institutions to give students access to their education records, an opportunity to have those records amended, and some control over their disclosure. The rules relate to educational records such as grades, when someone is acting within their capacity as a student. It does not apply if the student is kicked off a sports team because of his/her GPA. It does not cover directory information, parking tickets, employment, crime, etc.

1980 The U.S. Supreme Court defines the Central Hudson test to determine when commercial speech would receive First Amendment protection.

According to the court's ruling in *Central Hudson Gas & Elec. Corp. v. Public Service Commission of New York*, when deciding if the First Amendment should shield commercial speech, courts must consider whether:

- The expression of commercial speech concerns lawful activity and is not misleading.
- The asserted government interest is substantial.
- The regulation directly advances the asserted government interest.
- The regulation is no more extensive than necessary to serve that interest.

1989 In order to ensure college and university students get information about criminal activity on campus, Congress passes the *Clery Act* requiring universities to reveal all crime reports. Campus security must maintain a log of crimes committed on campus and distribute an annual report detailing crime statistics.

The federal mandate is named after 19-year-old Jeanne Clery, who was raped and murdered in her Lehigh University residence hall in 1986. Students had not been notified about 38 violent crimes that had occurred on campus in the three years prior to her murder.

The U.S. Constitution mentions only one industry by name as deserving special protection: The press.

1990   The *Student's Right to Know Act* helps (among other things) keep watch over financial aid by requiring most colleges or universities to compile annual reports detailing revenues and expenditures that can be attributed to their school's sports programs and graduation rates.

1992   Congress amends FERPA, making it clear that *campus law enforcement records* are not considered a part of a student's educational records and can be released to the public.

1998   Lawmakers further clarify FERPA rules, allowing the release of some *disciplinary records* from campus courts.

2008   Congress amends the Clery Act to require universities to publicize their emergency response plans and to immediately notify the campus community of confirmed emergencies.

Free Speech Today

The U.S. Constitution mentions only one industry by name as deserving special protection: The press.

The freedom of the press we enjoy today has taken time to develop. Before the Civil War, many states enacted statutes prohibiting any person from saying or writing that slavery should be abolished. And many local laws in the South allowed postmasters to censor abolitionist literature.

During the Civil War, President Lincoln closed the mails to "treasonable correspondence" and even ordered newspapers shut down and some editors jailed. His justification was that the South's rebellion directly threatened the life of the nation and he could not allow the press to incite uprising or cause desertions from the army if the country were to survive.

We have on-going conflicts over how far a free press can go. For instance, can pretrial publicity deny a defendant a fair trial, and should cameras be allowed in a courtroom?

Remember, the First Amendment ... is intended to protect individuals from actions taken by the government, not from actions taken by private citizens.

Remember, the First Amendment (and the rest of the Bill of Rights) is about what the state is not allowed to do. It is intended to protect individuals from actions taken by the government, not from actions taken by *private citizens*.

It is a violation of the First Amendment for a police officer to take a protester's sign on a public sidewalk, but it is not a violation of the First Amendment for some irate passerby to seize the sign (though it would probably be a violation of some other law, like theft or assault). Bottom line: The First Amendment is a limit on the power of the government to censor or punish expression. One of its primary goals is to stop the government from covering up embarassing information.

Campus free speech begins with the First Amendment. We all know about the First Amendment, right? How many freedoms are specifically mentioned in the first Amendment? Six? Seven? How many could you name without looking?

There are five freedoms mentioned in the First Amendment and they are:

Press, Speech, Religion, Petition, Assembly.

The First Amendment contains just 45 words. But in a recent survey conducted by the First Amendment Center, only 4% of those polled could name all five freedoms mentioned in the First Amendment. Only 55% could name free speech as one of the five. Less than 20% could name the freedoms of religion, press, and assembly.

FIRST AMENDMENT QUIZ

Test yourself to see how well you know what our Constitution says about First Amendment rights. Here's a test from the First Amendment Center.

1. Which of the following is NOT a right protected by the First Amendment? Press, Speech, Privacy, Religion, Petition, Assembly
2. Do Americans have the right to burn the American flag as a means of political protest?
3. Does the government have the right to restrict indecent material on the Internet?
4. Does someone have the legal right to shout "fire" in a crowded arena as a prank?
5. Do the federal courts have the right to send reporters to jail for refusing to reveal a news source?
6. Are there some student extracurricular groups the school may exclude?
7. Is it constitutional to teach about religion in a public school?
8. Do public school students have to salute the flag during a recitation of the Pledge of Allegiance?
9. Does the Supreme Court or Congress ultimately determine what rights are protected by the First Amendment?
10. In America, do the media need to get permission from the government before publishing critical articles?

(Answers are at the end of the chapter)

In a recent survey.. only 4% of those polled could name all five freedoms mentioned in the First Amendment.

Unprotected Speech

Not all speech is covered by the First Amendment. There are at least nine categories of unprotected speech. They include:

Obscenity, defamation, expression that is intended and likely to incite imminent lawless action (for instance, instigating a riot); fighting words (personally abusive language addressed to a specific person and likely to provoke a violent reaction); unwarranted invasions of privacy; deceptive or misleading advertisements or those for illegal products or services; clear and immediate threats to national security (for example, publishing information about troop movements during wartime); copyright violations; expression on high school grounds that causes a material and substantial disruption, is indecent or vulgar, or advocates illegal drug use. Some of these can only be punished AFTER publication, not restrained beforehand.

There is no right to shout "Fire!" in a crowded theater when there is no fire. There is no right to incite violence or promote illegal activity. And there are some iffy areas such as satire. If a college newspaper defames the president of the school, can the editor claim it was satire? The courts will ask one question: Would the average person instantly understand it as satire?

Student journalists should also be aware that the First Amendment does not protect misleading ads. Most of the time, if there is Federal Trade Commission action related to an ad, it is against the advertiser. But in a few cases, the advertising agency that created the ad has come under scrutiny. FTC or state laws related to false advertisements do not apply to the publisher who had no knowledge of the ad's deceptive content.

PORNOGRAPHY AND OBSCENITY

Are obscenity and pornography protected by the Constitution?

> Obscenity - not protected by the Constitution

> Pornography – is protected by the Constitution

Sexually explicit material is referred to as pornography until a court rules it illegal. Then it is considered obscene and unprotected.

JOURNALISTS' RIGHTS

There are no special federal rights for journalists. For instance, trespassing is not excused by saying, "I'm just trying to get a story." If it is illegal for a citizen, it is illegal for a member of the press. A judge may legally compel a reporter to reveal the identity of a source to whom the reporter promised confidentiality. Many journalists would say their ethics demand they disobey the court order, thereby breaking the law and facing the legal consequences.

For some journalists, it's a breach of professional ethics to reveal confidential information. For others, it's a question of duty to testify when called by the courts to do so. Either way, most journalists would view dependence on an anonymous informant as lazy reporting when information could be gathered through open channels.

If a reporter has verbally promised confidentiality to a source, the courts may consider this a contract between the parties. If that contract is broken, there could be legal recourse for the source. Sources can sue reporters for revealing their identities.

In 1991, the Supreme Court ruled (in a close vote) that journalists don't get a free pass for broken promises (*Cohen v. Cowles Media Co.*). Since then, some courts have sided with the source, others with the journalist.

The high court has recognized there are limits. A 1972 case (*Branzburg v. Hayes*) suggests that lawyers shouldn't use subpoenas to interfere with a journalist's relationship to sources. The case also gives states room to determine their own protections, and some have done so. Some states have *shield laws* protecting journalists from having to testify in court (and divulge sources) and some have court-recognized reporter's privileges. As mentioned earlier, there is no federal shield law.

FREE SPEECH ON CAMPUS

The U.S. Supreme Court has ruled that not only do all adults enjoy First Amendment rights, but even teenagers and young adults can receive the same privileges. The justices weighed in during a 1975 case about a city ordinance in Jacksonville, Florida, which attempted to prevent a drive-in theater from showing films containing nudity. The majority said speech "cannot be suppressed solely to protect the young from ideas or images that a legislative body thinks unsuitable. In most circumstances, the values protected by the First Amendment are no less applicable when government seeks to control the flow of information to minors."

Public universities have limitations on how school administrators can limit your speech. Private colleges can create many more restrictions. Public universities cannot legally retaliate against student-operated newspapers by cutting funding over content. Administrators cannot raise the grade-point requirement for student editors in order to disqualify a particular candidate. Nor can they cancel an existing order for new computer equipment, move the newspaper into less favorable office space, or take any other punitive action over content.

Even at schools where free speech is championed, people are not allowed to shout with a bull horn during final exams while standing next to classrooms.

A trailer for the documentary *Indoctrinate U* begins with a graphic that reads: *Welcome to the great Marketplace of Ideas.* This is what college campuses are supposed to be, yet they don't always turn out this way. The people made the film believe there are so many free speech violations on college campuses that it was worth making a movie about it.

New York's Hamilton College decided in 2005 to cancel a speech by a controversial professor from the University of Colorado at Boulder in response to threats of violence. In 2008, the San Francisco Art Institute closed a video exhibit rather than face threats of violence by animal-rights activists.

Sometimes, it is the students themselves who question the value of the First Amendment. Consider these comments from recent college essays about the value of the Amendment:

> "It is necessary that the government place restrictions on the notion of a free press and speech in order to ensure a safe and competent nation."

> "Paris Hilton and Kim Kardashian have been slammed by the media for leaks of sex tapes. Personally, I feel that Congress should step in."

> "A lot of the time people are allowed to say whatever they want as long as it doesn't disagree with the people in charge. The amendment should be changed to 'limit' speech and press."

"There should be provisions made in the Constitution to protect the famous."

"It seems to me the U.S. Constitution isn't fair. The press is protected by law and is given special rights."

"I feel that there should be a control on how much irrelevance is allowed in publication and broadcast."

"The press has too much power and too many privileges."

"I believe the Constitution is outdated and needs revision. It was written in an atmosphere and environment that was much different than ours."

CAMPUS SPEAKERS

Some school administrations have decided to limit off-campus speakers to just those who are sponsored by the school, faculty, or student groups. The fact that courts have said it's all right for schools to restrict speech when it would be a substantial disruption has led many universities to restrict *the time, place, and manner* of speakers and visiting groups. Even at schools where free speech is championed, people are not allowed to shout with a bull horn during final exams while standing next to classrooms. That would disrupt the educational process. But speakers can work with administrators to come up with an acceptable time, place, and manner that would be agreeable for all parties involved. However, this will only hold up if applied consistently. Administrators can't pick and choose, changing the rules for different groups.

In 2007, Massachusetts Senator John Kerry was visiting the University of Florida when undergraduate student Andrew Meyer repeatedly asked him a question at a public forum. University police decided Meyer was being disruptive and tried to remove him from the event, but Meyer resisted and was tasered by one of the officers. The meeting and Meyer's name might not ring a bell, but his reaction is probably familiar. Meyer shouted at the officer, "Don't tase me, bro!" A video of the incident, widely circulated on the Internet, is part of the reason the *New Oxford American Dictionary* selected "tase/taze" as one of its 2007 words of the year. Meyer's slogan wond first place in *TIME* magazine's *Top 10 T-shirt Worthy Slogans*. Whatever you think of Meyer's actions, if a student's "free speech" is disruptive, the university has a right to remove him or her in an effort to protect the free speech rights of the speaker.

Georgia's *Valdosta State* planned to build two new parking garages which student Hayden Barnes considered environmentally and fiscally irresponsible. Barnes protested in 2007 by creating a collage and posting it on *Facebook*. A letter from the institution's president was slipped under Barnes's dorm room door, informing him of his expulsion. A printout of the collage was attached. The school suggested that the title *S.A.V.E.-Zaccari Memorial Parking Deck* was a personal threat against the president. Barnes appealed but got nowhere. Eventually, he filed a lawsuit claiming his free-speech and due process rights were violated. A few days after the lawsuit was filed, the university's regents overturned Barnes's expulsion. The president announced not long afterward that he would retire six months earlier than planned.

Free speech is not only a verbal right; even the simple act of reading a book is an exercise of it. A student employee at *Indiana University-Purdue University Indianapolis* was found guilty of racial harassment in 2008 for merely reading the book *Notre Dame vs. the Klan: How the Fighting Irish Defeated the Ku Klux Klan* during his work breaks. The finding against Sampson was eventually overturned and his school record was cleared.

Pause for Discussion: Cyber Speech

Free speech issues are now moving into the areas of phone texting and social networking. If a student spreads false information about another student through *Facebook*, should a university get involved? What about cyberbullying? When someone stalks a student over the Internet or makes threats, is that a matter of free speech or should administrators step in to protect the student? What if a campus computer is used to make threats or harass another person?

Artistic freedom is also an issue, especially when it comes to performance art. What about college sports fans who use obscenities at sporting events located on college campuses?

Student Media

Several institutions have reprimanded student journalists for criticizing the administration. For instance, administrators on one campus told students they could not distribute a newspaper because of a controversial story it contained. The newspaper staff was told to literally cut the story out of the already-published paper because they would not be allowed to hand out copies as it was printed.

The student newspaper at the University of Wisconsin-Madison agree to post an ad in its online edition for 30 days that denies the Holocaust. Some 150 students and the school's chancellor urged the paper to refuse publication. The editor defended the ad, saying it is "bad for society to ignore such people." He argued that if a crazy idea is advertised, the community continue to do what they have done in this case, which is to "reject and denounce it."

Student journalists can take greater risks while still in school. Mistakes have fewer long-term consequences because of the security academic organizations provide. Since the early 1970s, no court has found the content of a college student publication objectionable enough to justify a school's claim that it constitutes a disruption of its activities. Yet, it is surprising how often administrators try to step in to control a publication.

The general rule suggested by the *Student Press Law Center* is that once a forum is recognized by a university, it cannot be shut down. And to date, no court has found a student-edited college publication to be a non-public or closed forum.

If administrators allow students to run the publication, editorial decisions must remain in their hands or it is a violation of their First Amendment rights.

If administrators allow students to run the publication, editorial decisions must remain in their hands, or it is a violation of their First Amendment rights.

The *Student Press Law Center* encourages student media to keep a *Censorship File* and pass it to succeeding editors and managers. The current editor might not need it, but his successor years later will be grateful. It should contain evidence of intent by school officials to take action against student media. For example, if an administrator calls an editor into a meeting to discuss a "lousy editorial," a summary of the conversation should immediately be added to a Censorship file. No matter how cordial relationships between student media, school administrators, and student government may appear at the moment, they can sour quickly. Administrators often use students' transitory status and lack of a an institutional history to their advantage.

Students should be aware that newspaper theft is a form of college censorship. Newspapers have been stolen from racks to suppress information, ranging from a homecoming queen's fans trying to preserve her image, to a professor wanting to withhold news from incoming students. For the legal protection of free publications, signs should be posted at newspaper stands indicating that taking any more than a certain number of copies is considered a crime.

Trends

FREE SPEECH TREND: SPEECH CODES

The First Amendment right to free speech has collided on the college campus with the desire to "protect" students against abuse. Do I have the right to offend you? Or do you have the right to not be offended? Speech Codes are extra limits to free speech imposed by colleges.

> At the *University of California, Santa Cruz*, you may have violated the school's sex offence policy if you use "terms of endearment" on campus.

> *Colorado State University* denied a request to hang posters in the residence halls showing a marijuana leaf. The policy cited has since been changed.

> The *University of New Hampshire* expelled a student from the dorms after he posted a flier that joked that female students could lose weight by taking the stairs.

Some campus policies have banished speech to tiny *free speech zones*. These marked-off areas might be only a few feet wide and long.

The *Foundation for Individual Rights in Education* (FIRE) claims it has helped to change 79 such unconstitutional and repressive policies at institutions. The group says 71% of public colleges earn what FIRE deems a "red-light" for unconstitutional speech codes. Just 11 institutions earn a "green-light" for having no policies restricting the free speech rights of its students.

Some would say these codes are telling students, "you are too weak to live with the freedom provided in the First Amendment."

FREE SPEECH TREND: ANTI-BIAS RULES

The federal courts have ruled that campus groups at public colleges and universities must adhere to the institutions' anti-bias rules.

The *University of California's Hastings College of the Law* refused to recognize the Christian Legal Society because the student group will not allow gay and lesbian members which violated the school's anti-discrimination policy. The Supreme Court sided with the college in a 2010 ruling. The majority found that the law school didn't violate the group's constitutional rights. The majority opinion supported Hastings' decision to permit "all organizations to express what they wish but no group to discriminate in membership." Dissenting justices wrote that the majority opinion rested on the principle that there should be "no freedom of expression that offends prevailing standards of political correctness in our country's institutions of higher learning."

FREE SPEECH TREND: WHEN TECHNOLOGY GOES BAD

JuicyCampus.com stirred controversy at colleges by allowing students to anonymously post comments about other students. The site went down early in 2009, but CampusGossip.com and others popped up to take its place before the end of the year.

What happens when someone posts threatening content on their *Facebook* page or puts inappropriate comments on someone's *Facebook* wall? Student affairs professionals can expect to face questions like this in the future.

Frank LaMonte of the Student Press Law Center says the number one future problem faced by school administrators will be *cyberbullying*. New Jersey's attorney general has said every school should have rules about it — even though other laws cover cyberbullying.

The Internet is putting tremendous power into the hands of the average citizen, which can be used for evil or good. Clay Shirky, author of *Cognitive Surplus: Creativity and Generosity in a Connected Age*, writes in *The Wall Street Journal*:

> "Increased freedom to create means increased freedom to create throwaway material, as well as freedom to indulge in the experimentation that eventually makes the good new stuff possible. There is no easy way to get through a media revolution of this magnitude; the task before us now is to experiment with new ways of using a medium that is social, ubiquitous and cheap, a medium that changes the landscape by distributing freedom of the press and freedom of assembly as widely as freedom of speech."

FREE SPEECH TREND: DON'T OFFEND ME, BRO

One might say, "If I'm insulted you shouldn't say it. No one should be ever be offended." That attitude goes against how the courts have interpreted the First Amendment.

The Free Speech timeline for this chapter includes a 2008 appeals court ruling that Temple University's speech code is unconstitutional. Here's what the lead counsel in the case had to say afterward: "First Amendment rights are precious and the mere fact that someone is angered or offended by your speech does not mean it loses its protection. In fact, it is the speech that offends or causes people to get angry that requires protection." Of course, someone must choose to take offense for something to be offensive. No one can force someone else to be offended. In other words, nothing can offend you if you don't allow it to do so.

FREE SPEECH TREND: APATHY — BUT WHO CARES!

University of Mississippi attorney Lee Tyner says, "I think the greatest challenge is student engagement. Not enough of our students are interested or involved in any sort of public discourse or debate. We also have some challenge in front-line staff understanding First Amendment freedoms." Waking students to their First Amendment rights and responsibilities is one of the critical roles of those involved in student media on campus.

"... it is the speech that offends or causes people to get angry that requires protection."

—David French

Recommendations

Student journalists should *identify* the free-speech-related policies and documents in effect at their university. If there are concerns with limiting free speech, be proactive in challenging policies, practices, and/or the culture of the university.

Research the history of free speech at your institution. Knowing that history may allow you to be sensitive to hot issues that may resurface. During interviews, regularly include a question about free speech policies and practices.

Keep the right to free speech in mind during story meetings and *talk* to students, faculty, administration, and peers about free speech happenings.

Stay current by *reading* news reports and professional journals related to free speech. Provide relevant articles to student services staff and university administrators.

Here are some specific recommendations:

• *Network* with the Law School, Student government, Student Services, and Administration to bring a national speaker to campus who can bring attention to the issue.

• Create a *Free Speech Link* on the university's front Web page with information for faculty, students, and visitors. Work with IT to enhance the search capabilities of the school's website so that a search for free speech will show links to the students' rights section of the school's policy handbook, the IT appropriate-use policy, and the Dean of Students office.

- *Host Free Speech Events.* September 17th is a good day to do this because it is Constitution Day. Colleges receiving federal funds are required to celebrate in some way. Here are some ideas:

> An issues alley could be temporarily created where various advocacy groups could set up booths along an area frequented by students.

> A First Amendment *Free Food Festival.* Here's how it works: A section of campus is roped off and free food is offered to students but only if they symbolically waive their First Amendment rights. They can't speak in line because there's no freedom of speech, they can't sit together because there's no right to assembly, they can't… well, you get the idea.

> *Open House.* Hold a First Amendment open house to educate deans, police and other campus departments on the laws related to FERPA, student media, etc. The student paper can explain how they choose stories, how to make corrections and the relationship with the Journalism Dept. — i.e., editorial control resides with the students because of their free speech rights.

> Incorporate a free speech topic into a new student orientation.

> *Market Free Speech.* Sell or give away t-shirts, put up posters and show video clips in the Student Union.

Campus Free Speech Resources

First Amendment Center - http://www.firstamendmentcenter.org/
F.I.R.E. - http://www.thefire.org/
Student Press Law Center - http://www.splc.org/

For Next Time

It's not unusual for a celebrity to threaten to sue over a negative story. Should there be more protection for celebrities battling the paparazzi than for the average citizen, or are well-known personalities fair game, having voluntarily stepped into the media spotlight?

ANSWERS TO FIRST AMENDMENT QUIZ

1. Which of the following is NOT a right protected by the First Amendment? *Privacy*

2. Do Americans have the right to burn the American flag as a means of political protest? *Yes*

3. Does the government have the right to restrict indecent material on the Internet? *No*

4. Does someone have the legal right to shout "fire" in a crowded arena as a prank? *No*

5. Do the federal courts have the right to send reporters to jail for refusing to reveal a news source? *Yes*

6. Are there some student extracurricular groups the school may exclude? *Yes*

7. Is it constitutional to teach about religion in a public school? *Yes*

8. Do public school students have to salute the flag during a recitation of the Pledge of Allegiance? *No*

9. Does the Supreme Court or Congress ultimately determine what rights are protected by the First Amendment? *Yes*

10. In America, do the media need to get permission from the government before they publish critical articles? *No*

From the John S. and James L. Knight Foundation

SIXTEEN
Media Law

Journalists can thrive by possessing a working knowledge of the fundamental building blocks of media law and ethics. This is one of the areas that separates the professional from the amateur. A lack of knowledge can either lead journalists into overconfidence or over-cautiousness.

Journalists are more attractive to potential employers when they possess a solid understanding of media law because it empowers a journalist to work to the edge of the law within an ethical framework. It is also a hedge against actionable legal entanglements. This chapter is a beginning framework, starting with the difference between libel and slander.

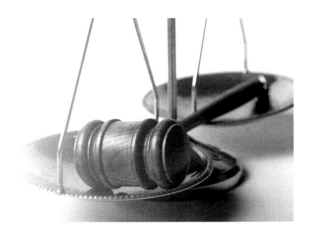

> Libel – the malicious publication of false information that damages a person's reputation.
> Slander – the oral or spoken defamation of a person's character.

Libel and slander are NOT protected by the Constitution.

A news report loses its First Amendment protection IF:

> 1. It defames a person.
> 2. Identifies that person.
> 3. It is published or broadcast.

A note on the second qualification. A particular representative in the House of Representatives would not be libeled by someone printing, "Congress is full of crooks," because no single politician is cited or identified in the statement. The question journalists should ask themselves when dealing with a questionable story is "Who can sue me?" If the answer is nobody, then there is no legal exposure and no actionable suit. Keep in mind, however, an article can still identify a person without using the person's name. Types of indirect identification include an athlete's jersey number, or a photo of a politician that accompanies an allegation-filled story, even if he isn't mentioned by name.

A news report is protected IF:

1. It is *true*, even if it damages someone's reputation.
2. It falls under *privilege*. An example of privilege is printing a quote from a public meeting.
3. It includes *fair comment*. Fair comment includes commentary, film reviews, etc. In movie reviews, a film clip is all right to use except for a "critical element" that gives away an ending or some other substantial aspect of the film. Fair comment is not the same as fair use. Fair comment covers your opinion while fair use covers the actual copyrighted material, allowing use of it for a range of purposes that are legal. For instance, if a celebrity dies, CNN would not have to ask permission to use segments of a movie illustrating the story. Airing the entire movie, would, however, not be covered.
4. Hyperbole is also a defense against libel, provided no one could take the statements literally.

Reporters can help themselves to avoid legal entanglements while covering a story by getting an accused person's response rather than just reporting the accusations. When putting together a story with serious accusations, it's often wise to wait for the response of the accused instead of publishing without it.

The Internet is providing new ground for accusations of libel. *Too Much Media* (which works with adult content sites) sued Shellee Hale after she posted comments saying the company was profiting from a security breach in its program. Hale claimed she was covered by New Jersey's reporter shield law (these state laws are designed to protect journalists who are doing their jobs). The court ruled against her, saying not all bloggers are journalists and she was not engaged in journalism. The court's opinion said, "New media should not be confused with news media. There is a distinction between personal diaries, opinions, impressions and expressive writing and news reporting."

The question of who qualifies as a journalist played in the case of Josh Wolf, as well. The blogger was jailed in 2007 for refusing to turn over a videotape he shot of a violent San Francisco demonstration held in protest of a G-8 summit meeting. A police officer was injured by a hooded assailant with a pipe or baseball bat during the event. Wolf, a student at San Francisco State who worked part time at a community college television station, caught part of the action with his camera. During his time behind bars, Wolf was cast by some journalists as a young champion of the First Amendment and who should have been protected by the state's shield law.

The Reporters Committee for Freedom of the Press was among the groups that filed briefs on his behalf. If you define a journalist as someone who brings news to the public, then Wolf seems to qualify. Other observers would say he was simply a person with a video camera who happened to record some public events. Wolf served 226 days in prison before being released by judge's order.

Actual Malice

The Supreme Court has ruled that even if some of the facts in a story are not true, the story is not necessarily libelous. There must be *actual malice*. In other words, it must be proved that the journalist knew the information was false before printing it.

False Light

False light is similar to libel. A television story about child molesters may show people walking down the street. If the voice-over implies the people shown are involved in some criminal activity, even by accident, this could be false light. Television reports often avoid showing faces for this reason. You'll see video of people walking away or only the feet of children.

Allegedly

Putting the word "allegedly" into every sentence won't help much if the person offended can prove the truth was known before the broadcast or publication. Even if a TV newscaster corrects a story on the air but the story remains on the station's website, there could be an opening for a lawsuit. The courts will simply look at the fact that the station neglected to remove information they already knew was false.

A student TV newscast ran a story about someone arrested for child molestation. "Allegedly" was not used and the accusation was not attributed. Instead of telling the audience, "Police say so-and-so did this," the anchor just flat out said "so-and-so did this." Even worse, the fact the man pleaded "not guilty" was not included. It appeared he had a strong case of defamation of character.

FOIA

Since the American government belongs to the people, the citizens have a right to know what elected officials are doing with their authority. That's where FOIA comes in. To promote the flow of information to help the democratic process, both federal and state governments have passed *freedom of information acts*. These legal documents specify the process by which media organizations (or private citizens) can obtain information from certain government agencies.

The federal FOIA applies only to portions of the executive branch, such as cabinet departments and regulatory agencies. The law does not apply to Congress, the Supreme Court, or the president's staff.

The U.S. Federal Government has often labeled information as classified that you wouldn't consider all that critical to national security. For instance, a joke in a 1974 CIA intelligence report referring to a possible terrorist attack on Santa Claus was withheld from the public for 25 years.

Since the American government belongs to the people, the citizens have a right to know what elected officials are doing with their authority.

PRIOR RESTRAINT

Prior restraint is the power of the government to prevent publication or broadcasts ahead of time. In the early days of the American colonies, newspapers were published only with the approval of the crown, but prior restraint is a rare event in the U.S.

A classic case of prior restraint involved the *Pentagon Papers*, a secret history of American involvement in the Vietnam War. The government study was classified as top secret, but was leaked to the press. The Nixon Administration got a restraining order to stop publication. The Supreme Court ruled that publishing the sensitive information did not present a clear and present danger, and decided in favor of the press.

PUBLIC FIGURES

A different set of rules applies to someone engaged in public activity. Private citizens have a right to keep confidential facts about themselves that would be acceptable to report about public figures. For instance, does the public have the right to know about the mental health of a politician? Revealing this type of information could help the public make a better decision in the voting booth. This would not be the case if a report reveals the HIV diagnosis of a private citizen with no public role.

There are two kinds of public figures; the "names you know" and the limited public figure, defined as someone who does something to draw attention to him- or herself. When reporting on private figures, a journalist might be protected in court if using as a defense that a supposed private act occurred in public view.

After a bomb exploded in Atlanta's Centennial Olympic Park during the 1996 Olympic Summer Games, temporary security guard Richard Jewell was praised for spotting the knapsack containing the bomb. He brought police to the scene and began clearing people from the area, probably saving lives. But his name was released by the press as the FBI's main suspect in the bombing, although he had not been formally charged. The news organizations cited unnamed sources at the FBI. Eventually, the Justice Department formally cleared Jewell of having any connection with the attack. Jewell filed and won a lawsuit against several news organizations, partly because he was considered a private citizen by the courts.

For information about state statutes regarding libel, go to the website of *The Reporters Committee for Freedom of the Press* (rcfp.org).

Undercover Reporting

The courts generally maintain that undercover reporting is legal, though not necessarily ethical, if it does not involve trespass.

One of the most publicized cases of undercover reporting took place in 1992 when the ABC News magazine *Prime Time Live* broadcast accusations against Food Lion.

Two producers gained employment at two North Carolina supermarkets without revealing their identities. They shot video showing unsanitary food handling and selling spoiled food. The company sued ABC, but not for libel. Food Lion wanted more than $2 billion dollars in punitive damages to "deter illegal conduct" by news organizations. A jury found ABC guilty of fraud and trespassing, awarding the supermarket chain $5.5 million which was dropped to $2 by an appeals court.

The first question in the next chapter's Ethics Quiz asks, "Is it ever right for journalists to be deceptive when working on a story?" Most students say "no," although most professionals surveyed agree to allow it under narrow conditions. It must concern an issue of great public importance, other alternatives must be exhausted, full disclosure must be given at some point, and the harm prevented outweighs the harm committed.

Copyright

The First Amendment protects the creator's financial interest in artistic expression.

Copyright rules apply to the Internet just as they do to other media. Material on the Net, even on electronic bulletin boards, belongs to the author. So its use, other than what falls under fair use, requires permission and possibly payment. Because material on the Internet is easily accessible, it is easily, freely, and privately copied. This renders it difficult, if not impossible, to police those who do copy. Another confounding issue is that new and existing material is often combined with other existing material to create even "newer" content. The Associated Press sued Shepard Fairey for copyright infringement, claiming an iconic poster the artist created called "Hope" was based on one of its photos. Fairey admitted the stenciled portrait started as a AP photo, but said he used the photograph only as a starting point, transforming it into an image with a new meaning and different message from the original picture.

Web monitoring company *Attributor* searched for all the articles published by 157 newspapers in the U.S. during a 30-day period in Fall 2009. It found more than 75,000 sites that reproduced articles without permission.

Once a copyright expires and the creator does not renew it, the material passes into the *public domain*. It can be used without permission.

Music licensing companies collect fees, not only from radio and television stations, but bowling alleys, supermarkets, etc. based on the users' gross receipts. If a business plays music, the writers and composers are entitled to compensation. The three big music licensing companies are:

      ASCAP – American Society of Composers, Authors and Publishers

      BMI – Broadcast Music Inc.

      SESAC - Society of European Stage Authors & Composers

A note for those involved in student media: Either the student newspaper or its student contributors hold the copyright on photographs and other content, not the school itself. This holds true even if the school provides some funding for the publication.

Keep in mind the Supreme Court ruled in 1918 that facts cannot be copyrighted. The facts of a case written in a news story cannot be copyrighted, while the way the story is put together is copyrighted.

Digital Rights Management

Digital media has a significant advantage over legacy media. When a digital piece of content is downloaded from a site, for instance, a digital book, this does not mean there is one less book for someone else to download or that more copies will have to be ordered. Unlike analog media, digital media files allow production of an infinite number of copies. Despite possessing a bottomless well, there are still laws governing the distribution of digital media.

Copyright kicks in immediately when publishing on the Web (even at zero views), unlike in newspapers where another party must read it first.

The Internet (with its file sharing) is forcing a significant reconsideration of copyright laws, which are usually referred to as DRM (*digital rights management*). Congress tried to map out what constitutes copyright infringement on the Internet in the *Digital Millennium Copyright Act of 1998* (DMCA). The Act puts responsibility on copyright owners to look for violations, with website owners expected to act expeditiously when notified of a violation. A site owner must designate an agent to receive complaints, post the agent's contact information on the U.S. Copyright Offices website and take immediate action when complaints come about claims of infringement.

While the Digital Millennium Copyright Act protects websites from content uploaded by third parties, it also requires site owners to take down infringing content if they are aware of it. This safe harbor protects the site owner against potentially huge exposure for hosting infringing works. This is the issue that led to a lawsuit between *Viacom* and *YouTube*. Viacom sued YouTube for one billion dollars, claiming "willful infringement of copyright" through posting video owned by Viacom. A New York judge dismissed the case in June 2010, saying YouTube's owner, Google, was protected by the Digital Millennium Copyright Act. Viacom immediately announced plans to appeal the ruling. A Los Angeles judge dismissed a similar lawsuit the previous year by Universal Music Group against video-sharing site Veoh for the same reason. He said companies are not required by the DRM to police their sites, only to remove copyrighted material when requested to do so by the copyright owner.

Posting a mug shot of Andy Pettitte taken from the *New York Yankees* website will probably not trigger legal action because the photo is understood to be intended for publicity purposes. If the shot comes from *USA Today* or a news source such as *Associated Press*, there would probably be a copyright issue. The rules for advertising are even tighter. Using Andy Pettitte's likeness in a promotional campaign without his permission would be a copyright violation.

Students borrowing from other works is also an ongoing battle in the classroom. Teachers sometimes use sites like *TurnItIn.com* to measure how much of a term paper is not original to the student. The site generates reports to help identify plagiarized compositions.

Copyright lawsuits over news stories are rare. When they do take place, the legal battle is typically between competitors, such as the *Dow Jones* 2010 suit against *Briefing.com*, which accuses the aggregate of pirating Dow content. It's worth noting that the Digital Millennium Copyright Act does not require content owners to issue take-down demands before filing a lawsuit unless the offending material was uploaded by third parties. The owner of the *Las Vegas Review-Journal* has taken it a step further by suing a blogger, a gambling site, NORML (the National Organization for the Reform of Marijuana Laws), and many others. The lawsuits came as surprises to the defendants since no warnings were sent prior to the legal action.

The Digital Millennium Copyright Act also impacts Internet music sites by prohibiting the advance posting of playlists since users could plan ahead to copy songs.

User-Generated Comments

Under Section 230 of the *Communications Decency Act*, you are not responsible for comments or what video users post on your website, as long as you are not the creator. The law treats sites as more of a bookstore than a newspaper. A bookstore is not responsible for the content of the books it sells whereas a newspaper is responsible for everything in its publication, including advertisements. But when the material is moved from the website to the TV newscast or newspaper, you lose your Section 230 protection. Websites may also moderate posted comments (such as removing profanity), but the changes should not substantially change the writer's intent.

Special Broadcast Issues

THE FAIRNESS DOCTRINE

The Fairness Doctrine required broadcasters to cover issues of public importance from different perspectives. Introduced in 1949, use of the doctrine ended during the deregulation of the 1980s, but it has come up in Congress several times since, and broadcasters are worried it may be reinstated. They say, rather than presenting both sides of an issue, the ruling led broadcasters to avoid ALL controversial issues.

Afraid of being sued by someone who complained all sides of an issue were not presented, broadcasters avoided any programming that might be called into question.

Afraid of being sued by someone who complained that all sides of an issue were not presented, broadcasters avoided any programming that might be called into question.

SAFE HARBOR

Safe Harbor is a time set aside during the broadcast day when children are not likely to be in the audience (typically 10 PM to 6 AM). Broadcasters find some protection when airing potentially offensive material during this time.

INDECENCY

Although obscenity and pornography are rarely issues for broadcasters, they frequently confront the issue of indecency. According to the FCC (the body that regulates broadcasting in the U.S.) indecent language or material depicts sexual or excretory activities in a way that is offensive to contemporary community standards.

The most famous case, *FCC v. Pacifica*, went to the Supreme Court. Comic George Carlin's *Seven Dirty Words You Can't Say on Television* routine was broadcast by a radio station. The court split 5-4 in favor of affirming the government's power to regulate indecent material on the public airwaves.

Another case of indecency on TV is the so-called Super Bowl wardrobe malfunction. The FCC fined CBS for Janet Jackson's breast exposure during halftime of the 2004 Super Bowl when fellow pop singer Justin Timberlake yanked at her costume. The agency found the network guilty of airing "indecent" material and levied a fine of $550,000. The courts overturned that decision because the FCC has a history of fining broadcasters for deliberately shocking an audience, but not for brief incidents in which the broadcaster did not know what was going to happen.

PLUGOLA AND PAYOLA

The FCC says a radio station that broadcasts material for which it receives compensation must identify the person or group sponsoring the broadcast. This sponsorship rule is designed to stop *plugola* — the on-the-air promotion of goods or services in which someone controlling the broadcast material has an *undisclosed* financial interest. Promotion of goods or services is legally permissible if the station management is aware of the interest and proper sponsorship identification is made on the air so there is no conflict of interest. Cases where recording companies have secretly rewarded DJs for playing and plugging certain records are examples of *payola*. A radio station can play a specific song in exchange for money, but this must be disclosed on the air as being sponsored airtime. Payola is a criminal violation subject to fines, imprisonment, or both. It can also lead to the loss of a broadcast license.

QUARTERLY NEEDS REPORT

Broadcasters are required by the FCC to keep a listing of programs showing the station is addressing the most significant community issues. This *Quarterly Needs Report* goes in the station's public file at the end of each quarter, four times a year.

RECORDING CONVERSATIONS

In cases of two-way communication where each party could reasonably expect privacy, such as wireless and landline phone calls, it is illegal to listen to the conversation without a warrant. In other words, bugging is illegal. An example would be leaving your smart phone in a room to record a conversation that takes place after you leave. If no party knows you are recording the conversation, you have violated the federal wiretap statute.

There are also state laws that apply. Some states require only one person involved in the conversation to agree to tape, while other states require both parties' consent. The situation can be complicated by involving the laws of more than one state. If you are in Georgia, which has one party consent, but record someone in California, which requires the consent of both parties, the courts recognize the California law as applicable. To find our your state's rules, go to the site of the *Reporters Committee for Freedom of the Press* (rcfp.org/taping).

Secret audio tapes of White House intern Monica Lewinsky in 1998 led to a sex scandal involving President Bill Clinton, who was impeached by the U.S. House of Representatives but later acquitted by the Senate. Linda Tripp, who surreptitiously made the recordings of Lewinsky during telephone conversations, was charged with violating Maryland's wiretap law. The charges were later dismissed.

Most wiretapping or eavesdropping laws include explicit exceptions for recording in public places because no expectation of privacy exists. However, in a few states, this understanding of the law is being challenged by police officers who have arrested people for video taping them in public places. These instances have been rare, and only in states requiring both parties' consent, unless the recording is obvious (i.e., TV crews carrying lots of large recording equipment)

Besides state and federal laws, there are extra rules about recording conversations when it comes to broadcasters which have been determined by the FCC.

At the beginning of telephone calls recorded for broadcast, the FCC requires the other party be notified. The rules are set up to deter shock jocks, while on the air, from calling people as a practical joke. The rule has been applied to all kinds of broadcasters, including reporters. "Implied consent" applies to callers of request and sports shows. It is presumed the person knows of the possibility that his or her voice will be aired. The FCC strictly enforces this rule. The agency fined a Mississippi AM station $6,400 for recording and broadcasting a telephone conversation without informing the other party of its intent to do so during the station's morning show, even though the person made the call to the station and had participated in previous calls that had been aired.

CAN I SHOW THIS VIDEO?

A news organization can broadcast illegally obtained video or audio as long as the outlet did not originate its creation.

When it comes to filming someone at work, courts have usually ruled that a person is entitled to expectations of privacy in a secure place, but not if the public can freely come and go from the area.

If a homeowner tells you to turn off the camera on private property and you are in a two-consent state, you have to turn it off. Some TV reporters with microphones will approach a homeowner's door while the cameraman films from the sidewalk. Recording video from a public sidewalk is legal but courts will say it is illegal if it isn't clear to the homeowner that recording of their voice is taking place, because the owner has an expectation of privacy.

Police "ride-alongs" present a different set of issues. Generally, the First Amendment gives way to private property. A warrant allows law enforcement to search a residence, not the news media. Reporters could be in trouble for taking photographs before the owner has an opportunity to order the media to leave. If a reporter is covering a fire or other crime, taking images of a private residence not directly part of the story could be problematic.

OTHER FCC REQUIREMENTS

Besides the issues already mentioned, the FCC expects broadcasters to (among other things):

> Receive and send EAS (Emergency Alert System) tests and emergency alerts.
>
> Give station identifications at the top of each hour.
>
> Notify the F.A.A. if a tower light is not operating.
>
> Disclose all contest rules to the audience and go by them.

FOR FURTHER HELP ON LEGAL ISSUES INVOLVING BROADCASTERS

BroadcastLawBlog.com, maintained by the Davis Wright Tremaine Law Firm

CommLawBlog from the Law Firm of Fletcher, Heald & Hildreth

For Next Time

Is it ever right for a journalist to be deceptive while working on a story?

SEVENTEEN
Ethics

"All of us who professionally use the mass media are the shapers of society. We can vulgarize that society. We can brutalize it. Or we can help lift it onto a higher level."   —Advertising Pioneer William Bernach

The law tells journalists what they can and cannot do. Ethics, on the other hand, is concerned with what is blameworthy and what is praiseworthy.

When NBC news received videos from the Virginia Tech shooter following his rampage on the campus that left 32 people dead including himself, a decision had to be made as to whether to play portions of those tapes containing his manifesto. Decision-making like this requires that we enter the world of ethics.

Whether TV reporters are required to perform stand-ups in packages or whether radio news is played at the top or bottom of each hour is a matter of preference based on what a station considers effective to reach its goals. When there is a moral issue at stake, then ethics comes into play. In news rooms, situations will force hard decisions. Defining ethical boundaries ahead of time will make those decisions easier and more clear-cut.

Central Park

In 1999, a lengthy debate took place between managers of *CNN's Headline News* network (now HLN) over whether to air video tape of young men dousing young women with water in New York's Central Park. While the video looked like a wet t-shirt contest, it clearly showed what was happening to the women. If you had been there that day as a manager, would you have recommended showing the video or considered it gratuitous?

CNN Headline News decided not to run the video at all. CNN ran small portions a few times when the story first broke. *FOX News* ran the video… over and over again.

Let's take another situation. Four people were killed when two news helicopters collided following a car chase in Phoenix, Arizona, in 2007. Should car chases be a part of televisions news? Does this really qualify as news or simply gruesome voyeurism, like fans who attend car races in hopes of seeing an accident?

Henry Blodget, editor-in-chief of *Business Insider*, a gossipy site that regularly uses gimmicks to attract readers, wrote an article titled "The Internet is Making Us Shallow and Vapid! (Or Maybe We Were Just Shallow And Vapid To Begin With)." He argues, "Since the dawn of media, someone has always been bellyaching about how media is taking society to hell in a handbasket... Every stop along the way, it has been alleged, the new media are dragging us into the gutter... perhaps it's time to float a new theory. We're already in the gutter. What we click on accurately reflects what we're interested in, no matter how much we think and protest and hope to the contrary."

Is Blodget being realistic or throwing out journalism ethics altogether under the banner of giving the public what it wants?

Code of Ethics

All major groups of media professionals have established formal codes or standards of ethical behavior, including:

> Society of Professional Journalists *Code of Ethics*
>
> American Society of Newspaper Editors' *Statement of Principles*
>
> Radio-Television News Directors Association's *Code of Broadcast Ethics*

In addition to industry professional codes, many media organizations have formed their own institutional policies for conduct. Local broadcasters often have policy books. In the case of the broadcast networks, these are enforced by Standards and Practices departments.

Newspapers and magazines standardize behavior through operating and editorial policies. Some media organizations have ombudsmen who serve as "judges" in disputes between the public and the organizations. The name comes from Sweden. In the early 1800s, it referred to someone who mediates between citizens and the government. Other media organizations have created *Media Councils*, panels made up of people from both the media and the public who investigate complaints against the organization and publish their findings.

Ethics Quiz

1. Is it ever right for journalists to be deceptive when working on a story?
   What if:
   It's an issue of great public importance?
   Other alternatives have been exhausted?
   There will be full disclosure at some point?
   The harm prevented outweighs the harm committed?

Does any of this change your mind?

2. Should journalists accept free samples? Gifts from organizations or individuals? What if a company sends a copy of a major film about to be released with a letter touting its unique computer graphics. Is it a story?

3. Should a travel writer ever accept a free trip from a resort, travel agency, etc.? If she does, should she mention it in her article?

4. If you meet someone for a cup of coffee to discuss a story, should you turn him down if he wants to pay for your cappuccino?

5. Should you give up your right to express political views, if you're in the news business?

   At the 2009 White House Correspondents dinner, President Barack Obama introduced himself by saying, "I am Barack Obama. Most of you covered me. All of you voted for me." The joke got laughs because many people regard the news media as politically biased while pretending to be objective. That's why some journalists even swear off voting in elections.

   Suppose you walked into *CNN* and saw a sea of stickers for Democrats, or *FOX News* and saw a sea of Republican stickers? Should political expression be kept out of the newsroom? *The Washington Post* once barred reporters from taking part in a march about abortion. Is this right? (It was a pro-abortion rights march). In 2002, a journalist for the *Houston Chronicle* was fired for writing an anonymous blog criticizing local politicians because it undermined the paper's image of objectivity.

   Where do journalists draw the line between objectively reporting on our democracy and participating in it? Should ethical journalists reveal their viewpoints, biases and affiliations as part of full-disclosure?

6. Would you publish the names of rape victims?

7. Would you publish the names of juvenile offenders?

8. Is a politician's private life ever off limits? What if the candidate is sleeping around? *The Oregonian* newspaper apologized to its readers for not publishing reports about Senator Bob Packwood's alleged sexual harassment charges until after he was re-elected. Should the paper have apologized?

9. Does the public have a right to know everything a news organization does?

10. A photographer working for *Reuters* took a picture of President Bush at the UN writing a note. He could not know what the note said, but an editor zoomed in on the page and found the message to Secretary of State Condoleezza Rice. It said he needed a bathroom break. Does this qualify as news?

(At the end of this chapter is a list showing how professional journalists responded to this quiz.)

How It Starts

Remember Jayson Blair? He's the *New York Times* reporter discussed in the chapter about newspapers who fabricated news stories. Recall how he said his deceptive writing got started? A source wouldn't give him a name, so he made one up. He didn't start by saying, "I'm going to fake an ENTIRE story." It started with just a couple of words. No big deal. But it gets easier to go further each time until you aren't sure how you got to where you are. Blair has said, "You cross the line again and again until you can't come back. Little by little, you become what you are chasing."

But it gets easier each time to go further until you don't know how you got to where you are.

It's worth noting that Blair apparently did not have a support system, a group of people who would hold him accountable, someone who would get in his face and tell him the truth. Instead, he withdrew and isolated himself from others.

The New York Times is not the only paper rocked by revelations of fabricated stories. In 1981, *The Washington Post* admitted that a Pulitzer Prize-winning story by reporter Janet Cook was false.

The movie *Shattered Glass* tells the true story of how reporter Steven Glass, for the *New Republic* began making up stories. He was caught fabricating an article about teenage computer hackers, and his firing sent shock waves through the magazine industry. How does a news organization prevent this sort of thing from happening?

Doctored Photographs

The magazine industry has largely come to believe there is an acceptance of photo manipulation on the part of readers. Readers expect a level of slickness, according to defenders of the practice. Cropping, coloring, combining, and otherwise altering an image has become the norm, rather than the exception. And it's necessary, they say, because of greater competition on the newsstand. Among the doctored covers that have received media attention:

> *Men's Fitness* showed Andy Roddick with enhanced bicep muscles.
> *Newsweek* magazine put Martha Stewart's face on a professional model's body.
> Jennifer Aniston's picture on *Redbook's* cover combined three different photos.
> *Washingtonian* magazine showed a chiseled Barack Obama in a red bathing suit. His swim suit was actually black.

Pause for Discussion: Photojournalism or Manipulation?

Are altered covers a serious ethical breach? Does it matter if the celebrity gives his or her approval? Should a publication refrain from any airbrushing? What about the *TIME* cover that appeared shortly after OJ Simpson's murder arrest in 1994 that darkened his skin, supposedly giving him a more sinister appearance? Do you think this is typical or the exception?

The Golden Mean

When journalists discuss ethics, they often mention Aristotle's Golden Mean as an example of how reporters can navigate through the murky waters of right and wrong. The Greek philosopher's views are misrepresented as advocating a commitment to moderation, suggesting the balance between extremes is the Golden Mean.

First, it should be noted that Aristotle never answers the question, "What ought one to do?" Instead, he offers the observation that virtue seems to be good for you. Just as antibiotics are good for you, being virtuous simply "does you good."

Now consider what goes into making an excellent chair. Would an excellent chair be one made of a moderate use of "chair" material? No, because this leaves out the question of function. Is the chair intended for work or comfort or a child? The Golden Mean may offer specific answers as to what to do in some cases, but there are other cases in which achieving it will depend on the person's purpose and goals. For instance, in answering the question, "How do I get to New York?" one person might say, "Take this route. It's scenic." Another might say, "Take this second route. It's faster." Which one is the "right" or "best" way? It depends, Aristotle would tell us, on your purpose. His view is that the goal of ethics is not knowledge, but action. Ethics is simply a brochure, offering guidance. It is not a rule book, which would be too long and impractical. The theory of the Mean is intended to serve as a recipe for virtues. Aristotle hopes to encourage virtuous (and thus happy) men.

ETHICS SURVEY: WHAT THE PROS SAY

1. Professionals are split on the issue of deception, drawing the line in different places. Some will participate in hidden camera investigations of organizations while others consider it unethical.

2. Yes, there is no law against journalists accepting gifts from those they report on. But almost every newsroom has a strict policy prohibiting its staff room from accepting anything of value because of the ethical desire to avoid conflicts of interest.

3. Yes

4. No

5. No

6. No

7. No

8. No. Journalists generally say politicians do not have the right to declare parts of their lives "off limits." A 2010 *Angus Reid Pubic Opinion Poll* found 55% of Americans agreed with the statement that a politician who commits adultery "lacks the integrity to hold public office" while 31% said adultery should not be a factor in judging politicians.

9. No. Although the public's "right to know" is sometimes cited by journalists as a guiding principle and goal, most news people would say the public does not have a right to know everything a news organization does. For instance, soon after the 9/11 attacks, many news organizations had video of people jumping from the World Trade Center towers, but chose to withhold airing the video at that time out of respect to the victims and their families, as well as a matter of taste.

10. Mixed

For Next Time

What is *news*? Can you define it? Or is news like what Supreme Court justice Potter Stewart said about obscenity in a 1964 ruling? While Stewart admitted having trouble defining it, he wrote, "I know it when I see it."

EIGHTEEN
Writing News

What Is News?

More than anything else, journalism is the effort to establish the truth of what matters to society.

Most news outlets have meetings before publication or a broadcast to decide what stories to cover and who'll work on them. Journalists are expected to bring ideas to the table.

Someone in a TV newsroom could make the suggestion, "I have a great story for us to do. There's this chicken farm in Texas that claims to have figured out how to run cars on bird droppings." The first question is going to always be, "Do we have any video?" TV news is video-driven. You'll never hear a TV anchor say:

> "Now we turn to a story about some baby ducks crossing the street. Now, we would show you the ducks but we don't have any video. Just imagine what they would look like…"

Cute ducks are a story on the local news because you can show them. That's why TV news organizations get desperate when a story lacks visuals.

If an anchor just sits, reading a teleprompter, it's boring television. When you watch *FOX News*, *CNN,* or local TV news, in a real sense, you are not hearing about the most important stories, but seeing a collection of the best video gathered that day. When TV news producers are putting together a show, they start by looking for supporting material. Do they have video? Can graphics be created to illustrate some aspect of the story? Would a phone interview or a studio guest help to bring the story to life for the audience?

Photo courtesy Flickr_MostlyDans

Cute ducks are a story on the local news because you can show them.

Walk around a network newsroom and ask producers, writers, and copy editors to define news. Chances are, they will struggle to articulate it, despite the fact they work with it every day. The dictionary says news is "a report of a recent event." In the 1800s, *New York Sun* editor Charles Dana defined news as "anything that will make people talk."

Here is one way to draw a circle around what we're going to call news: PICNIRET. Proximity, Impact, Conflict, Novelty, Influence, Relevance, Emotion, and Timeliness.

Any story that rises to the level of reportability must do so in one of these ways for your audience. The more of these characteristics it possesses, the more newsworthy a story.

PROXIMITY

A murder in Atlanta is not a story for small town media outlet in New Mexico. A murder on the local campus is news.

IMPACT

A new federal mining law is not significant news in Washington State. A new federal mining law is major news in West Virginia.

CONFLICT

A book club meeting is not news. A book club meeting where a fist fight breaks out over Harry Potter is news.

NOVELTY

Someone setting up to tailgate before a football game is not news. Someone setting up an unauthorized hot air balloon to fly over the stadium is news.

INFLUENCE

A friend saying President Obama should be impeached is not news. If the president of a university makes the same remark, that is news because of his or her influence.

RELEVANCE

The score in the USC football game is not significant news for a Virginia media outlet. The score in the local college game is news.

EMOTION

Baby ducks floating in water is not news. Baby ducks floating in water and covered in oil from a leak is news.

TIMELINESS

A natural disaster that took place six months ago is not today's news.

A natural disaster that took place this morning is today's news.

This is one effective way to figure out what constitutes news. You will probably develop your own definition of news over time. Whether it's similar to this one or not, get a clear idea of your target.

After deciding what information constitutes news for the day, the limits of time and space often require journalists to choose which of several stories to write. The weight of a story helps producers decide how much significance one story has over another. In TV, this comes into play when *stacking a show* (deciding which order to present the stories) and in print, deciding what to place on the front page or cover.

As you read this chapter, keep in mind there are two types of people who will always be listening or reading. One is the expert on the subject of your story who will be very judgmental and parse your every claim. The other is the casual reader or viewer. This person is curious, but lacks the time and doesn't want to put a great deal of effort into the subject. Your job is to write something accurate and weighty for the first person and something that will engage the second person all within in the same story.

What a News Writer Needs to Know

News writers should be well-rounded and have a working knowledge of the areas in which most news happens. These include:

The Federal System of Government

Know how the branches of government work and the divisions of powers between the federal and state governments.

The Legislative Process

Know the difference between a bill and a law and the process of how a bill becomes law.

The Judicial Process

Understand in general terms how courts work, the differences between civil and criminal cases, and the different jurisdictions between federal and state courts.

(Tip: Judges cannot comment, therefore never report that a judge had "no comment" about a case. They can only talk about cases in the abstract.)

The Electoral Process

The basic rules governing how elections are conducted and understand the role of political parties in the process.

The General State of Science & Technology

Have a basic understanding of the sciences and be able to recognize the importance of new developments.

Sports

Be familiar with major sports, the major professional and collegiate leagues, etc.

The Economy

Know the common economic terms. Understand how financial markets work and what government policies can influence the state of the overall economy.

Geography

Be familiar enough with U.S. geography to find specific locations on maps, and familiar enough with world geography to know which countries are on which continents. Who's near whom?

Popular Culture

Be familiar with current movies, network TV series, popular music, and celebrities in those industries.

The Military

Be familiar with the four branches of the U.S. armed services, have a general understanding of each one's primary mission and a working familiarity with military ranks and titles.

Law Enforcement

Have a working knowledge of how police conduct investigations, know different jurisdictions between local and federal agencies, and be familiar with the ranks and titles used by law enforcement agencies.

International Affairs

Be familiar with major international issues, understanding the role of international organizations like the United Nations, and be familiar with various forms of government.

The broader your base of general knowledge, the easier it is to tackle a complex story, sort through the facts and identify the elements that will best serve your viewers or readers.

If you don't know these areas, know where to find out. Learn to research by making use of the websites mentioned in the Online Newsgathering chapter. A journalist who is able to quickly find information wields power.

Stylebooks

First produced in 1953, the *Associated Press Stylebook* has grown from just 60 stapled pages to more than 450 pages in its current edition. It is the most used guide in the news industry for how to write stories for print or broadcast news (AP members and college students can get the spiral bound edition at a discounted rate). It's also available online at APstylebook.com. The online guide has the advantage of quick search and constant updates. The reference work is also available as an app for the iPhone and iPod Touch. The official Twitter account for the AP Stylebook (twitter.com/APStylebook) now has more than 44,000 followers.

Someone has set up a fake AP Stylebook Twitter feed, which anonymously provides tongue-in-cheek "style tips for proper grammatical writing."

Some samples:

> The correct title for an unmarried woman is "Ms." "Miss Jackson" should only be used if you are nasty.

> Dates should be formatted as MM/DD/YY except for the years 1990 through 1992, which should be denoted in "Hammer Time."

> Periods in RIP or not? That is a question that your heart is going to have to answer.

> Do not change weight of gorilla in phrase, "800-lb gorilla in the room." Correct weight is 800 lbs. DO NOT CHANGE GORILLA'S WEIGHT!"

> All mentions of the word "chameleon" should be preceded by five commas. In all other instances, they come and go.

> Do not use the phrase "sources have said" unless you can't get any real sources to say anything.

The real *AP Stylebook* now has a section on social media where it notes that "Web site" has become "website," while "Web" remains a capitalized proper noun when used as a shortened form of "World Wide Web."

Another news writing aid is ReligionStylebook.org. The *Religion Newswriters Foundation* put together this Internet site to help journalists get more info on how to write religious stories.

There are different rules for writing at every news shop, so be flexible. Develop your own ideas about "the way to do it," and be ready to implement your own plan when you're in charge. In the meantime, work within the system. First, learn the standard rules for print and broadcast. A professional should be able to switch between the two, depending on the needs of the news organization. For instance, *FOX News* does a lot of little things differently than AP. Keep in mind not all of this is in concrete. The *AP Stylebook* is not the Bible of Journalism. It's just the most common and highly regarded way to go about the business of communicating information in the news media.

Inverted Pyramid

The most popular way to go about writing a news story for print is the inverted pyramid. This simply means arranging the information from most to least important.

This style was adopted partly because it makes it easier to fit the newspaper space set aside for a story. If there's not enough room for the entire article, just drop the last few sentences. Adding an advertisement? Drop a couple more sentences. This option was more important during the time when cutting and pasting were a part of creating a newspaper. With today's software, moving information around in an article isn't as complicated.

The inverted pyramid is not used in broadcast news. Especially in TV news, stories are written in such a way it would be obvious to the audience if something was missing at the end. In fact, broadcast news writing often ends with a summary of the main facts of the story. Keep in mind that broadcasters must keep the attention of the viewers or listeners throughout a piece because the audience can't jump to another story when they lose interest, as print allows readers to do.

Nut Paragraph

A critical part of newspaper stories is a "nut paragraph." It's also known as a nut graph. This summary of the key elements of a story explains to readers why the story is being written. The nut can be the lead sentence or a transition from a specific example to the larger issue.

Here's how you might use it as a transition. A story begins by telling about Helen's health problems and then the nut graph comes. "Not that this is much comfort for Helen, but she is not alone. Health officials estimate that Americans…" So the nut graph puts her situation in perspective.

Putting together a nut graph first is always a good place to start when writing a newspaper story because your other material can work around it.

The Six Questions

Creating the nut graph revolves around the six questions:

who, what, where, when, why, and how.

SHOW, DON'T TELL

Don't tell the reader. Show the reader. Flesh out the idea. Don't tell me "John is funny." Describe the way people fell in the floor belly laughing at his jokes. Don't tell readers the speaker was angry. Describe how she pounded the lectern so hard she broke a finger.

USING THE SENSES

When possible, include all the senses to paint a more vivid scene.

Here are some examples of how using the senses paints a more vivid picture.

> Sight: Under the new snow, the street posts looked as though they had Mickey Mouse ears.
>
> Sound: When the penalty flag dropped, the hometown fans roared in unison, like a pride of well-rehearsed lions.
>
> Smell: The food court smelled like ripe garbage.
>
> Touch: The baby's hair feels like strands of silk.
>
> Taste: The steak tastes like charcoal.

LEADS

We would never begin a story this way: "The City Council met Tuesday." What the City Council *did* when it met is the news, not simply that the members met. When covering a meeting, a reporter's job is to tell readers what happened. Here's another lead that should never be written:

> President Obama had a tough day. He had orange juice for breakfast. And later, he declared war on assorted small countries in the Middle East.

The war angle would certainly play higher to create what is called a *hard lead*. Otherwise, the writer is committing the sin of *burying the lead*, putting the most significant part of the story below the first sentence. The lead should be reserved for the most weighty and unique aspect of a story even when it comes to single words. In the lead, "An alarm notified fire fighters yesterday of a blaze at the auto parts plant in Chickasaw," the use of alarm is not necessary.

Besides the hard news lead, there is the *soft* or *delayed lead*. The opening sentences might offer some anecdote or description, leading to a nut graph (within four or five paragraphs) which explains the larger picture. Soft leads can be harder to write than hard leads because it is easy to wander around the topic without making a point. Fast-breaking and important stories are not written with soft leads because there is no need to set up the information.

Another proverb for story leads: Clarity over cleverness. It's easy to get too cute or attempt to show off a sharp wit when writing a soft story but this can end up misleading the audience. Go for creativity with persuasiveness. Make it easy and effortless for them to grasp. This is especially true with broadcast teases and promos.

While most leads should be written in present or future tense, there are exceptions, such as the narrative lead. "Paul Jones always wanted to be a baseball player. He never expected to be called a hero."

You can also write a lead making a direct connection to the viewer's personal experiences. "If you've ever driven on the interstate and found yourself sandwiched between two semis, you know how frightening big rigs can be."

Some leads contain no specific facts at all. "We have breaking news out of Spain. A massive search is underway for a missing airliner."

In print news stories, the time is noted in the lead, but it does not come first. Instead of "Yesterday, the Smithfield School Board laid off 12 teachers because of budget cuts." it would be "The Smithfield School Board laid off 12 teachers because of budget cuts yesterday." Broadcast stories would either drop "yesterday" entirely to sound more immediate. "A dozen Smithfield teachers are looking for work. The school board blames budget cuts for the layoff."

Quotes are seldom used in leads but those that are should be short and to the point.

Once a lead is established, the next few sentences should support and explain it. These sentences should not wander away from the topic or jump into background information that might better fit at the end of the story.

ACTIVE VOICE

Take a look at these sentences:

    1. Something is happening to someone.
    2. Someone is doing something.

The first sentence focuses on the result of an action. The second focuses on the actor. That's the difference between passive voice and active voice in sentence construction. Active voice underscores the immediacy of unfolding events.

Scripts written in active voice convey a sense of action to the viewer.

The sentence is active voice when the person or thing expressing an action is the subject of the sentence. It's in passive voice when the person or thing receiving the action is the subject of the sentence.

Active voice is someone doing something. Passive voice is something being done to someone or something.

        Active: The governor gave a speech.
        Passive: A speech was given by the governor.

The action is the governor and his action is giving a speech. The actor comes before the action. And the identity of the actor should be stated. "The gunman was arrested," is passive and the actor is not even mentioned.

In many passive sentences the actor is missing.

Scripts written in active voice convey a sense of action to the viewer. They involve our audience in what's going on in the world around them. They underscore the immediacy of unfolding events. "Someone is doing something" is a model for broadcast writing.

Fixing a passive sentence can be as simple as following the classic order of Subject/Verb/Object. In an active voice sentence, the subject will always be the person or thing doing or expressing the action and the object will be the person or thing receiving the action.

Perhaps an easier way to remember to put the "act" in "active voice" is through A-C-T. ACT equals the actor, then the commission and finally the target. The key to writing in active voice is identifying the actor — the person, group, or even the institution that is taking action. Find the "someone" who is "doing something" and you're on the way to writing in active voice.

HEAR IT

> Celebrations today over a ninth win for Roger Clemens. He's the first pitcher to reach that mark this year.

This is a case of the "something is happening to someone" passive voice construction. While the focus of this story is Roger Clemens, he is not depicted in the copy as the principle actor. Instead, he is the "someone" that "something" happens to. To inject more energy into this script, focus on the people taking action rather than on the action itself.

> Roger Clemens and his fans are celebrating his ninth win. He's the first pitcher to reach that mark this year.

In this revision, people become the focus of the story, specifically Clemens and his fans. Framing the action of a story in human terms offers the viewer an instant connection.

The five W's can help identify the people taking action in a story. The first W is who and the second is what. When you identify who is at the center of a story and what he, she, or they are doing, you're well on your way to writing a script in active voice. The other W's, when, and where, and how are also helpful clues.

So What?

Look for the "wow" factor in stories: The piece of the story that's surprising, compelling or very practical.

Imagine you are dying to share a juicy bit of gossip with your best friend, but your friend's phone only allows 20-second voice messages. You hear the beep and breathlessly begin with, "Guess what?" Whatever comes next is your lead. You are summarizing the story in those brief seconds. Start with a "so what" sentence to get readers interested in the subject before hitting them with a load of facts.

It's the Felt Need angle. Here is an example:

> Instead of "The Fed is expected to raise interest rates again…"
> Try "It may cost you more to borrow money…"

See how something boring suddenly becomes something practical? Indicate how the story affects the lives of the readers or viewers.

Start with a "so what" sentence to get readers interested... before hitting them with a load of facts. Look for the wow factor.

The Face of Your Story

A high school teacher assigned a project where everyone in the class had to pick a country, write a report on it, and share what they learned. One student decided to talk about the country of Moldova because she became friends with someone from the small Eastern European country during her summer vacation. The student could have started her presentation with numbers about Moldova's population and GNP (Gross National Product), like the other students. Instead, she began with a specific person, her friend. She later offered the general information after humanizing the presentation. By working inductively, from the specific to the general, she put a face on the story. She even printed a photo of the girl from her *Facebook* page. The other students felt as if they knew her friend, and the place she lived was no longer an abstract series of numbers and facts.

Put a face on your story. Not every story will personally relate to every reader or viewer, but there is something important and interesting in every story. Look for the human element… what stands out to you?

Ownership

Writers are not only to put words on paper, but in the news business they have the added responsibility of taking ownership of their scripts and articles. When assigned a story, it belongs to the writer until it hits air, or is printed or uploaded. If there are updates during the writing process, it's the writer's job to get them into the script or article. If an important piece of information is missing, it is the writer's responsibility to step up and make a call, or throw it back at the producer or editor. Don't let it get to the audience with pieces missing. If the information is not enough to be considered news, writers should give that opinion to the producer or editor. Discuss it. Although management makes the final decision, part of a writer's job is to provide supervisors with input and feedback. It is a team effort. So when you are struggling to make deadline, don't hesitate to yell, "A little help here!"

Writers not only are to put words on paper but have the added responsibility of taking ownership of their scripts and articles.

Deadline Writing

There are many very skilled writers who could never make it in the world of news gathering. The constant deadlines imposed by the grind of 24-hour coverage requires a different kind of skill and attitude than weaving words together in a pretty package. Writers must crank it out. Half the battle is becoming accustomed to that pressurized routine. Someone trying to decide which field to move into for a career should weigh the deadline issue heavily. Writers who want more time may enjoy public relations more than journalism. Video shooters and editors may want to steer away from news in favor of documentaries in order to dive deeper into stories.

Subjective

Many news writers don't hesitate to break the rules mentioned in this chapter. Perhaps we should call these guidelines proverbs rather than rules, since they are often, but not always, true. Regardless of what we call them, newsrooms will come up with their own set of principles about what constitutes effective communication. Professional writers learn to switch hats, depending on the needs and goals of different organizations.

What one writer, copy editor, or anchor thinks is great writing, another might not like at all. Develop thick skin, knowing there may be a copy editor who will criticize your work every day. If your ego rides on keeping everyone happy, you're going to get frustrated and angry. Let other people have their opinions. You are a person of value even without the approval of others in regard to issues that do not involve moral choices.

Writing Techniques

Alliteration is taking several words beginning with the same consonant and grouping them together. There's a place for repetition. It helps drive home a concept. Notice all the B's in this story.

> For years Ron Smith studied boxing. He lived boxing and breathed boxing. But, on this day, he turned his back on boxing forever.

Parallel writing is the act of expressing two more ideas by using phrases or sentences of similar construction.

> In Arkansas, tempers are rising along with the waters.

The rule of threes is a useful device for writers. People remember concepts better if they are given in groups of three.

> The children spent their day working on reading, writing, and arithmetic.

A *simile* is the technique of comparing one thing to another, often using the words as or like.

> The wind tossed the trucks around as if they were small toys.

Hyperbole is well-placed exaggeration that paints a vivid picture. For instance, a writer might compare a rat to the size of a small car.

Special Broadcast Concerns

PRESENT TENSE

The most significant difference between writing for print and writing for broadcast is tense. Newspapers frequently use past tense while broadcasters avoid it, at least in the lead. Broadcast news attempts to stay in present tense as much as possible because of the desire for immediacy. Broadcast is all about what's happening RIGHT NOW. Don't tell me what happened yesterday. Tell me what's going on now.

You can get to the information that will allow you to write a script in the present tense by looking for the answers to two questions:

> What's Now?
> What's Next?

When you focus on those elements, you'll find using present tense in scripts comes naturally.

Suppose this is the story. "A small plane crashed last night in Memphis. Investigators are on the scene." How could it be changed to sound more "broadcast friendly"?

Instead of "last night" we talk about what's happening "this morning." "An investigation is underway this morning into the crash of a small plane in Memphis." Or maybe, "The pilot of a small plane is in the hospital this morning after he crashed in Memphis last night." Use "today" and "tomorrow" in broadcast writing where your focus is immediacy, but not in print, because you do not know when your readers will be looking at your article.

It's easier to write a script in present tense when news is breaking. "Police are on the scene…" "The Federal Reserve Chairman is telling Congress..." "The President is announcing his plan…" This is a story about what's happening at this moment. But how can a story be put into present tense when an event is over? Focus on elements of the story that haven't happened yet or which are ongoing. For example, here's the lead on a wire story from a Friday morning. The actual event happened on Thursday, but the implications are ongoing. The wire service cast the story in past tense.

> President Obama on Monday ordered the Justice Department to seal all documents seized from a congressman's office for six weeks as the Justice Department and Congress work out a dispute over the FBI's weekend search.

This script was used on television Friday morning using the same information, but was presented in a way that demonstrates the story is still unfolding.

> President Obama is giving the Justice Department and Congress time to settle a dispute. The disagreement centers on last weekend's F-B-I search of a representative's office. The president has ordered a six-week seal on documents the F-B-I seized in the raid.

Notice that FBI includes dashes for easier reading. That's a part of the broadcast writing style. Any words that are meant to be read together should be hyphenated in a script.

While presenting the same story elements as the wire service report, the script puts the viewer squarely in the middle of the story and illustrates how it is evolving and developing.

Writing in present tense can be especially challenging when using video that was shot on an earlier date. The temptation is to describe the events depicted in the video. The result is a script that can sound outdated. Here's an example of how not to use video from an event held the day before (Viewers are seeing video of mourners at the Speedway):

> Hundreds of NASCAR fans flocked to the Atlanta Motor Speedway yesterday for a tearful tribute to Dale Earnhardt. Earnhardt died in a crash Sunday during the last lap of the Daytona 500. A private funeral is scheduled this morning for family members and others close to the NASCAR driver. A memorial service will be held Thursday in Charlotte, North Carolina. It will be closed to the public, but televised.

How could we get this story's lead into present tense and still use the video? By focusing on the facts that are ongoing in nature and events that haven't happened yet. Here's one alternative:

> Racing legend Dale Earnhardt is being remembered at private and public services. A private funeral is today, and there are also public memorial services at race tracks around the country. Yesterday's service in Atlanta drew hundreds of fans. Another memorial will be held tomorrow in Charlotte, North Carolina. That service will be closed to the public, but televised. Earnhardt died in a crash at the Daytona 500 last weekend.

In this case, the ongoing fact of mourning brings the script into present tense. The factual elements that have not yet happened, the funeral and memorial services, give the viewer a sense of being up to the minute on the story, yet still includes reference to the video.

Broadcast stories often begin or end with what will happen next or offer a summary of where things stand. For instance:

> It's not known whether any of the missing passengers were Americans.
> The airline is contacting the relatives of the missing passengers.

FORCED PRESENT TENSE

Many writers will start with a past tense lead. Then, fearing the wrath of news managers, the writer simply changes the tense of the verb from past to present. The result is "forced present tense" or "TV speak." Here's an example:

> A Memphis bank is robbed this morning… and the gunman gets away.

While this lead is in present tense, the problem is that it doesn't sound natural. When was the last time you sat down to dinner with your mom and said, "Hey Mom, a bank is robbed this morning?" No one talks that way. This style of writing might be appropriate for a tease but not for the story itself. The first rule of broadcast writing is to be conversational.

The way to fix it is to ask those two critical questions: What's now? What's next?

What is happening right now: Police are looking for the gunman; the bank is processing its security camera pictures; etc.

What will happen next: The gunman will or will not be caught, the bank will release its security photos, the bank will reopen tomorrow with business as usual, etc.

The best and most effective lead will also be the one that focuses on the human element. Here are some present event examples.

> One Memphis man is recovering from a frightening experience this afternoon.

> This has turned out to be a day one Memphis man won't soon forget.

> Police are searching for a gunman who held up a Memphis bank this morning.

Here are some future event examples:

> When Otis Armstrong returns to work tomorrow… he'll have one amazing story to tell his friends.

> Police hope evidence to be released tomorrow will help them catch a crook. Otis Armstrong's grandchildren will be hearing about this day for years.

Some exceptions to the present tense rule in broadcast news go beyond the scope of this chapter. The general rule is to put a lead in present tense if it is possible.

Attribution

In print news, attribution can go at the beginning, middle, or end of a sentence. For instance:

> "According to police, the alleged assault happened shortly before 8 p.m. on Halloween."

> "The alleged assault happened, according to police, shortly before 8 p.m. on Halloween."

> "The alleged assault happened shortly before 8 p.m. on Halloween, according to police."

In broadcast news stories, the attribution will always go at the beginning of the sentence. Otherwise, the listener has to go back and put the quote with the attributed speaker while the anchor moves to the next sentence. This is unnecessarily confusing. Also, broadcasters would change "according to" to "says" and place dashes between the letters "p" and "m". The sentence would read, "Police say the alleged assault happened shortly before 8 p-m on Halloween."

Not every fact needs attribution. There is no need to attribute facts that are not in dispute and are considered a matter of common knowledge (such as the sun rises in the East). However, attribution is helpful when a statement is controversial, based on opinion, or because the person has authority and attribution will give weight to the statement.

It's best to put attribution after a quote when starting a print paragraph. Quotes are often more effective leading off a paragraph. However, when the person being quoted is more important than what the person is saying, then attribution should come first. Most news writers have no ethical problem with minor editing and deleting throwaway words from these quotes (such as deleting a speaker's "well" or "you know").

Conversational

Broadcast copy shouldn't sound like it was written at all. Writing for TV or radio is writing something to be heard, not read. We must write the way people listen. This is sometimes referred to as writing for the ear. The goal is avoiding words that make you sound like you are reading instead of just talking intelligently about an important topic. The story should sound conversational, and this is true for the Internet, as well. Find ways to relate the topic to the audience. However, just because broadcasters use "you" in stories, that does not mean slang, colloquialisms, or incorrect grammar are acceptable.

Imagine an anchor saying, "The regulations regarding alcohol consumption at sporting events on the campus are being modified." Yawn. But what if she said, "The rules about what you can drink at the football stadium on game day is about to change." The first lead sentence sounds boring. The second would get your attention.

Here are some ways to make it conversational:

> *Keep it short.* Aim at keeping your sentence to 15 words or fewer. Stick to one idea per sentence and if it takes more than one breath to say it, it's probably too long. The anchor shouldn't be gasping for air. For print stories, try not to exceed more than 25 words in each sentence.

> *Use Contractions.* We talk in contractions, so use them occasionally in broadcast writing. The time to avoid contractions is when "not" is important to understanding the story. Rather than "President Obama isn't going," use "is not" to make sure it is clear he's not going. An anchor slur can confuse viewers.

> *Use fragment sentences.* This can be abused, but a few well-placed fragments can make for more powerful copy.

> *Keep it simple.* While writers shouldn't talk down to their audiences, there's no reason not to keep the cookies on the lowest shelf so everyone can enjoy them.

You probably wouldn't say, "Hey mom! A Big Time Airline's 737 with 57 passengers on board disappeared from radar shortly after takeoff from Buenos Aires this morning, sparking a major search by the Argentine Air Force." That's neither short nor simple. Instead, you might say, "Hey, Mom! Did you hear about that plane crash in Argentina?" So our lead might be "We have breaking news out of Argentina: A massive search is underway for a missing jetliner."

Identifying People

Broadcast news handles names differently from print news. Small town papers may include the name of the person in the lead no matter what, but most newspapers and TV networks will just start with "An Ohio Man" or "A Springfield teenager" depending on whether the average viewer would know where Springfield is located. Then, the name may be given on the next reference.

When it comes to spokespersons, newspapers will often include their names and titles, but broadcasters will leave that information out unless the person is prominent or identifying the speaker adds credibility to a quote. A newspaper story that begins, "Sean Smith, spokesman for Time-Warner Cable Inc. said…" may be simply become "Time-Warner Cable says…" for broadcast news. If a TV story uses a spokesperson speaking on camera, then the person must be identified either in text or verbally by the reporter. Shorten the title as much as possible, especially if you are showing someone on television because the graphic identifying the person will have a limited character count for his or her title. The same is true for locations. Broadcasters seldom use addresses. Usually the name of a city or neighborhood is sufficient.

If a public figure is not well-known to the audience, then a story might begin, "A Mississippi Senator says…" However, the same story for a Mississippi audience might read, "Senator Trent Lott says…" Whether the audience considers the person in the story a prominent figure helps to determine how to identify the person.

Print articles often include the age of a person who's part of the story. In broadcast and online, the only time to include the age of a person is when that fact it is an essential part of telling the story. For instance, give the age of a 12-year-old college graduate or an 80-year-old snowboarder. Otherwise, it's unnecessary, as is identifying someone's race, unless it is part of the story.

Words to Avoid

Keep the subject close to the verb and avoid *to-be verbs* when possible. *Are* and *is* must be used often, but can become crutches. Instead of, "Bob is marching in the band every week," drop the *is* and write, "Bob marches in the band each week." Use action verbs when possible.

Other words to avoid include *of, by,* and *has been.* Many of these unnecessary words can be eliminated simply by flipping a sentence's phrases.

"John Smith of New York" becomes "New York's John Smith."

"Investors were not comforted by the company's chief executive officer" becomes "The company's top man did not comfort investors."

Instead of "The crowd had been warned by the police," try "The police warned the crowd."

Avoid pronouns. A broadcast story is difficult to follow if the writer often uses *he*, *she* or *it* when the audience didn't catch the original reference or several names are mentioned in the story. Repeat proper names, using the news maker's last name on the second reference, never just the news maker's first name. Again, avoid names entirely in the lead unless the person is well known.

Avoid *quote/unquote*. You've heard news reports where the anchor says, "President Barack Obama says, quote, I am against the use of tasers on children under the age of two, end quote." That's a bit formal-sounding. Sometimes you'll want to use it, but there are other devices, such as, "He put it this way..." or, "In his words..." or "With these words..." If the quote is very long, turn it into a graphic so the viewer can read along. When quoting only two or three words, there is no need to even use terms indicating a quote. The anchor's inflection can suggest the quotation to the audience.

Avoid emotionally charged or biased terms. Just like in newspaper writing, pick language that is as neutral as possible. For instance, instead of using *pro-life* and *pro-choice*, use *anti-abortion* activists and *abortion rights* activists.

Avoid *after*. The word *after* is often used when writers want to put the most significant of a series of events first. For instance, a story might read, "Police arrested two suspects after chasing them ten blocks after they robbed a convenience store." Besides putting the lead in past tense, the *after* makes the sentence too long and forces viewers to hold onto one idea while detailing other events that happened before it. If *after* comes up often, you are probably putting too many ideas into one sentence. That's fine if someone is reading text, but unnecessarily complex for listeners. Sometimes *after* can be dropped simply by using the "one thought, one sentence" approach. Break up your ideas. The new lead might read, "Two men are behind bars on robbery charges. Police chased them for ten blocks from a convenience store."

Avoid *continues*, *remains*, and *still*, especially in teases and leads. These words imply nothing new is happening with the story. Why should your audience stick around?

Avoid "this morning" in a broadcast lead that runs in the evening because it suggests there's nothing new since this morning or that the reporters aren't out digging up information.

Avoid dependent clauses when writing scripts for broadcast news. The opening words are meaningless without what comes later. The listener can be confused. Use independent clauses instead. For example:

> With the strong backing of Governor Minner, a second state spending limit bill is scheduled for final Senate action today.

Here's a better way to introduce the story.

> The Senate will vote today to make deeper cuts in state spending with strong backing of Governor Minner.

Anchor Voice

Putting words into someone else's mouth in such a way that they come out sounding natural is not an easy task. Talk to the anchor and find out what they like and don't like in their scripts. This will make it easier for them to read your scripts over the air. Does she like her scripts typed a particular way? Get on the same page when it comes to style. Don't write scripts in a way that's either too casual or too formal for the anchor. Some news readers are more open to delivering jokes or sarcasm in a fun way. Other anchors don't like a surprise, but will be all right with it if they are given a heads up. When an anchor stumbles over phrases, make a mental note so you'll have a better idea how to write specifically for him or her.

Numbers

Keep numbers to a minimum in broadcast stories, preferably one to a sentence and only a handful in a story.

Whenever possible, translate numbers into terms people can understand.

> The landfill is the size of two football fields.

Spell out numbers from one to eleven. Some organizations only write out up to nine or ten. Use number symbols from 12 to 999.

Use a combination of figures and words for thousands, millions, billions, etc. Here are some examples:

> She won 13-point-six million dollars in the lottery.
> He spent 20-thousand dollars at the track last night.
> Two-million children were born with birth defects.
> He got one-thousand-243 votes in the election.

The exact number of people killed in a plane crash is important, but that's not the case with most numbers used in broadcast news copy. The precise number is usually not as significant as the general idea. It's easier to grasp "a budget of nearly two-million-dollars" instead of "a budget of one million-865-thousand-dollars." This also goes for giving locations in broadcast stories. Landmarks are better reference points than exact street addresses.

Do not use Roman numerals in copy. Make it: World War Two, King George the Sixth, Pope John the 23rd. Roman numerals may be used on screen titles if they are part of a familiar name: World War II.

Spell out casual expressions: A thousand times no! Thanks a million. He walked a quarter of a mile.

Follow an organization's practice in using words or numerals in proper names: Twentieth Century Fund, Big Ten.

The idea behind writing out numbers is to keep the anchor's eyes moving across the screen at a steady pace. If you are continuously slowing, stopping, and speeding up, your reading is likely to become choppy. Although these efforts are considered broadcast standard, the bottom line is do what works for the news anchor. If a certain style helps her communicate better, then that's the way to go. Don't get caught up "going by the rules" and fail to keep the larger picture in mind.

If your ego rides on keeping everyone happy, you're going to get frustrated and angry.

Pronouncers

When an anchor may not know how to pronounce someone's name, a city or something else odd or unfamiliar, writers add a "pronouncer" or "prono." It sounds the word out for the anchor. So, a reference to a town in Louisiana might be, *Lafayette* (LAF-ee-et) but if the story is about a Mississippi county, the pronouncer would be *Lafayette* (lah-FAY-it).

Background

A problem in telling the same story over and over is how much background to give the viewers. The typical viewer is a person who keeps up with current events. So, we can rely on them to know what we're talking about in recent news stories. We don't need to set up a story over and over describing how it first happened. Once the basic facts of a news event have been reported, we can trust them to be remembered. A quick one line reference is often all that is needed. It's not necessary, for example, to tell the entire story of September 11th each time the story is referenced in a script related to the attacks. Think of it this way: Telling a story that requires a reference to the Civil War would not need a detailed description of what that war was about, or even when it occurred. The Civil War is considered common knowledge.

Writing Teases and Headlines

Writing great teases for TV and headlines for story links is an art. It takes a different kind of thinking than writing news stories. It's more creative and requires writers to step out of the box.

An effective way to grab a viewer's attention in a tease is through the "hook and promise" concept. Research shows that the pattern helps to hold viewers across commercial breaks. The format is simple. *Hook* the viewer with some unique, interesting aspect of the story, then *promise* something specific they will get when that story airs.

Don't be sneaky or trick the audience whether writing teases for broadcast or links on the Internet. Rather, state clearly what they are going to be given. Remember: Clarity is better than cleverness. A tease full of puns or clichés doesn't offer much substance. Headlines should tempt, not tease. Make people want to KNOW what's on the other side of the link, not WONDER what's on the other side of the web. However, that doesn't mean you shouldn't be creative. The hook should grab viewers and pull them into the story. Consider the following as the first line of a tease:

> The Fed is expected to raise interest rates again…

The information is factually correct, in present tense and it's a story that affects the majority of viewers. However, this can be written to better engage the viewer and make the story hit closer to home.

> It may cost you more to borrow money…

There is the hook. It's brief, concise and brings the viewer into the story. Not only does the hook pique interest here, but it also shows how this story will directly affect our viewers.

Seal the deal by adding a promise. The promise should be specific. Not "Details coming up," or "Just ahead," or "After the break." These phrases are too generic. Tell the viewers what they will see or hear when the story airs, and give them a reason to stick around. Don't make people try to figure out what you are talking about. Tell them why they will want to watch this story on this channel. Teasing is not a guessing game.

Specific does not mean wordy. Give viewers just enough information to keep them interested. Don't give away too much of the story. That's like giving away the punch line of a joke.

Ask yourself, "What's unusual, surprising, or interesting to me about this story?" Then tease that angle. Just like the hook, promise something viewers can relate to. Just make sure you are not using the same wording in the story lead.

Going back to the previous example, consider this hook and promise:

> It may cost you more to borrow money. Find out how high your interest rates could go.

The first sentence is the hook: Why the audience should care about the story. The second sentence is the promise: Here's what you'll find out if you stick around.

When teasing a story, get to the emotion and describe it. People care, they just don't always realize it. Help them see why a story matters, and don't use words that will allow them to filter the story out.

Writing headlines for online news has the added goal of catching the computer-generate algorithms of search engines. In this game, straightforward, short headlines crammed with hot names beat clever phrasing that alludes to the topic. *The Huffington Post* shows its grasp of search engine optimization with headlines like this one, combining two high searched names with innuendo: "Obama Rejects Rush Limbaugh Golf Match: Rush 'Can Play With Himself'." The article may reel in both blue and red staters. When Michael Jackson died, CNN.com found switching a couple of words to parallel Web searches about the pop star's death produced many more hits for the site.

Do We Really Need Writers?

Below are the opening lines of three stories written about a recent college base-ball game. Two are from schools' sports information departments. The other was produced by software that takes box scores and spits out news articles. Which one was created by a machine rather than a person?

1. "The University of Michigan baseball team used a four-run fifth inning to salvage the final game in its three-game weekend series with Iowa, winning 7-5 on Saturday afternoon (April 24) at the Wilpon Baseball Complex, home of historic Ray Fisher Stadium."

2. "Michigan held off Iowa for a 7-5 win on Saturday. The Hawkeyes (16-21) were unable to overcome a four-run sixth inning deficit. The Hawkeyes clawed back in the eight inning, putting up one run."

3. "The Iowa baseball team dropped the finale of a three-game series, 7-5, to Michigan Saturday afternoon. Despite the loss, Iowa won the series having picked up two wins in the twinbill at Ray Risher Stadium Friday."

Number two was composed by the computers of *Narrative Science*. The Illinois company specializes in "machine-generated content" first developed at Northwestern University. The goal is to branch out from sports game summaries and general news articles covering subjects like medical studies and crimes statistics.

If a news story is cobbled together using a machine, is it still journalism? And will positions now held by reporters eventually become the domain of computer algo-rithms, or is this a clever but limited tool to gather information?

For Next Time

Have you seen or read media created in countries other than the U.S.? What are the major differences between the American news media and the news produced in other nations?

NINETEEN
Global Media

Books Around the World

Most books are no longer published in the U.S. Of the top 50 book publishers, 43 are headquartered somewhere else. A German company owns Random House and an Australian company owns HarperCollins.

In Europe, publishers are looking for new ways to get their books into the hands of readers. A German publisher is re-purposing cigarette vending machines around the University of Hamburg as book dispensers, offering graphic novels and travel guides written by local authors.

Yet there are at least 17 countries in which less than half the population is literate. This includes 14 African nations. Without the ability to read, large groups remain impoverished, untouched by the print media and unable to educate themselves.

Newspapers Around the World

Newspapers outside the U.S. have mostly fared better financially than domestic publishers. Non-English papers often face less competition from online news aggregators and other Silicon Valley whizzes.

For instance, more than 70% of Germans read newspapers regularly. Newspaper revenue has held steady in the country since 2004.

German newspapers have been hurt by the recession, but not by the kind of rapid structural changes seen by America newspapers. Circulation of dailies fell 19% in Germany between 1998 and 2008, according to the German Newspaper Publishers' Association.

Central European publisher Axel Springer recently recorded the most profitable first quarter in its history. In the Czech Republic, an insurance company invested in a chain of small coffee shops which serve as newsrooms for its papers. The stories are local while the organization's Prague headquarters provides a national report.

Brazilian papers have completely shrugged off the recent economic downturn. The total circulation of Brazilian newspapers has expanded in the past ten years, thanks to inexpensive new papers focusing on sex and crimes. In 2003, three of Brazil's top ten papers were tabloids. Now, half are tabloids. It is a global trend to give readers what they want to read, as opposed to what media outlets suggest they ought to read. Thus, newspapers are becoming more distinctively defined and customer-focused. Rather than trying to bring the world to as many readers as possible, they are carving out niches for themselves.

Japanese newspapers, the world's biggest by circulation, are slowly losing readers. But they have an enormously long way to fall and ought to be cushioned by the media conglomerates of which they are a part. The circulations of the best-selling U.S. papers are dwarfed by the daily newspapers in Japan, the largest of which reaches more than 10 million readers.

Although *Naspers*, South Africa's biggest newspaper publisher, is nearly 100 years old, it is ambitiously moving online. While making most of its money from print and pay-television, Naspers' funds are shifting toward the purchase of online firms.

Some experts point to Europe as a model for the U.S. because these publications made cuts in scope and quality of coverage as have American papers.

European newspaper companies have experimented with new technologies, formats, and promotions. Yet these innovations have something going for them not shared by their American counterparts. A majority of the population uses the public transportation system, which is highly saturated with nearby newsstands. These conditions are available to only a few U.S. newspapers in major cities.

Movies Around the World

More than eight out of ten dollars made from movies goes to the American film industry, but it only produces 15% of the world's movies. India produces the most movies, twice as many as the U.S. Japan, China, and Brazil each have thriving film industries.

The market for films has become more global during the past decade. Since language barriers are not as significant in action and special effects films as they are in dialogue-driven movies, they are especially popular in international waters. American movie makers can overlook mediocre U.S. box office draws if overseas revenues can make up the difference. Sony's movies took in $1.5 billion at U.S. theaters in 2009, but made a record $2.1 billion in other countries.

Besides language, there are cultural barriers that moviemakers face overseas. *Anna and the King* (1999) was not shown in Thailand because it was deemed critical of the country's royalty. The Academy Award-winning film about a talking pig named *Babe* (1995) faced opposition in Malaysia because of the Islamic prohibition on eating pork products. *Kite Runner* (2007) was largely filmed in Afghanistan but banned in the country during the Taliban's rule. *The Passion of the Christ* (2004) was banned in Morocco, Burma, and Malaysia.

Radio Around the World

While radio has faded into the background among U.S. media, low cost, battery operation and low power consumption has made it the preferred media in developing countries. Radio is the most important medium in Africa. A 2009 survey by the International Center For Media Studies says people in the developing world trust radio more than any other source of information. In testimony before Congress, lawmakers were told a terrorist group in the Middle East had declared that in the fight for Iraq, "Media is half the battle." Radio is a major force in the region with Muslims who put it ahead of their religious leaders in terms of trust, in terms of trust, according to the survey.

Some countries impose rules at odds with American views on media freedom. French law requires that 40% of all music broadcast by its radio stations be in French. Iran bans all Western music from radio and television.

In the radio chapter, we discussed how shortwave radio was used in the 1920s by the major European colonial powers to connect with their various colonies in Africa, Asia, and the Middle East. Not only did colonial powers make use of international radio, but anti-government or anti-regime radio were also an important segment of international broadcasting. These are called clandestine stations. These secret stations often operate outside of the borders of a country to which it is aimed, keeping its studios and tower beyond the reach of government officials who would want to shut it down.

During World War II, radio stations operating from Britain and other Allied nations encouraged German soldiers and sailors to sabotage their vehicles and vessels rather than be killed in battle. The war also brought America into the business of international broadcasting. The U.S. government began what would become the *Voice of America* (VOA) in 1940 to support the allied war effort and counter enemy propaganda. The *Voice of America* promotes democracy around the world, but some media critics believe the federal government should not be in the business of spreading pro-Western views around the world through radio.

In the 1960s, *Pirate Broadcasters* illegally operated stations broadcasting to British audiences from offshore or foreign facilities. The movie *Pirate Radio* tells the story of rogue DJs who blast rock music from a boat in the middle of the Northern Atlantic in defiance of the British government.

During the 2009 Beijing Olympics, *Reporters Without Borders* set up a clandestine FM station in China. In September 2008 the FCC shut down nearly a dozen pirate radio stations and fined each of the operators $10,000. Most of the stations were using the FM band in locations that varied among Florida, Oregon, New York, and Cleveland. Cleveland?

Television Networks Around the World

Many developing countries lack the wiring necessary for cable television and depend on satellite transmissions though some countries, like Malaysia, have criminalized owning a satellite dish.

Consumers in countries such as India are acquiring second and third television sets, while Australia has one television for every two people because the country is large and many of its people live in remote places. Developing countries like Uganda have almost no television presence.

American productions dominate television viewing around the world because the U.S. developed strong distribution channels early in the medium's history. American TV offers well-composed, well-lit shot with actors properly positioned within the frame. Home-grown shows may be more culturally relevant, but they can't compete with Hollywood's expensive and carefully crafted product.

Discovery Communications, one of the largest video distributors now derives a third of its revenue from places outside of America. FOX International Channels pulled in more than $1 billion in 2008-09.

The *Cartoon Network*, which is part of *Time Warner*, is sent into 145 countries in 14 languages. *Nickelodeon* is the most distributed kids channel worldwide and can be seen in more than 320 million homes

But that's nothing when you compare it to *MTV* which can be seen in 366 million households. There's *MTV Latin America, MTV Asia, MTV Australia, MTV Brazil, MTV Japan, MTV Europe, Germany, Holland, India, France, Nordic, Poland, Romania, South East Asia*, etc.

Although MTV produces local content, it is largely a distribution engine for American programming. MTV India, for example, is dominated by local acts but MTV Poland is a vehicle for international music. Series like Jersey Shore, a show about young Italian-American, are released here and outside U.S. at the same time.

There are rules for American productions airing in other countries. *The Simpsons* is widely distributed across the Middle East, but all references to Duff Beer in the cartoon have been changed to soda. Moe's Bar does not appear at all.

The Qatar-based *Al Jazeera* network is the most powerful news and current events channel in that part of the world, well ahead of its Saudi-owned rival, Al Arabiya. Al Jazeera claims to reach half of all Arabic-language homes, while its English-language channel reaches Asia, Africa, and Latin America. Pro-Western Arab governments often accuse it of bias.

Opportunities are opening for television distribution partly because it is no longer perceived by foreign governments as the number one cultural threat. Iran blamed social media, not the BBC, for widespread protests in 2009. The spotlight of Chinese government censorship is now on Google rather than Hollywood.

Television and cable distributors have another concern to deal with in the meantime.

They are wrestling with how to address the growth of online video. *Freeview* offers British audiences about 50 channels for free. SNL Kagan says the number of households receiving free digital terrestrial television more than doubled in Italy between 2007 and 2009. Experiments with charging for content are already underway in Europe. French outfit Canal Plus allows users to buy additional access to sports and films. German broadcaster RTL allows people to catch up on recent shows at no cost, but charges them to view older episodes. Some episodes of prime-time shows are available from RTL several days before their television debut.

Many consumers in emerging markets appear to be increasingly prepared to pay for television online. As American cable operators know, few people drop pay-TV once they have it, and may buy more expensive packages.

Digital TV is also making inroads in Europe. The International Television Expert Group says the 42 million viewers in 2009 watching over-the-air digital broadcast TV will grow to 59 million by 2013.

Video Games Around the World

There are concerns over video game addiction and ratings worldwide. Players are fighting for access and governments are battling to keep a lid on excess.

A South Australian Attorney General has said he thinks he and his family "are more at risk from gamers than we are from the outlaw motorcycle gangs who also hate me and are running a candidate against me." He has the power to veto changes to the country's rating system. Australia is the only Western country without an adult rating for games.

South Korea has imposed a gaming curfew to try to crack down on what authorities call an epidemic of video game addiction among the young. The Culture Ministry announced anyone under 18 would be blocked form accessing three popular online computer games after midnight. One couple was charged with letting their infant starve to death while they raised a "virtual child" on the Internet.

The Internet Around the World

It is nearly impossible to make use of what the Internet promises in countries without adequate phone lines or consistent electric power. For nations where the Internet is available, it provides immediate information, framing issues in a compelling way.

The Internet is shaking up the media landscape with both left and right-leaning governments promoting legislation designed to rein in online expression. An Italian court held three Google executives responsible for a video posted to YouTube that showed teenagers bullying an autistic classmate. It sentenced each executive to a suspended six-month jail term. China's government is growing increasingly sensitive to any online threats to its authority, developing an extensive system of monitoring and censorship to block material deemed subversive. Chinese troops are ordered not to have blogs or personal websites. And yet the Internet is still the most open and lively forum for discussion. The Chinese online population is now more than 400 million, the most in the world.

Despite all that hand-wringing over the dangers of technology, many governments from South Korea to Sweden seem to regard universal fast broadband access as a human right to be paid for out of general taxation. The excitement over the 2010 World Cup illustrates how the world is embracing the new technology. Network operator Akamai says the games now hold the record for the most video requests ever, passing the inauguration of President Barack Obama, which previously held the record.

One of the remarkable changes now taking place online that shows the Internet's widening appeal is the increasing use of native languages. English will soon lose its dominance on the Internet. InternetWorldStats.com says 27.7% of people used English as their first or second online language at the end of 2009. Chinese is not far behind with 22.6% and Spanish comes in third with 7.8%.

Mobile phones are considered a valued resource in areas of the world where access to the Internet is uncommon. In Africa, 40% of the population now have mobile phones. Since bandwidth is still thin, headlines are sent out as text messages. It's possible the most dramatic effects of this explosion of information have yet to be felt in areas like Southeast Asia and Africa.

Social Networking Around the World

Market researcher comScore says the use of social networks grew 38% worldwide in 2008. According to Nielsen, the number of users on social-networking and other community sites across the U.S., Australia, Brazil, and several European countries, jumped 31% to 301.5 million people between August 2008 and August 2009.

Google's social media service (Orkut) is popular in India and Brazil while Facebook is big in Canada. Brazil has the second-highest number of Twitter users after the U.S.

There are now more Facebook users in the Arab world than newspaper readers, according to a survey by Dubai-based *Spot On Public Relations*. The agency says there are more than 15 million Arab subscribers to the social network. The total number of newspaper copies in Arabic, English, and French is just under 14 million. Facebook is so commonly used in Australia that court notices can be served through it. In Denmark, half the nation has active Facebook profiles.

Pakistan banned Facebook in the Spring 2010 when a Facebook group called *Everybody Draw Mohammed Day* was launched which encouraged drawings forbidden by Islam. Protesters took to the streets to rail against Facebook. How did they organize the demonstrations? Yes, you guessed it—Facebook.

Facebook is halfway to its goal of 1 billion global users. The company plans to double down efforts in China, Japan, Korea, and Russia in order to get there. In most of those nations, the site only has one million users. Most people around the world use the service for the same thing—engaging with a community of selected family and friends.

In January 2010, eight of the world's top 20 Twitter-using cities were outside America, according to the marketing firm, *HubSpot*. Twitter has become a gathering place for dissidents in China. The newly elected president of Chile has asked all of his cabinet members to start tweeting. Politter, a site dedicated to Twitter and Japanese politics, reports 485 politicians in the country have Twitter accounts. A survey by the University of St. Gallen found that 577 German politicians had opened Twitter accounts. The microblogging site has seen an explosive rise of more than 200,000 active accounts in Venezuela, one of the highest rates per capita of Twitter users in Latin America.

Free Speech Around the World

According to *Reporters Without Borders*, more than a third of the world's population live in countries where there is no press freedom. These people mostly live in countries where there is no system of democracy, or where there are serious deficiencies in the democratic process. Freedom of the press is a problem for most non-democratic systems of government, since strict control of information access is critical to their existence. Most non-democratic societies use state-run news organizations to get propaganda to citizens.

...more than a third of the world's population live in countries where there is no press freedom.

Some journalists are willing to work in dangerous areas of the world where life-threatening situations are a daily routine. They tell stories that would otherwise never see the light of day. Journalists working in these areas operate on the fringes of what is considered acceptable and often become the targets of government-induced intimidation. This can range from simple threats to their professional careers (such as professional blacklisting) to more dangerous concerns: death threats, kidnapping, torture, and assassination. At least 71 journalists were killed in 2009, which is the highest death count in the 30 years the *Committee to Protect Journalists* has been keeping track. Twenty-nine of those deaths came in a election-related ambush of reporters and others in the Philippines.

The *International Federation of Journalists* says more than 130 journalists and media personnel were killed on the job during 2009. Two dozen died accidentally while the others were singled out because of their profession. That's up from 109 media deaths in 2008, and 175 in 2007. The most dangerous locations were Somalia, the Philippines, and Mexico. Iraq has been the most dangerous place for the media during the past seven years.

Legal Issues Around the World

Iceland's parliament voted unanimously in 2010 to create what are intended to be the strongest media freedom laws in the world. *The Icelandic Modern Media Initiative* has international implications because it creates a safe haven for publishers and their servers. It may take a few years before the full impact is felt and what an "offshore freedom of expression haven" means to journalists worldwide.

Wikileaks was involved in promoting this law, which could give journalism organizations some measure of legal protection for anonymous sources if all communications were routed through Iceland. The investigative journalism site already routes submissions through Sweden where anonymous source investigations are illegal. There's more about Wikileaks in the Internet chapter.

Journalists Around the World

Voice of the Village is a rural news bulletin in India which uses a mobile phone as the broadcast medium. The news is generated by the villagers and broadcast in their local dialect by native journalists, something which was previously not possible because of widespread illiteracy, which rendered newspapers and SMS alerts ineffective. It focuses on hyperlocal news reported by local citizen journalists.

Advertising Around the World

Ad revenue fell worldwide in 2009, more than 10% from the previous year. Media-buyer *ZenithOptimedia* says the situation is changing and advertising will grow 3.5% worldwide during 2010 compared to the previous year. That would put worldwide ad revenue at $448 billion. The strongest growth is taking place in North America and Europe. The situation may improve after that since global ad spending expected to climb 4.5% in 2011 and 5.3% in 2012. Developed markets will grow by 2.4% in 2011 and 2.9% in 2012. Developing markets will grow even more: 9.1% and 9.8%, mostly from Asia-Pacific and Latin America regions.

Television is expected to get more than a 40% slice of the ad pie in 2012, up from 39.2% in 2009. The Internet takes the number three spot after newspapers. Internet ad spending will grow 13.1% in 2010 followed by larger gains in 2011 and 2012.

TWENTY
Conclusion

Every news gatherer is speculating how best to ride the digital wave sweeping across the media's horizon. At the moment, it's easier to see what's broken than what will replace it. Traditional media are being forced to jump off a bridge without knowing whether there is a net below. But journalism will survive the death of some of its institutions because there will always be story-tellers.

Here's what you should know from reading the previous pages. The distinction between media is becoming less relevant as we move forward. The containers aren't important. Many students moving into print or broadcast positions will discover Web jobs as their point of entry into professional journalism. People are no longer passive viewers and readers; they navigate their way through content at their own pace and whim. That's why building discoverability into our stories can give future audiences the ability to construct a meaningful narrative.

Barbara Ehrenreich told UC Berkeley Journalism graduates recently, "…We are *all* on a mission here. That's the meaning of your journalism degree. Do not consider it a certificate promising some sort of entitlement. Consider it a license to fight."

The tools to navigate this battle are adaptability, curiosity and perseverance. Develop proactive attitudes and seek to take the initiative. Why let someone else decide your fate? Live dangerously. Stretch yourself a little beyond what you think you can do. If you want to get ahead, then over-deliver. While quality journalism is possible as a work of solitary labor, it is often a collaborative effort. A digital future will still require real world relationships even if you earn your living blasting targets with words.

A quote from the Greek philosopher Aristotle hangs in my office: *It is the mark of an educated mind to be able to entertain a thought without accepting it.*

To appreciate the art in a museum, you walk around the pieces, taking them in from different angles. Even if the piece is not to your taste, there are parts to value if you look closely. Approach college, career and news with the same attitude. Walk around the ideas that confront you, looking at them from different angles. Gain nuggets of truth even from perspectives you don't embrace. Doing so helps clarify your own positions.

Embrace uncertainty and love the possibilities.

Live dangerously. Stretch yourself a little beyond what you think you can do.

Bibliography

Albarran, Alan B., *Management of Electronic Media: 3rd edition*, Belmont, CA: Wadsworth/Thomson, 2006.

Ariely, Dan, *Predictably Irrational: The Hidden Forces That Shape Our Decisions*, New York: HarperCollins Publishers, 2008.

Auletta, Ken, *Googled: The End of the World As We Know It*, New York: Penguin Press HC, 2009.

Baran, Stanley, *Introduction to Mass Communication 6th ed.*, Boston: McGraw Hill, 2010.

Black, Jay, and Bob Steele, Ralph Barney, *Doing Ethics in Journalism: A Handbook with Case Studies 3rd ed.*, Needham Heights, MA: Allyn & Bacon, 1998.

Bradbury, Ray, *Fahrenheit 451*, New York: Ballantine Books, 1953.

Bridges, William, *Transitions*, Cambridge, Mass: Perseus Books, 1980.

Briggs, Mark, *Journalism Next*, Washington, DC: CQ Press. 2010.

Brown, James A., and Ward L. Quaal, *Radio-Television-Cable Management 3rd Ed.*, Boston: McGraw-Hill, 1997.

Cappon, Rene J., *The Associated Press Guide to News Writing: The Resource for Professional Journalists*, Lawrenceville, NJ: Arco, 2000.

Carter, T. Barton, and Juliet Lushbough Dee, Martin J. Gaynes, Harvey L. Zuckman, *Mass Communication Law in a Nutshell 4th ed.*, St. Paul, MN: West Publishing, 1994.

Carr, Nicholas, *The Shallows: What the Internet is Doing to Our Brains*, New York: W.W. Norton & Company, 2010.

Christensen, Clayton, *The Innovator's Dilemma: When new Technologies Cause Great Firms to Fail*, Boston: Harvard Business School Press, 1997.

Dilts, Ralph L., and Jon Paul Holsinger, *Media Law 4th ed.*, Boston: Mcgraw Hill College, 1994.

Dominick, Joseph, *Dynamics of Mass Communication 10th edition*, Boston: McGraw Hill. 2008.

Dominick, Joseph, *Broadcasting, Cable, The Internet, and Beyond: An Introduction to Modern Electronic Media, 6th ed.*, Boston: McGraw Hill, 2007.

Eastman, Susan Tyler, and Douglas A. Ferguson, *Media Programming: Strategies and Practices 7th ed.*, Belmont, CA: Thomas Higher Education, 2006.

Gomery, Douglas, *A History of Broadcasting in the United States 2nd ed.*, Needham Heights, MA: Allyn & Bacon, 1994.

Hanson, Ralph E., *Mass Communication, Living in a Media World*, Boston: McGraw Hill, 2008.

Harrower, Tim, *Inside Reporting*, Boston: McGraw Hill, 2007.

Herrick, Dennis, *Media Management in the Age of Giants: Business Dynamics of Journalism*, Ames, IA: Iowa State Press, 2003.

Kleppner, Otto, *Otto Kleppner's Advertising Procedure 9th ed.*, Englewood Cliffs, NJ Prentice-Hall, 1986.

Kovach Bill, and Tom Rosenstiel, *The Elements of Journalism*, New York, Three Rivers Press, 2008.

Lanier, Jaron, *You Are Not a Gadget*, New York: Knopf, 2010.

Lanson, Jerry, and Mitchell Stephens, *Writing and Reporting the News, 3rd ed.*, New York, Oxford Press, 2007.

Lessig, Lawrence, *Remix: Making Art and Commerce Thrive in the Hybrid Economy*, New York: Penguin Books, 2008.

Lindstrom, Martin, *Buyology: How Everything We Believe about Why We Buy Is Wrong*, New York: Random House, 2008.

Morville, Peter, *Ambient Findability*, Sebastopol, CA: O'Reilly Media, 2005.

Ogilvy, David, *Confessions of an Advertising Man*, New York: Atheneum, 1988.

Othmer, James P., Adland: *Searching for the Meaning of Life on a Branded Planet*, New York: Doubleday, 2009.

Packard, Vance and Mark Crispin Miller, *The Hidden Persuaders*, New York: Ig Publishing, 2007.

Patterson, Philip, and Lee Wilkins, *Media Ethics 6th ed.*, Boston: McGraw Hill, 2007.

Pavlik, John V., and Shawn McIntosh, *Converging Media, 2nd ed.*, New York: Oxford Press, 2011.

Pringle, Peter, and Michael Starr, *Electronic Media Management 5th ed.*, Oxford, UK: Focal Press, 2006.

Quinn, Stephen, and Stephen Lamble, *Online Newsgathering: Research and Reporting for Journalism*, Oxford, UK: Focal Press. 2007.

Remond, James, *Balancing on the Wire: The Art of Managing Media Organizations 2nd ed.*, Atomic Dog Publishing, 2004.

Rodman, George, *Mass Media in a Changing World*, Boston: McGraw Hill, 2008.

Sagolla, Dom, *140 Characters: A Style Guide for the Short Form*, Hoboken, NJ: Wiley, 2009.

Schramm, Wilbur, *The Process and Effects of Mass Communication*, Urbana, Il: University of Illinois Press, Revised ed., 1971.

Shook, Federick, and Dan Lattimore, *The Broadcast News Process 6th ed.*, Englewood, CO: Morton, 2001.

Shook, Federick, *Television Field Production and Reporting 5th ed.*, Needham Heights, MA: Allyn & Bacon, 2008.

Silverglate, Harvey A., and David French, Greg Lukianoff, *FIRE's Guide to Free Speech on Campus*, Philadelphia: Foundation for Individual Rights in Education, 2004.

Stauber, John and Sheldon Rampton, *Toxic Sludge is Good For You: Lies, Damn Lies and the Public Relations Industry*, Monroe, ME: Common Courage Press, 2002.

Sterling, Christopher and John Michael Kitross, *Stay Tuned: A History of American Broadcasting 3rd Ed.*, New York: Routledge, 2001.

Student Press Law Center, *Law of the Student Press 3rd Ed.*, Arlington, VA: Student Press Law Center, 2008.

Taleb, Nassim Nicholas, *The Black Swan, The Impact of the Highly Improbable*, New York: Random House, 2007.

Wasik, Bill, *And Then There is This: How Stories Live and Die in Viral Culture*, New York: Viking Adult, 2009.

Weinberg, Steve, *The Reporter's Handbook: An Investigator's Guide to Documents and Techniques*, New York: St Martin's Press. 1996.

White, Ted, *Broadcast News Writing, Reporting, and Producing 4th ed.*, Burlington, MA: Focal Press 2005.

Wilkinson, Jeffrey, and August E. Grant, Douglas Fisher, *Principles of Convergent Journalism*, New York: Oxford University Press. 2009.

INDEX